CW00357481

Made Without Managers is an insightful explo
hierarchy. Mayden's groundbreaking appro
consistent honesty about the challenges al
valuable and inspiring aspects of their story. ʳᵒˡᵈ ... ... ,
people who went through the change, Mayden share their truth so that we can
all learn from it.

Ceri Newton-Sargunar, agile behavioural coach, Mondo Media Ltd

Mayden is a remarkable organisation, and *Made without Managers* is a
remarkable book. A great source of inspiration to anyone who seeks greater
autonomy, and to invite the full collective wisdom of their people in pursuit of
the firm's purpose.

Ben Simpson, co-founder/director of Organisational Vitality,
and chairman and director of Deming Alliance

In the quest to discover better ways of working, Mayden was signposted to
us by the Corporate Rebels. As a direct result of Mayden, we have witnessed
a shift in mindsets of some senior leaders and have begun trialling new
approaches to how we work. We will be including this book in our libraries,
and also delivering a copy to every team trialling new ways of working.

Jayne Price, head of continuous improvement for the Science and
Technology Facilities Council, part of UK Research and Innovation

I have to say that I enjoyed the book a lot. It fits well with the conception of
what an organisation ought to look like in order to be capable of managing the
tension between exploration and exploitation of opportunities and capabilities.
It draws the reader in, grounding each chapter in a practical problem.

Dr Tim Wakeley, senior lecturer in business economics and
associate dean (education), Bath School of Management

This may be the most useful book on the subject of managing a business that
I have ever read. Mayden avoided falling into the trap of picking some 'flavour-
of-the-month' with an appealing label. Instead they started with underlying
principles, experimented and learned, and built their own operating models
over time. Great!

Denis Bourne, co-founder/director of Organisational Vitality

Mayden is truly one of my inspirations, one of the few companies in the UK that works without managers. How can that work, you might wonder. Find out in this book exactly how it works. You too will be inspired.

Henry Stewart, chief happiness officer, Happy

In *Made Without Managers* Team Mayden share their profoundly inspiring experience of succeeding without (much) structure. Mayden's story showcases the importance of empowerment and community in organisational success – a must-read for cynics of contemporary organisational life.

Professor Stephen Brammer, dean of Bath School of Management

Made Without Managers is one of the most unpretentious business books I have ever read. It is equal parts moving and funny, common sense and inspiring. It beautifully brings to life the unique transformation journey of one organisation that will provide huge value to others on a similar path.

Lisa Gill, Tuff Leadership Training and *Leadermorphosis* podcast host

Mayden's journey has been built around a compelling vision, highly motivated employees and the art of the possible. What Team Mayden have in abundance is a strong connection to their purpose and an equally important empathy with each other – two essential ingredients for today's ever-changing world.

Paul Goddard, agile coach and certified scrum trainer, Agilify

There is lots written that paints a competing picture of where future organisations could or should be, but very little that takes us by the hand and walks us through the journey. This is a 'warts and all' account that will give you the inspiration to take the first steps.

Dr Graham Abbey, chief executive, Farleigh Performance

At a time when the world is crying out for change, this is a book about a group of people that really listened. But more than that, they acted on it! This is an inspirational account of an organisation doing things differently. Written by practitioners, for practitioners – but informed by a growing body of academic work and worthy of consideration by anybody and everybody who wants to think in new ways about organising in the future.

Dr Richard Longman, The Open University

MADE
WITHOUT
MANAGERS

One company's story of creating
a self-managing workplace

**TEAM MAYDEN
ALISON STURGESS-DURDEN
DR PHILIPPA KINDON
CHRIS MAY**

Made Without Managers
ISBN 978-1-912300-50-1
eISBN 978-1-912300-51-8

Published in 2023 by Right Book Press
Printed in the UK

Contents

This book is dedicated to every one of Mayden's employees, past and present, who have inspired, challenged, championed, questioned and pioneered our way of working. They have been the reason for creating a different kind of workplace; an organisation created by its people in service of their customers and each other.

Foreword

Margaret Heffernan, CEO and writer

Whenever I talk to executives about self-managed businesses, the first challenge is always: what about underperformers? As though this were the single most important aspect of running a business. The question in itself is so revealing: a fear that, left to their own devices, the workforce would skive off, a fundamental belief that people come into work to do a poor job. And so executives continue to rely on hierarchies and performance management to ensure that they get their money's worth from the people they employ.

Those hierarchies carry their own problems. Everyone in them swiftly learns that success depends on pleasing the people above them. This incurs a costly side effect: rather than thinking for themselves, they develop instead the core capacity to anticipate their boss's desires. In other words, they learn to think like everyone else. No wonder Britain continues to suffer from a chronic productivity problem: preventing bad work is nowhere near the same as fostering good work.

In an age when complexity and volatility make it near impossible to know what's coming next, disabling critical and imaginative thinking is a terrible mistake. Whether it's a pandemic, an economic, employment or energy crisis, supply chain issues or staffing shortages, when these extreme events hit a business, it needs more ideas, imagination and creativity, richer contributions not from a few but from everyone. Indeed, during the Covid-19 pandemic, many companies were forced by events to get a taste of working differently. Far from the action and unable to travel, managers had to trust their people to make good decisions. Many expressed huge surprise at how well business continued – but why? If you hire good people and ensure they have the information they need, shouldn't you expect them to know what to do?

The gradual trend towards self-management has been a slow, steady indicator that there are better ways to address today's turbulent environment than through expensive, lugubrious and soul-destroying bureaucracies and surveillance. After all, the whole premise of organisational life is that groups of people, working together, can come up with more ideas, craft better solutions, than individuals working alone. But that capacity depends critically on how freely those people can collaborate. So, unsurprisingly, some of the most creative companies in the world operate along principles similar to Mayden's. They are not all small. Or simple. Some are global businesses. Others work locally and export widely. Many have been working this way for years, others are just starting. Some of them are described in this book, sources not of competition but inspiration and shared learning, proof that there are no immovable barriers to working the Mayden way.

This book is as blissfully far from the heroic CEO's panegyric as it is possible to get: not the hackneyed hagiography of the superhero whose genius alone demolishes obstacles, but a richly textured narrative of collective learning and discovery. It isn't the first book on self-management and it won't be the last. But it does something very important, which is to fill in the gap between aspiration and achievement. Full of practical examples of problem-solving, it convinces not through rhetoric but by laying out in everyday detail how work gets done well. And with delight.

And work should be delightful. We spend around 100,000 hours in our jobs, so we give to them the single most precious thing that we have: time. The one thing can never be replaced. So it shouldn't be frightening. It should be and it can be fulfilling for everyone. And when people grow, the business grows.

Meet the chapter authors

Dave Bould

Dave joined Mayden in 2010 as our eighth member of staff. He started out as a software engineer fresh out of university. Dave has had the unique opportunity of growing along with Mayden for more than a decade and his role has evolved over time to solutions architecture, applications architecture and technical leadership. In his spare time, Dave enjoys kickboxing, running, HIIT (high-intensity interval training) and spending time with his family.

Taryn Burden

Taryn joined Mayden in 2016, originally as an administrator. These days, she curates and facilitates our efforts to build the kind of company we all want to work for. Taryn is an accredited trans-formational coach and is working towards her ICF certification. She hails from South Africa and lived in the States before settling in England. In a previous life, Taryn was a DJ and voice-over artist. She is a foodie who loves baking cakes for everyone and holding a *braai* (barbecue) or *potjie* (a stew cooked over an open fire in a cast iron pot) – whatever the weather.

Rob Cullingford

Rob has been with Mayden since 2012 and was instrumental in introducing the scrum framework and agile ways of working. A software engineer for many years with a passion for creativity and problem-solving, he's been a scrum master since 2013. Rob loves playing cricket for his local team, walking and travelling – the last two tie in with Rob being a cartophile.

Dr Philippa Kindon

Philippa's focus is business development in the broadest sense. She's forever seeking ways to improve our work and our processes, and to make Mayden the best company to work for. Philippa has a PhD in Identity in the Workplace from the University of Bath. She is also one of our coaches. In her time outside work, she loves spending time with her family – being the mum of two, this generally entails being a taxi and cheering from the sidelines at various sports grounds.

Chris May

Chris is Mayden's founder and has three passions: using data to improve health outcomes, helping those around him to thrive, and chocolate. In the little spare time he has, Chris loves to write and has written one novel with another well on the way. At Mayden, Chris has been building the kind of company people want to work for, with an agile, open working culture, a flat structure and shared responsibility; somewhere where everyone can flourish.

Michele Rees-Jones

Michele owns Mayden's internal coaching initiative, having joined the company as a marketing freelancer many moons ago. Michele quickly realised that Mayden was and is a company where she could happily work every day. She fell in love with coaching when the company offered her the opportunity to train, and she never looked back! Michele is now a professionally accredited business and personal coach. She is a mum of two and loves nothing more than camping by the coast in the summer with family and friends.

Alison Sturgess-Durden

Alison is one of our four directors, overseeing both organisational and business development. Alison joined Mayden after a career in the health service and has been key to building Mayden's open, self-managing culture. In any spare time she has, Alison likes to snuggle up with a book, take her dog for long walks or spend time with her adventurous family.

Ruth Waterfield

Ruth loves collaborating to find solutions to puzzling problems, whether that be as a developer or as a scrum master, to bring positive impact to the lives of others. Ruth has been with Mayden since 2017 after graduating with a Mathematics degree from the University of Bath. Another foodie, Ruth has a minimum of five different kinds of pasta in her cupboard at any one time and bakes a mean macaron.

Introduction

Dr Philippa Kindon

My journey with Mayden began in a classroom. I met Chris Eldridge, one of Mayden's directors, on the board of governors at the primary school our children attended. Knowing I had been a student of management, specifically organisational behaviour, he thought I'd be intrigued by Mayden's management ethos and way of working. His hunch about Mayden and me might also have had something to do with the lemon drizzle cake I brought to the meeting; I would later learn that Mayden often runs on its stomach! Given that my doctoral research explored identity in the workplace, I jumped at the chance to be interviewed for a role in the business. Poring over the company's website in preparation, I began to learn what it did (something to do with mental health, patient records and software), but I also began to glean how Mayden was doing it. Flat structure. No managers. Agile. Exciting! I wanted in.

Welcome to Mayden!

I soon became better acquainted with what Mayden was about. Mayden started in Chris May's 'den', the attic room of his home and hence our company name. It was there that he founded the company as a healthcare analytics consultancy in the year 2000 at the height of the dotcom boom. Informed by his experiences and frustrations with healthcare IT systems while working in the UK's National Health Service (NHS), Chris M could see the potential offered by web-based software applications, so he went

1

ahead and employed Mayden's first software developer. By 2004, a small development team had moved into regular offices and started work on the software platform used to run a system for quality-assuring cancer services across the NHS. A few years later, a chance meeting at a healthcare conference resulted in Mayden being commissioned to develop a prototype electronic patient record (EPR) for a new kind of psychological therapy service in the NHS. A case was made to the UK government that if access to psychological therapies for common mental health disorders (such as depression and anxiety) improved, many receiving therapy would not only get better, but become able to return to work (Clark 2018). The government agreed to fund two pilot NHS 'talking therapy' services on the condition that these and other key outcomes were collected as evidence. Dr Ben Wright, clinical lead for the National Demonstration Site in east London, recognised that his team would need an EPR capable of supporting such data capture. On crossing paths at the conference, Ben asked if Mayden could help. And so, in 2008, the NHS's Improving Access to Psychological Therapies (IAPT) service was born, and, soon after, the first iteration of Mayden's EPR, iaptus (see iaptus.co.uk). The IAPT programme proceeded to report outcome measures that helped make the case for it being rolled out across the country. Where IAPT went, iaptus aimed to follow and was often successful as it was chosen by many NHS teams.

At the time of writing, Mayden employs more than 100 people and has a turnover approaching £10 million. We are based in the World Heritage city of Bath in the west of England. iaptus has around 40,000 users working in over 200 clinical services, including 100 NHS organisations. Between them, our clients deliver two thirds of NHS IAPT services in England as well as other psychological therapy services at home and abroad. We have clients in Australia, where a similar programme to IAPT has been rolling out, and will soon go live in Canada and Ireland. iaptus has also started to be adopted by other clinical disciplines. We are holding more than 7m patient records for our clients, and counting. Some years ago, we set up our own academy to train software developers to address our struggle to recruit talent. iO Academy is now a commercial success in its own right, helping those leaving education and career changers to move into software development.

Two interviews after first chatting to Chris E, I too found myself part of the Mayden team. The role I was offered was different to the one originally envisaged. The team could see my skills and experience would be a better fit for a different gap. I was thrilled, of course, and accepted the offer to become the company's 'executive programme manager'. It's a job title I rarely use (except for online registration forms that require a job title) and even then the 'executive' was dropped almost as soon as I started. Within three months the executive team I would be supporting was disbanded, deemed too hierarchical. In most companies this would be a threatening and scary time. You've just got through the door and the team you work for no longer exists. You're out again, right? Well, not at Mayden. What happened instead turned out to be an opportunity to work on the most rewarding programme of my career to date – developing a whole new way of working.

What this book is about

This book shares one company's experience of an extraordinary approach to work. First, it's about how a 'flat' organisational structure works in practice – one without middle managers that doesn't rely on the hierarchical authority of a line manager over subordinates to get things done. People are expected to manage themselves. I love the story in the box below told by two of our placement students. In so many ways, it sums up much of what this book is about, as they compare their experience of our way of working to the conventional corporate one they had already had in a previous placement (I also love the fact that those with the least experience and freshest eyes have the honour of telling you their story first).

Emily Quinn and Lottie Bodley Scott, undergraduate placement students, University of Bath

We both joined the market discovery team at Mayden for a six-month placement from the University of Bath, where we were studying for a degree in business. Having worked for large corporates in our first placements, in our final year we decided to have a look at a small enterprise. Little did we know that this would take us into the wonderful world of flat management structures.

Emily: I completed my first placement at an internet services company that specialises in providing cybercrime disruption services. This was my first real experience of a corporate job, so I wasn't sure what to expect. It quickly became clear that following instructions from my superiors and paying attention to detail was really important, that hierarchy was how things got done. Because of my set role, there were few opportunities for additional personal development and exposure to more areas of the business, which, I assumed, was normal for a placement student.

Lottie: Similar to Emily, I worked at a large corporation during my first placement – a professional services network. This was my first time working from 9 to 5 in a fast-paced environment. After the first few months, I was clear where I stood in the hierarchy and whose work I should prioritise.

Emily: When researching Mayden in preparation for my interview, the idea of working within a flat management structure was something I'd never thought about or even knew existed. This uncertainty left me feeling nervous about how it would shape the placement: Who will be my manager? Who's going to tell me what to do? How will I know if I've done well enough? Little did we know that this culture shock would provide such a motivating and rewarding experience. From day one, we were welcomed by everyone, and straight away felt part of the company. In place of a directly involved line manager, daily team meetings with our teammates in market discovery were key to keeping our work on track and getting the support we needed.

Lottie: After a while we grew in confidence to start flexing our self-managing muscle. One of the things we were proudest of was developing the 'FAVE-WAVE-DAVE' tool for the business. It was our idea – we weren't asked to do it – but it quickly allowed the team to conduct an 'analysis and visionary evaluation' (AVE) of different opportunities that might be beyond (further, wider or deeper) in relation to our core market.

Emily: While having a chat with some of my university friends who were completing their six-month work placements, the subject of line managers came up. My friends were all working in corporate environments and were expected to follow instructions from line managers. Lottie and I have had a totally different experience in our Mayden placements. When I mentioned that I was working within a flat management structure, my friends were surprised and intrigued to know more. One of them commented how rare such arrangements are, especially for an inexperienced placement student. Not having a hovering superior symbolises the trust placed in you to get the job done. Another reflected on this structure: 'It must surely benefit employee wellbeing, given how much you are enjoying your placement, with that level of autonomy.' Seeing how shocked they were made me think about why there's such a lack of awareness of flat management structures.

As students completing business degrees, we see that leaders of the future need to become more aware of how businesses **can** work. The autonomy we've had, which relies heavily on trust, was handed to us from the get-go. This is rarely something that an employer would do for a placement student straight away, but it has made our experience so rewarding and given us a huge confidence boost.

Twenty years ago, I was in Lottie and Emily's shoes – an undergraduate student of management at the same university in the south-west of England, which I then followed with postgraduate studies, leading eventually to a PhD. Even as an undergraduate hoovering up what my eminent lecturers had to say about management theory and practice, I had a niggling sense that something wasn't quite right in a world where people were classed as liabilities rather than assets in the accounts. Surely people are a company's greatest asset and should be thought of and treated as such? My continuing interest in the field gave me an emerging awareness of alternative ways of organising, and I noticed a number of university departments setting up centres for the 'future of work', Bath itself being one. People were questioning the conventions of organising. Paradigms appeared to be shifting.

Over the years, having moved to implement an alternative way, Mayden has received considerable interest in our way of working from other organisations and thought leaders, as well as academics. The Health Foundation's Q Community (q.health. org.uk), representing the finest in improvement practice in the NHS, have sent delegations to learn from us. A few years back we were added to the Corporate Rebels Bucket List of 'pioneers, rebels and revolutionaries... who change the status quo of frustrating workplaces' (corporate-rebels.com/bucketlist). Seven years since we last had middle managers, including two years of pandemic-driven remote working, we feel we have gathered enough experience to be ready to share our particular journey. Given the lack of practical insight and case studies from anyone actually doing this, particularly in the UK, we have been encouraged by others to write about how we work.

One of our aims in writing is to get beyond the hype. We've all heard companies bragging about their revolutionary new remote working policies. 'Work from anywhere!' Spotify announced to its staff (and the rest of the world) during the Covid-19 pandemic of 2020. But it looked as if employees still needed to get approval from their manager to do so. So far, so normal, in terms of the flexible working legislation we've had in the UK for many years. We're conscious that this way of working can be long on attention-grabbing headlines ('unlimited annual leave' or 'set your own salary', anyone?) and short on the practicalities. And sometimes the details are prosaic and familiar, yet shouldn't disguise the substantial differences in mindset and ethos that lie beneath, giving it a whole other complexion. We seek to shed light on such matters.

When I started at Mayden I was delighted to have the opportunity to be directly involved in crafting a workplace that would become a case study on the future of work. The crafting process is the second thing this book is about – the journey we went on to discover and implement it. Director Alison Sturgess-Durden will take you through Mayden's journey in the next chapter. For now, the point is this: if you're in the business of allowing your employees to manage themselves, you come to realise that also means allowing them to design the organisation itself. Self-management doesn't start with a prescription from on high as to how exactly it should be done. It needs to continuously emerge from the community itself. This book is therefore also about that process: how an organisation figured out how to organise itself, not just the solutions it has arrived at. The work I personally came to focus on came out of a watershed Mayden staff day in November 2016 when, picking up the threads that had already emerged in our software development teams, we began to collectively define our way of working at Mayden – to make it better at serving its customers, and be the type of company we all wanted to work for. I helped to nurture the programme of organisational development that followed after that day.

Implicit in this is that the journey Mayden went (and continues to go) on, and the particulars of our way of working, will be different to any other organisation's. Your organisation is made up of a different bunch of people, holding to their own values, pursuing a particular purpose, dealing with distinctive challenges and struggles at a certain point in time. I return to this in our final chapter with Taryn Burden about how and where you might start your own journey if inspired to do so. What this book is therefore *not* about is providing a 'playbook' of how to do it. At some points our lack of prescriptiveness may even frustrate you. But we do hope to provide some overall guidance about pursuing your own approach, while giving insight from our unique experience.

And, of course, Mayden itself is by no means 'done', which is the final thing this book is about. We fully expected the writing process, and extensive involvement from so many of the team, would help us reflect on our own progress and where we need to go next. We're grateful for this opportunity to reflect! One of Mayden's four organisational values is transparency. As you will discover, our way of working cannot operate without it. As well as sharing our overall story, the book includes plenty of tales about where we've gone wrong. We're not writing it to boast about our success. We want to be transparent with you so you can learn from our struggles and mistakes, but also to show that whatever path you take it should be one of constant iteration, improvement, failure, review, learning and growth. We are sharing our experience in the spirit of mutual learning, not because we think we have all the answers. Indeed, we ask you to think critically about what you read about Mayden and draw your own conclusions.

How we've written the book

Two of our other guiding values at Mayden are contribution and collaboration. Naturally, we decided to produce this book accordingly. This is not another book by another CEO. You'll read chapters written by a variety of authors who work at Mayden. Between us we have incorporated stories and quotes from other employees that bring further perspectives. We've taken this multi-vocal approach for the very reason that this way of working is not owned or directed by one person or group. There isn't a single organisational narrative (see Gabriel 2015). By tuning into many voices, you're more likely to get an authentic sense of how things are.

Whenever we talk to others about our way of working, we've noticed how the same questions tend to follow. We're guessing you'll have some of them yourself. So, we decided to dedicate each chapter to one of those frequently asked questions, such as 'Isn't it complete chaos?' (referring to the practicalities of how the right work still gets done), 'Who's to blame when things go wrong?' (how we deal with mistakes and failure) and 'How do you get promoted?' (what progression looks like).

The book is arranged into three parts. Part 1 tells our origin stories. These are the personal accounts of some of the people who were there at the genesis of our way of working and had a significant impact on shaping it: our founder, Chris M; one of our directors, Ali SD; and Rob Cullingford, with Ruth Waterfield and Dave Bould from the software development team. Part 1 therefore provides three different perspectives on the catalysts for what we did and how things unfolded. While this creates a certain amount of overlap in the authors' accounts, our intention is to provide you with richer insight while allowing each author to share their particular perspective.

In Part 2, we delve into the practicalities. Each chapter focuses on different parts of the overall management system (or 'scaffolding' as we refer to it) we've created that, together, help us function without managers. Finally, in Part 3, as already mentioned, we will reflect on where we anticipate Mayden will go next, while encouraging you to consider how you might take some of this away and start your own journey. We hope you accept the challenge. Before we get into the detail, let's start with an overview of the way of working I'm talking about.

Mayden's way of working in a nutshell

So, what is this management system? What is the scaffolding we've erected in place of people hierarchy and line management? If you remove hierarchy and leave the organisation unstructured and unsupported, you get confusion, frustration, inertia or diversion. As you'll read shortly, we know from experience! There's a reason only the tiniest creatures manage without a skeleton, and we were no longer a micro enterprise when this began. It's just that people hierarchies are not the only organisational skeleton available, and the absence of such a hierarchy doesn't mean an absence of structure altogether. Mayden has sound structures and processes to create organisational order. They're just not a hierarchy of line managers.

We sum up our way of working like this: we manage the work, not the people. We've done nothing short of deconstructing hierarchy and line management, looked closely at the functions they serve, and come up with a different way of achieving those things, of organising the work and ourselves. We've summarised this translation in the table below. It starts with everyone having clarity about two essential organisational guides in place of a manager: the purpose and strategy (Chapter 6), and values and ethos (Chapters 5 and 3 respectively). They're essential if everyone is to be able to work and make decisions that align with where we're going, and in the Mayden way. The directors (which, spoiler alert, we still have – see Chapter 10) are responsible for setting this overall direction and expectations. They then get out of the way and leave self-managing teams to work out how to best deliver work in line with those things.

Next, scrum, an agile framework for implementing projects, gives us a clear and commonly shared approach to prioritising and delivering work by a group of peers (you'll learn about scrum and agile in Chapter 4; in the meantime, the boxes below provide a high-level overview). Everyone has a clear role and responsibility for owning elements of the workflow rather than for supervising others' work. Indeed, individual progression at Mayden comes from owning more complex and impactful work rather than increasing the number of people or departments you manage through climbing the organisational ladder (Chapter 12).

Agile

Agile can be described as an iterative approach to software development, but is now used in other industries too, articulated by a set of values and principles as set out in the Agile Manifesto (agilemanifesto.org), which is as follows:

'We are uncovering better ways of developing software by doing it and helping others do it. Through this work we have come to value:

- individuals and interactions over processes and tools
- working software over comprehensive documentation
- customer collaboration over contract negotiation
- responding to change over following a plan.

That is, while there is value in the items on the right, we value the items on the left more.'

The Agile Principles can be found in Appendix section A to this book.

These roles and responsibilities for the work determine who the decision maker is in the case of each decision. Whole-company strategic and high-cost decisions are reserved for the directors; otherwise our decision-making process helps all other decisions to be made in the best place within the organisation (Chapter 7). Crucial to enabling people to make decisions is the open sharing of information around the business (Chapter 6) and a no-blame culture (chapters 3 and 13) that encourages everyone to take responsibilities, exercise their autonomy and remain accountable to each other.

Scrum

A lightweight framework of roles (product owner, scrum master and developers), practices and events (sprint planning, daily scrum, sprint review and sprint retrospective) that helps teams deliver products in short cycles (sprints), enabling frequent and regular feedback, continual improvement and the ability to adapt to change – see scrumguides.org.

Scrum team

A small, self-managing group of people consisting of a scrum master, a product owner and developers. The team should have all the skills necessary to successfully deliver the work it commits to each sprint. Although there are different roles within a scrum team, there are no hierarchies.

Sprint

A short, fixed period of time (a month or less in length) during which a scrum team commits to delivering product backlog items. They are cyclical in that a new sprint starts immediately after the end of the previous sprint, and are of the same length.

Product owner

This person represents the customer within the team. They are responsible for shaping and communicating the product vision and goals, for maximising the value (or return on investment) of the product and for prioritising the product backlog. Effectively they are responsible for **what** is going to be worked on, **who** it is for and **why** it is worthwhile; they are not responsible for **how** work will be done.

Scrum master

Serves the developers, product owner and wider business by training and coaching agile and scrum practices and adoption. They guide the scrum team to higher levels of self-management, cross-functionality and effectiveness and work to remove anything impeding the team's progress. They're coaches, facilitators and champions of teamwork.

Sprint planning
An event, marking the start of a sprint, where the scrum team determines which product backlog items they are going to commit to delivering in the sprint and how they are going to deliver them.

Daily scrum/stand-up
A short (15-minute) daily event where the scrum team inspects its sprint progress and produces a plan of action for the day.

Sprint review
An opportunity for the scrum team and stakeholders to inspect the outcome of the sprint and the progress made towards the product goals, and adapt the product backlog in response.

Sprint retrospective
A meeting at the end of each sprint where the team reflects and inspects and adapts its practices, processes, behaviours, interactions and attitudes. A chance to increase quality, effectiveness and team health.

Product backlog
A prioritised list of desired improvements for, and value to be added to, a product in order to achieve the product's goals.

User story
A short description of a desired improvement to a product written from the perspective of an end user or customer. They articulate how the improvement will add value and promote conversation. They're not part of the scrum framework, but originated with Extreme Programming (XP) and are often adopted by agile teams.

In the absence of line management and people hierarchy, the importance of facilitation and coaching – of teams, individuals and as a day-to-day practice towards one another – cannot be overstated. We have invested not only in scrum masters in our scrum teams, but team coaches in our other self-managing teams (Chapter 6). They don't manage the work or the people, but 'hold the space', questioning, challenging and encouraging groups of peers to keep moving forwards. Everyone can also access an individual coach to explore work, personal development, relational or other issues they face, identifying solutions and taking ownership of their contribution and progression (Chapter 9). Free-flowing peer-to-peer feedback facilitates continuous improvement (Chapters 6 and 12).

Finally, the directors provide whole-company assurance, monitoring company-level metrics, getting involved only where necessary or helpful. As the table below shows, with all these things in place to manage work and support individuals in managing and developing themselves, there is little left for line managers to do. Nevertheless, we still have them – our directors. Chapter 11 explains how the residual line manager role is about those remaining HR matters that cannot be managed by individuals or within teams.

Put the whole together and you have the apparatus of our way of working: managing without managers. Most of the constituent practices may not seem that revolutionary. The difference, we believe, is the extent to which we have embedded them, to the point that they are able to largely replace tiers of middle managers. But we've also learned the other crucial difference comes from the mindsets of those practising them – from our beliefs about one another's ability to manage ourselves, an ethos concerning how work should be and the shared values guiding how we work with one another and our customers. But why and where did this all begin for us? Let's start with stories from those who were there at the beginning.

Table: Conventional line management compared to Mayden's way of working

CONVENTIONAL LINE MANAGER FUNCTION	AT MAYDEN
SETS AND SUPERVISES WORK – decides what should be worked on, by whom and often how.	Directors set strategic direction and expectations (including strategy, the value to be delivered and the values to be upheld in the process), then get out of the way and allow those owning the work and projects, and self-managing teams, to work out how to deliver in line with those.
	We manage the work, not the people. Managers do not manage people in order to manage work. People get on and manage their work. People 'own' (take responsibility for) work and projects. They make extensive use of agile practices to provide a common framework for delivering work. They negotiate with self-managing delivery teams (software development, marketing, data services, etc) over what user stories and other tasks go into the forthcoming sprint of work, all in the knowledge of the overall direction and expectations. Self-managing teams agree among themselves the best solution to each story or task in order to meet required outputs and outcomes. The decision-making process enables the most appropriate person to make decisions about the work and decisions can be challenged. Scrum masters and team coaches facilitate the engagements, and information needed to manage the work is freely available.
MANAGES PERFORMANCE AND DELIVERY – determines key performance indicators, checks progress, takes corrective action.	Self-managing teams work out how best to deliver the outcomes and value required from the work as well as the priorities for their available capacity. They regularly account for progress and outputs to the whole company in the sprint review (e.g. fortnightly). Teams are responsible for keeping their own metrics to know how well they are functioning and that they're continuously improving, and make those metrics visible to others in the business. Individuals are expected to manage themselves and their contribution. Directors play an overall assurance role, focusing on monitoring whole company KPIs. They step in under exceptional circumstances when their support, advice or further direction is needed.

EVALUATES INDIVIDUAL PERFORMANCE – of subordinates, commonly in the form of the annual appraisal.	Regular retrospectives (at the end of each sprint) are used by self-managing teams to evaluate what went well and areas for improvement – for teams and individuals. A culture of peer-based feedback gives each employee regular insight into how their contribution is valued and where it might improve.
SETS REWARD – makes salary recommenda-tions based on their evaluation of individual performance through the appraisal process.	Directors at Mayden remain responsible for setting salaries, based on roles, responsibilities, contribution and industry benchmarks, as well as setting other rewards and benefits. Regular surveys check employee satisfaction with rewards and benefits and when changes are needed they are implemented.
SETS PERSONAL OBJECTIVES – has the most say about where the employee is expected to improve and develop.	The individual 'owns' their personal development. They're free to set what personal objectives they wish, based on feedback and in light of what's important to Mayden (direction, expectations). Coaching helps with goal setting, planning and achievement.
SUPPORTS PERSONAL DEVELOPMENT – providing coaching, mentoring or access to training and opportunities to support the achievement of personal objectives.	While individuals 'own' their development, Mayden makes resources and support widely available – coaches, mentors, training budget and opportunities to try different work and roles.
MANAGES EMPLOYEE RELATIONS – responsible for adherence to HR practices and employment law, and takes management action in relation to the individual employee where needed.	Many individual employment matters are managed by teams, e.g. agreeing annual leave and much of recruitment. Directors retain authority for making any revisions to contractual terms of employment and HR policies and procedures, and remain the escalation point for more complex or serious individual HR issues.

A week in the life of a Mayden employee

Hi! I'm Isabel. I've been working at Mayden for five years as an account manager. I've recently started experimenting with a new role where I can be more proactive in working with our customers. Before joining Mayden, I had worked in various customer-facing roles within hospitality, retail and security services. I had no idea about the software or healthcare industries, and I had no experience working in an agile or flat-structured environment. I thought the story of a typical week in my working life at Mayden might help any of you in the same position to understand how it works.

Monday

I had a call with a key customer about a piece of development. I'm gathering user feedback to share with the internal group of User Experience, product and technical specialists working on the feature. It is this cross-disciplinary group of peers who will decide the best design, not our manager. I love that I could flex my role to bring the user voice even more directly into our decision making, and that the people closest to the customer and technology get to make those decisions.

Tuesday

With one of my teammates, I interviewed a final candidate for a vacancy we have in the team – the new recruit will be a peer of ours. Our recruitment coordinator has supported us through the process and afterwards my colleague and I agreed on our preferred candidate. We answered questions Chris E (our director) had about our recommendation, who then, on behalf of the company, and having never met the candidate, went ahead and made her an offer. She immediately accepted!

I joined our daily team stand-up which we call 'Hey at Midday'. We share what we did the day before, what we're doing today, and if we have any blockers stopping us from getting on. Then it was straight into the iaptus sprint review to hear what our developers had produced and deployed in the software in the last two-week sprint. It's always a big, busy meeting, with nearly 50 people. There were lots of questions about how new features work from account managers, product owners and the directors.

Later in the afternoon our team had a session with Philippa, who sometimes coaches us as a team. When she does this, Philippa 'holds the space' for everyone if uncomfortable but important conversations are needed about how we're working together. We always find it best to work through problems together instead of escalating these to a manager figure. It means issues can then be resolved on a personal level and we can move on. Sometimes those conversations benefit from being supported by someone like Philippa. Today she's facilitating a retrospective about how we worked together over the past couple of weeks. That usually means playing some games together that help to surface issues without being confrontational. They're fun and set the right mood for being open with one another. We've witnessed how well agile and scrum work in other teams, but our work is quite different, so we're still working out how it translates to the work we do.

Wednesday
It's the point in the month when our team publishes customer support statistics to show how we've performed. We updated our team page on One Place (the company's intranet) and sent a link round to the whole company. Straight away, people started getting back to us to praise the outcomes we've achieved for the customer and to ask questions about the data and our work. It's encouraging that they are so interested in what we do, and their questions make us accountable for what we are doing, which is why being transparent like this is so important.

In the afternoon I went along to a new working group spun up by various colleagues who realised they were sharing the same pain around some aspects of Mayden's decision-making process. The working group chair kept us focused on defining the problem and identifying solutions. We could talk for hours!

Thursday

The day started with an alert that a few of our clients were having unexpected problems accessing our iaptus software. This doesn't happen very often, but when it does, a response swings into action involving those needed depending on the issue, such as customer support and the software developers if a fix in the software is needed. We have a well-oiled process where those with the information and the expertise are able to act in the best interest of the business and make the decisions needed to resolve things for customers quickly. The directors do not need to be involved in these moments unless the problem is really significant. I was the first to jump in, talking to clients about the issue which I flagged to our developers and systems. They responded immediately and deployed a fix. I called clients back to confirm all was well.

I made it to our 'Directors' Digest' meeting where the whole company gathers to share updates and celebrate success. One of the directors plays host and in today's session we heard an update about new business we've won and what that means for achieving our business plan and financial results.

Friday

This morning we had a strategy group meeting. Anyone from the company can attend. The directors have drafted a strategy and have invited everyone to comment. I went along to understand the proposal better and have my say – I want to make sure our customer service continues to inform and reflect where we are going.

I asked for a coaching session about how I should discuss and communicate my new role with my colleagues. I realised that people hear things in different ways. The coach I talked to encouraged me to consider each person's communication preferences, with insight from their personal colour profile, a tool we use to understand each other's differences. I walked away with a plan of action around how best to approach the conversation with different internal stakeholders.

Mayden's 'Ministry of Fun' hosted an autumn evening, featuring seasonal food and drinks and a craft fair for Mayden employees to sell their handmade goodies. The proceeds went towards a nominated charity. It was a great way to end the week!

So, that is fairly typical of working life for me. On my very first day at Mayden, I unfortunately wasn't warned about the sticky lock on the bathroom door and actually got stuck in there; it took four people to get me out! Little did I know that I'd just started in a workplace where I would be given my freedom in more ways than one. Five years on, I enjoy working in an agile environment and love the collaboration that goes on between teams. It was a struggle becoming a self-managing team but with the help of my colleagues and coaches, I have adapted and thoroughly enjoy it.

Mayden: a timeline

2000   Mayden House Ltd established by Chris May and run from his attic at home. Undertaking data analytics and business case projects for the NHS.

2001   Chris M takes on his first software developer to work on some client projects.

2003   Wins contract to develop digital tools to support the National Cancer Programme.

2004   Mayden moves into its first office premises in Biddestone, Wiltshire.

Software development becomes the company's main focus.

2006   Launches news service Healthcare Today.

Wins contract to build an electronic patient record (EPR) with East London NHS Foundation Trust for IAPT pilot service.

2008   First contract win for our new iaptus EPR.

2009   Mayden wins 20 more IAPT clients.

2010   The tenth employee joins Mayden.

£1 million turnover hit.

5,000 users now active on iaptus across 40 clients.

2011 Mayden acquires its 100th client.

Employee number 20 joins.

Mayden expands into second premises in Wiltshire.

2012 Number of patients registered on iaptus hits one million.

2013 Turnover hits £2 million.

Children and young people's version of iaptus launches.

Mayden also launches bacpac for single-handed practitioners.

The 40th employee joins the business.
Whole development team goes through scrum training and sets up their first self-managing scrum team. First iaptus development sprint May 2013.

Work on Mayden Manifesto – our first attempt to deliberately work on our culture.

2014 Mayden moves into new office in central Bath.

Starts putting new way of working into daily practice.

2015 Turnover hits £3 million.

Our three middle managers move on to other things and are not replaced or covered during their absence. We decide to embrace self-management more widely.

The 50th employee joins Mayden.

Government funding awarded to launch Mayden Academy training software developers (later to be rebranded iO Academy).

2016 Organisational values identified, and workshops with each team explore their meaning.

Staff survey – poorest results on record.

Purposeful work kicks off the design of our way of working without managers at a whole-company staff day in November.

2017 Mayden ready to diversify from our core market into new markets for our products and services.

iaptus launches in Australia.

Working groups continue to design elements of our organisational scaffolding, e.g. feedback and decision making.

Executive team is disbanded in favour of work-based groups – strategy, way of working, innovation, etc.

Training delivered for the first cohort of individual coaches.

IAPT Connect 2017, our first major customer conference, is held.

iO Academy wins People's Choice Awards (SPARKies 2017 celebrating all things tech in the west of England).

2018 Mayden shares our way of working with NHS representatives through the Health Foundation's Q Community site visits for NHS Improvement specialists.

Annual turnover exceeds £4 million for the first time.

Employee number 70 joins.

Mayden moves into its fourth office, The Old Dairy, in Bath.

Winner – Development Team of the Year (UK IT Awards 2018).

2019 Turnover hits £5 million.

Now at 80 employees.

Finalist – 'Top Small to Medium-sized Undergraduate Employer' Award (NUE Awards 2019).

iO Academy wins Tech South West Bristol and Bath cluster (best tech support company).

2020 Turnover hits £6 million.

Mayden makes the Corporate Rebels Bucket List.

Whole company decamps to working from home during the global coronavirus pandemic.

We launch video conferencing within weeks to support our customers treating patients remotely.

Office fish (Swim Shady, Splash Gordon and Guppy Goldberg) take up residence at The Old Dairy then swiftly have to paddle to Aimée Tahko's house for the duration of lockdown.

Sixth best coding bootcamp globally in August 2020 for iO Academy.

2021 Turnover hits £7 million.

The 100th employee joins.

Mayden wins 200th iaptus contract.

We celebrated our 21st birthday party.

Finalists – UK IT Awards 2021.

Sixth best coding bootcamp globally for the second year running for iO Academy and highly commended for best education initiative by Tech South West.

2022 120 employees.

Turnover hits £8.5 million.

First in-person staff day since 2019!

iaptus prepares to launch into Canada and Ireland.

PART 1

Origin Stories

Chapter 1

Do you need managing?

Shifting management paradigms

Alison Sturgess-Durden

My management pin-up

I'm a manager by trade − a general manager. After graduating from university, I didn't train in law or accountancy. I chose management. In the NHS. It was tough. As well as the high-pressure working environment of a busy hospital, in my first post I found myself managing administrative staff more than twice my age with decades of experience. By the age of 25 I was promoted to general manager, one of only seven in the hospital, now with clinical personnel reporting to me too. I was on a career path, having completed the NHS General Management Training Scheme (GMTS). The NHS had bought into 'general management' in the 1980s following the Griffiths review (Griffiths 1983). By the mid-1990s when I joined, many senior posts in healthcare organisations were filled by career managers rather than health professionals who may have progressed, or fallen, into management.

There's a lot to the discipline and profession of management in its own right − operations, strategy, procurement, finance, contracts, employment law, compliance, governance and risk, information management, customer service, PR, marketing, sales and commissioning, communications, project delivery, organisational development, performance management, quality improvement... I could go on. The issue is that 'management', encompassing all these activities, is inexorably linked with *line* management. When I say the word 'manager', chances are you're not thinking of someone who manages these different kinds of *work*, you're thinking of someone who manages *people* – someone who can tell the others what to do because they are their superior. It's about the chain of command, ensuring effective management control throughout the organisation, and is the standard operating model of most workplaces. It's perfectly sensible; indeed, it's difficult to imagine what possible alternative there could be to the clear and simple system that we are so accustomed to. The NHS followed the standard model, placing professional managers in the chain of command over other staff because they were, well, managers, despite the other staff members' evident expertise. That was even when those managers had significantly less experience than the staff they were managing, as was the case with me and many of my fellow management trainees. It didn't make a lot of sense to me then. It still doesn't now.

It was somewhat improbable, therefore, that during my first year in the NHS I learned of another way. We were in the throes of a significant crisis at the hospital, and the executive management team cancelled their trip to the annual NHS managers conference to stay back and deal with the pressures at the hospital. They gave their tickets to two colleagues and me – three junior but up-and-coming women whom the team thought would be inspired by rubbing shoulders with the most senior healthcare leaders in the country. Bags packed and full of excitement, we boarded the flight to Glasgow and felt destined to be hospital executives ourselves one day. Being so keen and ambitious, we went to all the talks. That's when I first came across Ricardo Semler (see Semler 1993). In his keynote address to the conference, the youthful and charismatic business leader from Brazil wooed me with stories of Semco, the conglomerate he headed up, which had no managers. It blew my mind. I was smitten! Ricardo literally became my management pin-up. I put his picture up on my office wall as soon as I returned from our trip. But as my career got under way and I became engrossed in business-as-usual in the hospital, I forgot about Ricardo. During some office move or other (and there were many), his poster came down and never made it back up onto my next office wall.

Fast-forward 16 years, and in 2011, after a number of years in healthcare followed by a break to have my family, I found myself starting work at Mayden – employee number 20. I didn't know anything about software development and little about running a business, but I was experienced in healthcare, the sector in which Mayden operated. The company offered me the world in terms of flexible hours around my young family and the master's degree I was studying for. The job seemed like a good stopgap, an opportunity to learn how things were done in the commercial world until my children had grown up and I was able to return to my NHS management career. Little did I know that the software world's passion for how work and people are organised would lead me back to Ricardo, and that at Mayden I would learn some of the most valuable management lessons of my life.

Shifting paradigms

Let me ask you a question: do you have a manager?

And another question: do you manage other people?

One last question: do you need managing to work effectively and perform in your role?

Yes, yes, no? Thought so.

But, I hear you cry, *you* don't need managing, but I really should meet some of the people who work in your organisation!

In fact, the first thing people ask after hearing about Mayden's way of working is often, 'Ah, but what about the poor performer?' And sometimes, sadly, 'What about the bully?'. Unless your recruitment and culture are particularly challenged, I'd hope that these are what are known in software as 'edge cases' – infrequent exceptions. We've certainly had those at Mayden. One individual single-handedly changed the culture of their team, and not in a good way, the day they started working for us; it changed right back the day they left (not long after). But behind the 'what about...' question is an assumption that we need to organise workplaces as if *everyone* is one of those exceptions and needs managing, rather than working in a way that works best for everyone else who make up the majority.

The adults we employ in our organisations manage a vast array of things for themselves when they're not at work. They maintain relationships, contribute to their local communities, budget, give advice and seek counsel, volunteer, lobby for political change, deal with adversity and unforeseen circumstances and think about the future. They don't have managers making them do it or checking whether they're doing it right. They get on with it largely by themselves. So why, when they step into the workplace, do we assume that they leave their self-managing superpowers at reception? Why do we give adults a manager as if they're children in need of supervision? When you stop and think about it, it's actually quite weird. At work, the convention is to manage work by having managers who manage people to do the work. Why not cut out the intermediary and let everyone get on with just managing the work?

We are more than half a century on from Douglas McGregor's Theory X and Theory Y (McGregor 1960). It distinguished between an assumption that employees avoid responsibility and need to be controlled and coerced to work effectively (Theory X), and the opposing assumption that employees have an intrinsic interest in and are motivated by what they do (Theory Y). So much recent management thinking has been about engaging, empowering and coaching employees. Yet Theory X would appear to be more prevalent than modern managers might like to think, institutionalised in our organisational hierarchies that maintain the underlying premise that everyone needs managing.

As Philippa has already mentioned, life beyond hierarchy has been gaining attention from practitioners and academics alike for some time. Both are drawing on the experiences of companies that have gone before, further and deeper than Mayden, companies as diverse as Patagonia (outdoor apparel, USA), Favi (automotive parts manufacturing, France), Morning Star (tomato processing, USA), Buurtzorg (district nursing, the Netherlands) and, of course, Semco. Some have been around for decades. Contrary to popular belief, this is not a new management fad, and it's being used in some very large and highly regulated sectors, as these examples include.

Why Mayden works this way

For these reasons, the case for a different way of working may seem compelling in its own right. But I recall some advice we received a few years back from Brendan Martin of Buurtzorg Britain & Ireland. He counselled us not to get caught up in pursuing a flat organisational structure for its own sake, for ideological reasons, and certainly not because it seems cool and exciting. Rather, we should be careful to adopt an alternative to hierarchy only if we believe it is a better mechanism for achieving our organisation's purpose.

Mayden provides patient management software to the health sector. Our purpose is this: to change what's possible for clinicians and patients. Two of our expressed differentiators (how we set ourselves apart from others in our industry – see Zook and Allen 2011) are customer service and innovation. There was much that was wrong in our industry and how our competitors operated when we set our own purpose and differentiators, from

29

user interfaces that thwarted healthcare staff and often got in the way of patient care itself, to the length of time it took for new features in the software to be developed, with the service disruption caused by infrequent and therefore significant system upgrades when these developments were eventually deployed. We wanted to be different. When our customers needed us, we wanted to make sure they were able to speak directly to someone who could really help, who understood our product intimately and how the customer used it, and could respond to find solutions to their problems. We wanted those closest to our customers to have the tools and freedom to do what was needed to help the customer, quickly. We needed a way of organising that allowed us to respond, adapt and innovate to make sure our products and services constantly changed what was possible for our customers. These aims, ultimately, are why we decided to pursue a way of working beyond hierarchy.

Dr Ben Wright, lead clinician, Newham National Demonstration Site 2005–2010

Fifteen years ago, we were launching a new psychological therapies service as a national demonstration site for the NHS IAPT programme. I found myself in an ocean of paper. We had boxes and files of patient records stacked up and we were drowning. I was having to do the IAPT returns for the service for the national demonstration site on a spreadsheet and I knew this couldn't continue.

I was walking around an NHS conference thinking, 'What am I going to do? I am in such a hole.' I was pretty dejected when I arrived at Mayden's stand and saw that they produced software supporting cancer services. I chatted to Chris M and, on the back of an envelope, I sketched out the system I needed.

We met a few more times and worked on the opening technical specifications, which kept growing. We then had this really intensive development cycle while we produced the first iteration of the software. The developer I was working with would produce some functionality and I'd give feedback on what was working and what wasn't. I was able to review and influence the product's development along the way. To Mayden's credit, they pulled the rabbit out of the hat and produced a fantastic product.

Mayden continues to evolve iaptus in response to users' suggestions. It consistently gets 95–98 per cent satisfaction rates, which is unheard of in the clinical systems domain. It's just an amazing system that's enormously popular – and it saves lives. The volume at which iaptus enables clinicians to manage their cases means that patients don't have to wait long to be seen after they first engage with the service. It allows services to manage vast numbers of patients, tracking where they are in their care pathway and flagging how long they've been there, which makes a tremendous difference to patient safety.

I've worked with Mayden since 2006 and have found that they share our passion to give our patients outstanding care through their software. For their employees, being part of Mayden means you are making a powerful contribution to the lives and wellbeing of millions of patients.

Modern management practices emerged in the industrial age. There are many metaphors for organisations, 'machine' remaining a common one where engineering principles have been applied beyond the manufacturing process to the organisation itself (see Morgan 1986). University schools of management and management consultancies have carried out billions of pounds' worth of research and business learning and advising on how to do management better. I've studied in the former, and worked in the latter doing just that. In the relatively short time that management has been a professional discipline, thinking has changed radically. It has shifted from the mechanistic approach of F.W. Taylor's ideas for optimising efficiency in the organisational machine (Taylor 1911), to today's creative, adaptive and networked workplaces that meet the needs of customers in a world full of uncertainty and innovative possibilities. Yet in all that time one rather mechanistic feature of organisations has endured: people hierarchies. In fact, when visiting the preschool section of my local science museum, I was horrified to find an exhibit about the construction sector depicting electricians and roofers in a simple hierarchy under a site manager. Children, at such a young age, were being taught it's simply how work is organised.

For those of us who have worked in a typical hierarchy, we know they are far from that clear, far less ordered than the simple lines on the chart suggest, as this apt cartoon illustrates:

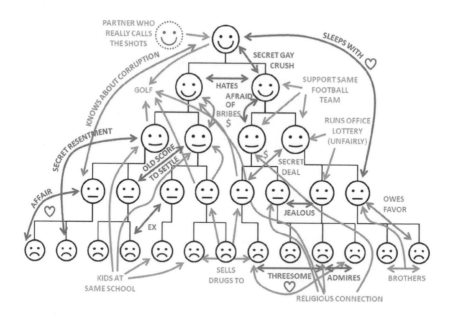

The Real Organisation Chart by Integration Training and Mark Walsh.

In the following chapters, Chris M will explain more about his own misgivings about hierarchy, but one story sticks with me by way of illustration. I was more amused than affronted the day I met a consultant pitching for business at Mayden. The meeting had been arranged on a busy day and Chris M and I were both running late. In our absence, the person from Mayden leading on the project got things under way with the consultant. When I entered the room (late), I was introduced as 'Alison, one of the directors'. From that point on, the consultant ignored my colleague who they were some way into a conversation with and proceeded to only address me. Then, when Chris M walked in some time later and was introduced as the managing director, I was duly ignored for the rest of the meeting in favour of Chris. Little did the consultant realise that the project lead was actually the most important person in the room as it was they who were closest to the problem we needed solving and would be making the decision about awarding business. Nor did the consultant realise all three of us had noticed what had happened.

Organisations are full of ever-changing humans, forming relationships that ebb and flow. They are situated in a complex world, with constant pressure to adapt and evolve in response to changing customer needs and other changes in the social, political, economic and physical environment. Nothing stays the same for long. Organisations are about continuously making, breaking and reassigning connections between people, knowledge and resources that are not necessarily distributed according to seniority. Enabling these connections is especially important if the organisation is to adapt, innovate and respond to customers, as our purpose requires us to. The fixed lines of a people hierarchy therefore seem to be from another industrial age because, well, they are. Maybe it's time to accept that and work with the complex and adaptive nature of organisations rather than continue to cling to the illusion of control hierarchies may comfort us with.

But relinquishing traditional forms of management control,

rightfully intended to maintain quality, cost, customer service and good governance, seems like an impossible risk. That is until you consider the people you are freeing up from line management control: the adults you thought competent and trustworthy enough to employ in the first place to take responsibility for all those management concerns which they are closer to than you – taking responsibility for themselves, for each other, for the business and ultimately for the customer.

Our journey into a new way of working

When Mayden started, we had no idea what kind of organisation would come to be created. As the company expanded with the roll-out of the iaptus software, we did what most companies do as they grow – we installed managers. By 2015, we found ourselves with three middle managers – one technical, one for marketing and the third for customer support. But before I reveal what happened to them, I need to rewind a little. In 2013 we were around 40 employees strong and struggling with two fundamental issues: delivering software updates on time to our customers and maintaining our organisational culture in an expanding workforce. In direct response to the first, and central to our purpose and mission for our customers, Mayden adopted scrum as an agile software development framework. I will leave our software developers to tell you about that and what it means later. Suffice to say, it turned out to be a brilliant solution to the first of our problems, delivering projects effectively. It also introduced the concept of the 'self-managing team' to Mayden, a small group of developers *facilitated* by someone called a scrum master rather than *managed* by a team leader.

Regarding the second issue, that of our culture, until then everyone had just known what it was like at Mayden. Because there weren't many of us, everyone worked closely with everyone else, including Chris M, so the culture spread by osmosis. With the number we now were, that effect was starting to fade. In order to help where osmosis was failing, I began working with everyone to define the culture more explicitly. The 'Mayden Manifesto' was crafted – a little booklet explaining our culture, including a 'credo' summarising the kind of mindset we were looking for from everyone (see Appendix section B). It was based on feedback from a series of workshops I held with teams and influenced by the agile practices being adopted by our development teams. Who knows whether it was all part of our growing pains, the mix of people we had recruited at the time, or that Chris M was right in saying that by drawing attention to the culture, we were killing it. But that deliberate exercise to define our culture and how we wanted everyone to work was shut down, and everyone was left to 'just get it'.

By this time, half the business was in a self-managing software team due to the move to scrum, and the other half (those not directly involved in developing software) were not. Then, in 2015, for one reason or another, all three middle managers moved on to something else within or outside the business. One went overseas, one on maternity leave, and the third moved to a different role within Mayden. While discussing with me what to do about the vacancies, Chris M confessed to some profound misgivings about hierarchy and middle management. He was concerned that layers of management would distance new recruits even further from the culture he aspired to maintain, and mused about whether there was another way. Was this an opportunity to work differently across the whole business, inspired by the experience our software teams were having in adopting scrum? At that moment I remembered my pin-up, Ricardo. I dashed home, dusted off my copy of his book, *Maverick*, and started reading. We didn't refill those management vacancies. Instead, we decided to pursue our journey into managing without managers, and to expand self-management across the business.

Our software teams at least had the framework of scrum practices to support them in being self-managing, while the other teams who'd lost their managers didn't even have that. The scrum teams were struggling themselves to negotiate where their self-management stopped and the directors' leadership of the organisation started. But as with the work on our culture, and taking the idea of self-managing at its word, everyone was essentially left to figure it out for themselves. It was painful. People were confused, they didn't know how decisions were made, and that meant too many decisions were left to directors, who then became a bottleneck to progress. We effectively became more top-down than ever! I recall a poster from my childhood picturing a bunch of chickens (presumably of the soon-to-be-headless variety) which read: 'Everybody thought somebody was doing it because anybody could but actually nobody was.' It seemed to sum up where we'd got to – a flat structure with no middle managers, but a distinct lack of clarity about how things got done without them.

> I think about the transition from a hierarchical company to a flat structure and Mayden's way of working with self-managed teams. In my experience of coming into a team not long after that change had happened, I think people felt the support hadn't been there or they weren't really aware of how to get the support to find the way of working... We found it hard to take it on ourselves and say: "We can change this"... I think we've made massive steps in the last few years, sometimes forwards, sometimes backwards but sometimes you have to go backwards to go forwards.
>
> **– Pat Wood, account manager**

Then we hit the wall. In 2016, we had our worst-ever annual staff survey results. They weren't terrible, but for us they were an all-time low. Even though some questions showed improvement following work we had undertaken on the areas in question, such as vision and strategy, other questions scored lower than ever,

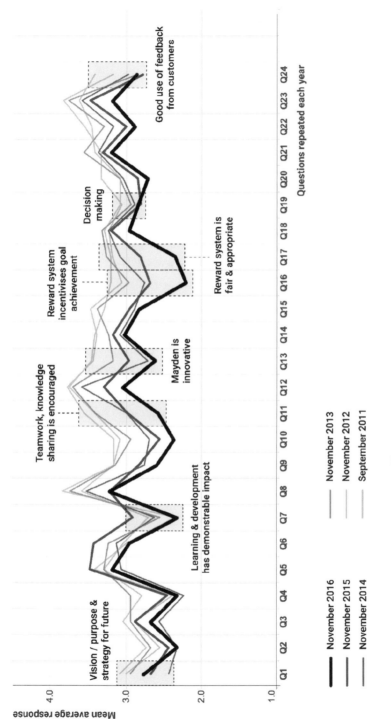

Staff Survey Results, November 2016

such as those around learning and development and our reward system, and importantly innovation and customer service.

One memorable comment left in the survey read: 'WE NEED MORE MANAGERS.' Similar comments told us the flat structure wasn't working, with teams pulling in different directions while decisions were still being made behind closed doors 'by management'.

We were in a no man's land between the disempowerment of top-down management and the ineffectiveness of an immature flat structure. Having previously decided not to work on our culture for fear of killing it by prodding it, we now had the need, and the permission, to work on our way of working. We recognised by now that if we removed the scaffolding of hierarchy, we still needed scaffolding, only of a very different kind. We were about to start construction.

We've taken inspiration and advice from many examples of this way of working, together with emerging concepts such as Teal (reinventingorganizations.com) and codified systems for managing without managers such as Holacracy (see holacracy.org and Robertson 2015). However, Mayden hasn't subscribed wholesale to any of the models out there. We decided to find our own way through what would work for us in service of our customers, hierarchy or no hierarchy. We have experimented, tried and failed and have evolved and adapted our implementation of scrum and a flat structure that works for us.

We began with our organisational values. Even before the staff survey, and continuing to sense the need for something like the credo we had tried a few years previously, we undertook some work in early 2016 to define our values and make them known to everyone at Mayden. They seemed a useful place to start without running the risk of addressing our culture directly. You'll read all about this in Chapter 5. This work naturally led us to identify all those areas of the business where we were not living our values; those were the areas we decided to prioritise in clarifying how our way of working needed to be defined and work better. This work began at a whole company staff day in November 2016. The staff survey results were presented, Chris M gave an impassioned speech about the kind of organisation Mayden needed to be, given our purpose, and everyone rolled their sleeves up and started prioritising which aspects of our way of organising without managers needed attention. Our first working groups quickly spun up after that – self-selecting groups of people from around the business looking to (re)design different organisational processes in place of line management. Early working groups included management arrangements, decision-making and feedback culture. The chapters in Part 2 will explore all of these.

And so we proceeded, mindful that if we were going to allow our employees to manage themselves, that would mean allowing them to figure out what our organisational arrangements needed to be – sometimes leaving us directors gritting our teeth and sitting on our hands while everyone took time to try, fail then break through with more impact than if we'd told them what we thought would work in the first place, and often coming up with something better in the end.

There have been times when the company has struggled with a general level of dissatisfaction among employees. The benefit of the Mayden culture is that everyone pulls together through these difficult times and helps identify and resolve the underlying issues. Not long after moving to a flat structure, there was a time when overall morale was at an all-time low (which incidentally was still high, just low for Mayden) and a number of long-term employees were not enjoying their work at the company anymore. This was identified reasonably quickly, and a lot of effort was invested in improving things. It took some time to return the company to previous levels of morale but it was a necessary process. We have ended up with stronger teams, more effective processes and an even better culture.

– Dawn Woods, product owner

Final reflections

To say it hasn't been easy would be an understatement. The pain we experienced when we left everyone to 'just get it' was replaced many times with struggles to figure out a workable alternative to hierarchy. Sometimes it was hard to convince everyone (including ourselves occasionally) that we hadn't lost the management plot. There were days when I was done, and thought it would be so much simpler to just bring back managers. We discovered how indoctrinated we all are with hierarchy – through family life and schooling to previous work experiences – and how hard it was to override such an entrenched convention. Even in challenging it in these pages I feel as if I'm leaving the house with my management skirt caught in my proverbial knickers! But we saw the fresh shoots of energy and engagement in our employees from the alternative as we remembered the way we had struggled with the pitfalls of hierarchy.

Mayden isn't trying to be radical or progressive. We're just trying to create a workplace where employees are treated like the adults they are and enjoy conditions where they can bring their best work. I think of us as rather moderate and pragmatic in what may appear to be a revolutionary way to work. For the reasons we've covered, it doesn't seem that radical to us; it seems like common sense. Maybe you can't subscribe to some of what you will read about here, and who knows if we are on the cusp of a paradigm shift in how organisations are organised. I hope we will at least cause you to question the extent of our reliance on people hierarchies, and to consider that there may be other – better – ways to organise work and workplaces.

Let me hand over to Chris M, who is going to explore this further.

Chapter 2

Why would you give away so much power and control?

A founder's story

Chris May

Beginnings

My personal journey with new ways of working began, not very auspiciously, as a postgraduate student. I was visiting a brick factory in the east of England. It was the biggest producer of bricks in the country and the whole manufacturing operation proved to be very slick until, at the end of the day, we paid a visit to the last department in the workflow: dispatch. Here we found one (very fit) middle-aged man taking bricks from the end of a moving conveyor belt and stacking them on a pallet. He was very good at it, but I quickly realised that this was what he did, minute by minute, hour by hour, day after day. It was repetitive, tedious, boring, and I remarked as much to our tour guide. I was quickly corrected. I was told that this was what he wanted to do. He apparently didn't want to think or have responsibility or ownership. The routine and rhythm provided in his role stacking bricks – and then going to the pub at the end of his shift –

was all he desired from his work day. He was fulfilled; he was happy. I was not.

Fast-forward two years. I was settling comfortably into my first proper job as an engineer at Cadbury's chocolate factory in Bournville, Birmingham (an inspiration behind Roald Dahl's delightful Charlie stories) when I was unexpectedly made line manager of the Creme Egg production line. The plant operated 24/7 in a four-shift pattern covering nights and days: four days/ nights on, four days/nights off. Shift A was underperforming compared to the other three shifts. They wanted me to find out why and implement remedial actions to bring the not-so-A-team (some 50 production workers) in line with the other production crews. For several weeks I observed how the team performed their respective operations and gradually worked out what the problem was. They were bored. The vast majority were doing the same jobs day in, day out. Whether sorting, boxing or shrink-wrapping the eggs, life for everyone on the production line had become mind-numbingly tedious. Some were taking extraordinarily long toilet breaks; others had figured out how to cheat the clocking in/out system. To alleviate the tedium, many had become remarkably innovative at avoiding doing anything productive. The answer, I decided, was to alleviate the monotony by varying the work, rotating people around the various roles so they could try different things. This would increase their interest, provide new challenges, improve teamwork, and all with the additional benefit of complete flexible cover for sickness and holidays in every part of the operation. I expected an initial drop in productivity, but believed the long-term gains would outweigh the short-term cost. Furthermore, I delegated the task of scheduling who would work where to the production staff themselves.

It was a disaster. Almost immediately, arguments broke out on the shop floor – about who should work when and where, what various machine settings should be, and the debatable competencies of colleagues. Chaos abounded and my experiment was quickly abandoned in favour of maintaining the productivity at the previous – albeit relatively low – level. I did manage to make some improvements in other ways, but never did get Shift A's output to match that of the other three teams.

What was my mistake? I have since concluded there were three. First, I am an engineer, trained to treat everything like a machine with moving parts. In this case, some of those moving parts were human, so I attempted to account for this in my assessment of the situation. But I was young and naive and underestimated the human aspects of the problem. Secondly, I believed, and still believe, in treating people how I'd want to be treated. That's a good thing; it's a fundamental tenet of building social capital with others. But it led me to assume, in my naivety, that all people were just like me. As a member of the human race, I assumed I was fairly typical in wanting autonomy. I didn't like routine and valued flexibility, which I understood had to work both ways. Once I became familiar with my work environment, I generally didn't need to be managed. I saw what needed to be done and just did it. Sometimes I was even good at problem-solving! But it turns out that people are not all like me. In fact, I'm not always like me either.

On a whole range of issues, individually we sit on a spectrum between two extremes, and the aggregation of all these factors makes each of us unique. This includes the self-motivated and the apparently not-so-self-motivated. The latter exist, of course, and can display talents and capabilities far beyond my own; they're just not good at galvanising themselves at work and need someone – a manager – to do it for them. But could this trait really apply to a whole production team? Thinking that this was the case was my third mistake. Realising now that the workforce doesn't simply fall into the polarised camps of those who need managing versus those who can organise themselves, I wonder what else might be going on. Could it be that employees' behaviours, including their ability to motivate and manage themselves, are conditioned by their environment, and not the other way round? Was I contending, unaware, with the wider organisational context in which Team A was operating that worked against them taking responsibility and thwarted my best intentions? Ultimately, did my experiment with Team A fail because I designed the new system for them instead of allowing them to design it for themselves?

Roles are varied and people are complicated, whether you're stacking bricks or packing chocolate on a production line, or a manager trying to figure out how to make the productivity of such people even better. We can all have unconscious biases and world views that we impose on others. And while it is perfectly possible for one set of humans to design the perfect operating environment for another set, the chances of designing something that is suboptimal is higher. Surely it is better to simply agree what's required and let people work out for themselves how to deliver that in a way that is best for them and the organisation?

In case you're already lost, the summary conclusions from my experiences are these. Any operation involving humans will be both unique and messy. However, most – but not all – would like autonomy in their work. Most – but not all – are perfectly capable of exercising that autonomy to manage the work themselves. Most – but not all – would be able to thrive autonomously at work if given the right conditions for them. And most – but not all – are perfectly capable of designing their work environment to provide those conditions.

Do you work to live, or live to work? Whichever end of that particular spectrum you favour, when it comes to work, the ideal for employers and employees alike is that employees are passionate about the work they do and want to excel at doing it. I believe that the culture we've created at Mayden, where employees are expected to organise themselves rather than be managed, will work for the majority of people that we could potentially employ, but wouldn't work for others who'd prefer or need to be directly managed. In other types of organisations, it might appear that those cohorts are reversed, that most need to be managed. I prefer to think that given the right working conditions – whether flat or hierarchical – most people can thrive, and if we want to bring out the passion and motivation in everyone we employ then we should design our work environment to help them flourish. I believe that means challenging some established beliefs, including some that point to the essence of our humanity. Here, then, are the seeds of ideas that grew to inspire and challenge my thinking when developing Mayden's work culture.

Evolution

In his thought-provoking book, *The Righteous Mind*, the social psychologist Jonathan Haidt (2012) describes humans today as being 90 per cent chimp and 10 per cent bee. According to evolutionary theory, as humans we share a common genetic ancestry with chimpanzees. In the tree of life, we're each twigs from the same branch and share around 99 per cent of our DNA with our evolutionary cousins. Chimps build hierarchies. In the wild, power structures form in which the strongest apes rise to the top of their local troop and a pecking order of males and females develops underneath them. It isn't all about physical strength. Chimps are highly intelligent and it's intriguing to note that the collective noun for a troop of chimps is a shrewdness. Apes aren't alone in this – many other mammals build societies with similar hierarchical power structures. Bees, on the other hand, build cooperative colonies. Each type of bee (worker, drone, queen) has a role that isn't part of a power structure. Even though there's only one queen in each colony, it's not a leadership position, but instead a unique role that happens not to be shared by any other bees. Bees work for the collective. They collaborate, rarely put themselves first, and, if necessary, are willing to die for the colony.

The percentage of chimp to bee that Haidt uses is of course

illustrative, not literal. He argues that as we've progressed, humans have found that simply winning the competition to exert power and control over other human beings isn't the end of the story. As groups increasingly competed with other groups down the millennia, the successful tended to be those who worked together, eschewing their local hierarchies if necessary, and instead promoting innovation, collaboration and cooperation to overpower and defeat the enemy. Even better when that enemy is no longer seen as such and is persuaded to become part of the collective. It transpires that an effective team is more than the sum of its parts or their individual egos (a conclusion you can see played out every season in the English Premier League where rich teams of world-class soccer players are frequently beaten by teams of players who are individually inferior but better organised). We might be genetically programmed for hierarchy, yet find that the sense of achievement of working with others towards a common goal provides some of the most rewarding experiences of our lives. This transition for us humans, from 'chimp' to 'bee', is reflected in societies that become ever more social, caring and mutually supportive as the years progress. How can we also grow our organisations like this?

Behavioural preferences

I am an introvert. While I'm mostly able to perform in a crowd when required, I find it drains me and I'll eventually need to retire to a dark and silent room to re-energise. As Susan Cain notes in her best-selling book, *Quiet: The Power of Introverts in a World That Can't Stop Talking* (2013), one third of the population shares this trait with me. The other two thirds are extroverted, meaning they gain energy from being around people and find that being alone saps their energy. This division, however, is not quite accurate; it's really a continuous spectrum along which we all sit at some point, with a bias towards one extreme or the other. People with extreme introversion or extroversion are rare. People are loosely characterised as being one or the other based on any predisposition to one over the other. On a scale of 0 to 10, where 0 indicates extreme introversion and 10 extreme extroversion, I consistently measure around two to three; very much in the introvert range, but not extreme. I share Cain's concern that workplace hierarchies tend to favour extroverts. In general, extroverts are better at making their voices heard, commanding attention and building social capital in a work setting. Introverts, on the other hand, will at times tend to gravitate away from other people, yet despite their lower levels of social energy, have equally as much to contribute.

Even so, the wider point is that a tendency towards introversion or extroversion is only one dimension in a number of behavioural preferences that we can exhibit. People are different in many ways that affect how they behave. There are many systems we can explore to discover the rest (such as Myers-Briggs, Insights, Ocean and Enneagram to name a few). What really matters is that organisations need to be designed to bring out the best in everyone. In a knowledge economy we employ people primarily for their brains, and if those brains don't get the opportunity to express themselves, then that's both tragic and wasteful for both the organisations and the individuals. So, how do we design our organisations to help everyone thrive, whatever their disposition?

The power of communities

One of the first books I turned to when exploring different ways of working was *Holacracy* by Brian J. Robertson (2015). This offers what might be the most widely known blueprint for organising without hierarchy. It usefully identifies the fundamental DNA that we need to engage with when exploring different ways of working. (Unfortunately, you can make a lot of different animals with that DNA, and the one that *Holacracy* presents as being *the* alternative to hierarchy was too prescriptive for me. But read it and decide for yourself.) I was particularly struck by a passage where Robertson talks about the productivity per capita of communities (villages, towns, cities) in relation to their size, compared to that of corporations, surmising that in the former productivity increases with size while in the latter it decreases. I will leave economists to contest the analysis, but it got me thinking about the very idea of how communities and corporations are organised differently, and how much can be achieved by the former without the conventional structures of the latter.

As Robertson reflected, cities have law enforcement, rules and procedures; you can't do anything you want. You have to pay your taxes and bills; you can't transgress a wide range of other laws designed to make the city function well for everyone and the authorities will intervene if you do. But otherwise, large populations of citizens are free to live their lives and they achieve things! Therein lies the power of community in a free society – individuals combine and interact, trade and collaborate in myriad ways without pervasive, centralised control. In companies they don't; rather, a central management bureaucracy usually grows up in proportion to the organisation's expansion. For me, this was a radical realisation. If communities of largely responsible adults can achieve so much without that, why can't our companies, also populated by largely responsible adults, operate more like communities?

The problem with hierarchies

I'm not against hierarchies in organisations in principle. But they do have inherent problems that need to be recognised. Here are a few I have experienced:

+ **The iceberg of ignorance:** Widely attributed to Sydney Yoshida (1989), one research study is purported to have found that executives in the place he studied only saw 4 per cent of the problems in the organisation, senior managers 9 per cent, team leaders 74 per cent and staff on the ground 100 per cent. Whatever the numbers are in reality, it is self-evident – and certainly my experience in organisations large and small – that as managerial layers separate groups from the work, issues and people, visibility and understanding are lost. The more layers of separation, the more this will be the case.

✦ **Information hugging:** Hierarchical structures lead to individuals climbing to the next rung of the ladder. There are fewer spaces on each rung than people on the rung below, so individuals are naturally set up to compete with each other for those limited opportunities to climb. In those circumstances, why would you help those against whom you are competing? So instead of making everything transparent, individuals are incentivised to hold on to information to gain an advantage. After all, information is power, and power is what we're trying to obtain. So, information is not shared, communication is poor, internal politics runs rife, and the only thing that's clear is a lack of transparency.

✦ **Stifling talent:** As an employer, I invest a lot of money in attracting and utilising the best talent I can find. If those brains are buried at the bottom of a multi-layered hierarchy, then the chances are I'll never hear those voices and the contributions they're able to make, not just at the level they're employed, but at any other level. As founders and leaders, we're arrogant and wilfully negligent if we allow those voices, with their brilliant ideas and insights, to be stifled.

✦ **The manager premium:** Imagine a department head has five people reporting to them. That's a fifth of their salary per report. If most of what the manager is doing is managing the others in the department, that's a hefty overhead. I'd rather spend the money expanding teams to deliver more product or service than pay people to manage other people who can probably manage themselves.

+ **The rise to incompetence:** In a hierarchy that works well, once you become proficient at your role, you'll be looking to take on the next challenge and should hopefully be promoted (to the next level). When you excel in that role, you'll be promoted again... and again. As long as you keep excelling, as you take on challenge after challenge you'll be promoted until you reach the point of your personal limitations. Known as the Peter principle (after educational theorist Laurence J. Peter), those who become promoted beyond their abilities risk becoming stuck on the highest rung they reach, in a fixed post within the rigid structure. In my experience there's nothing worse than a manager who's stuck in a role in which they're incompetent, in a hierarchy in which there's nowhere else to go.

If we recognise any of what I have said so far as presenting questions for our organisations, what can we do about it?

Conclusion

These are the seeds that forced me, as the founder of Mayden, to ask questions about whether conventional ways of working were designed to bring out the best in everyone. But where could I turn instead? It seemed at least to mean discarding the traditional hierarchical structure that would have me at the top, exercising the ultimate power and control over everyone and everything we do. But for these seeds to germinate, they needed to be planted in fertile ground. Organisational cultures don't just happen. They grow from something more fundamental. In the next chapter I'll suggest that it's an organisation's ethos that forms the roots of its culture and what that looks like at Mayden when we dig below the surface.

Chapter 3

What replaces power and control?

Ethos

Chris May

Ethos isn't something that's often talked about in business. You hear a lot about purpose and vision, mission and goals, plans and targets. Enlightened organisations have also invested time and energy defining corporate values that they hope will underpin culture which, according to a quote widely attributed to Peter Drucker, eats strategy for breakfast. I think of ethos as being in this mix somewhere, but what do I have in mind, and how does it fit in?

I see a company's ethos as the foundation on which all these other things are built. It comes from the Greek word meaning moral character. In the context of how we manage, ethos is the belief system about people – employees and customers, indeed any stakeholder – and what role they play in the life of the business; their dreams and desires, their motivations, ability and aspirations, how they naturally treat others and would themselves like to be treated. This belief system creates an attitude of mind present at the genesis of a new business venture and which has the power to influence almost everything that follows.

I believe the nature of a company's ethos is therefore an important question to ponder. I've seen at Mayden how a view of the world has fed through to the values and culture – and ultimately the more familiar construct of brand (how the organisation is perceived by those outside it). At the same time, it's difficult to create an intended work culture if the underlying ethos is in conflict with it. Similarly, a brand strategy portraying benevolence in all its various forms won't survive for long if the foundational ethos, and in turn culture, is self-serving, while a weak brand can be invigorated by taking on the character of a strong and healthy organisational ethos. Once established, the perception of a company's ethos might therefore be difficult to shake. You'll know of companies you don't like, sometimes because you've personally had a bad experience with them, or more often because of their reputation. Bad service in itself doesn't create the negative perception you might hold. Every organisation makes mistakes from time to time. It's how your complaints are dealt with that really makes the difference. And it's often in times of trial and adversity that the underlying ethos really shines through.

One of the enduring mysteries for me about an organisation's idea of ethos is that it can apply to the organisation even though it doesn't seem to apply to many individuals within it. At work, I've seen people behave in ways that would otherwise be alien to them. Equally, individuals might behave counter-culturally (in both good and bad ways) but it will not necessarily affect how the organisation is viewed as a whole. And that's really the point: when you have a single experience that's not what you expect, you view it as counter to the organisation's ethos, not that the ethos has changed. Once established, it seems ethos does have a degree of stickiness that's difficult to shift.

Ethos isn't culture but instead underpins it, providing the moral backbone by which the culture and working arrangements are supported. The behaviours, customs and practices that follow, both among employees and between employees and customers, then create the culture. So how does this look in practice, and where does an organisation's ethos come from?

Mayden's ethos

The first question is perhaps best answered using a real-life example, so let's look at Mayden's ethos. In doing so, the roots of the approach we've taken to work will become clear. Before I begin, it's worth acknowledging the intangible nature of ethos. I should mention that ethos doesn't appear in any of our company literature. In fact, this is the first time we've attempted to write it down. The very act of producing this book has caused us to dig deep into the origins of our way of working. I have long held a sense of some key beliefs – an ethos – that the company was founded on, an ethos that forms the roots from which the culture and way of working you are going to learn about in the rest of this book could grow.

I would define Mayden's ethos as characterised by the following beliefs and mindsets:

+ the golden rule
+ trust
+ organise for the majority
+ no blame
+ share the rewards
+ abundance mindset
+ flexibility
+ reciprocity
+ data driven.

I'll explain each in turn.

The golden rule

Proclaimed by Jesus of Nazareth during his Sermon on the Mount, and described by him as the second great commandment, the common English phrasing of what has become known as the golden rule is: 'Do to others as you would have them do to you.' This foundational ethic is not only present in some form in many religions and cultures, but would seem to be common sense in any decent society. The problem is that it's conspicuously absent from many workplaces. To understand why this is, we might need to be honest with ourselves as to what we believe about the motivations of the people we work for, those we work with and those who work for us. These beliefs, whether we're consciously aware of them or not, will affect our own behaviour and how we interact with our colleagues. This in turn affects the perceptions of those around us and their consequent behaviour. In this way, the golden rule – or doing the opposite – has a self-fulfilling quality. Negative beliefs promote negative behaviours where I'm not treating others as I would wish to be treated. That drives a negative response and a downward spiral that can rapidly permeate an organisation, creating a culture of disrespect, mistrust, fear and low morale. The opposite is also true – positive attitudes and behaviours towards others, which result in treating others as you would wish to be treated, will engender positive responses and evolve a cycle of beneficence, creating an organisation that's emotionally mature. The golden rule applied at Mayden means we have an underlying belief that people can and should respect and look out for each other and themselves. By adopting this core maxim and treating individuals accordingly, it turns out, in my experience, to be *mostly* true.

Trust

The elephant in the room here is trust. Trust, or rather a lack of it, is the primary reason, I believe, why many organisations have ended up where they are: leaders not trusting and therefore seeking to control subordinates, and subordinates not trusting their leaders. For both parties, trust is built on the consistent demonstration of integrity and capability. We need to have confidence that the people we work for and with are competent to perform their roles and have the organisation's best interests at heart. If we don't trust someone, is it because we think they're incompetent or simply untrustworthy? One danger is that the two are conflated. That is, we can act as if we don't trust someone's integrity when really it's their competence we're concerned about, or vice versa. No one is perfect, but too often it's the shortcomings in the integrity of highly capable leaders – those who are supposed to represent our role models – that let them down, even as they behave in ways that demonstrate a lack of trust in their subordinates. I believe people generally know when they're behaving with a lack of integrity, but it's a shame when they then assume that everyone else must be too. Capability, on the other hand, isn't in short supply. Most people have the potential to be excellent at their roles if given the freedom and responsibility. Returning to the golden rule, how do people like to be treated? Mostly, they like to be trusted: trusted to be conscientious, trusted to be competent, trusted to organise themselves. Everything follows from that.

So, should employees be trusted? Trust takes time to build, and we therefore need to decide our initial default setting. Do I assume trustworthiness and hope to have it confirmed? Or do I assume that people cannot be trusted until they prove that they can be, by which time my lack of trust has probably already lost them to cynicism? Our initial attitude risks becoming a self-fulfilling prophecy; whatever we expect is often what we get. Happily, in my 20-plus years at Mayden, when I've chosen to trust a colleague and adopt this ethos from the outset, I've found them *generally* to be trustworthy. In this respect, it has to be the organisation that makes the first move. New recruits to Mayden often arrive from organisations where trust was in short supply, and they will be tainted by their previous experiences. They will have researched – and hopefully experienced – Mayden's culture during our recruitment process, and will have entered Mayden with a lot of goodwill. But the organisation will need to confirm that it's worthy of their trust, and this is largely achieved by demonstrating that it trusts them. If people can be trusted, you then have to question the extent to which you need to manage them.

Organise for the (competent, hard-working) majority

Mostly true? *Generally* trustworthy? The two beliefs described so far – adopting the golden rule and an assumption of trust – are all very well, but life has taught us that this isn't how *all* people behave. But if it can be true of most – the competent and hard-working employees who make up the majority of the workforce – why do we organise our workplaces as if *everyone* is like the few who don't behave that way? As well as the line management control, in previous workplaces I've been in I've seen the volume of HR policies and procedures guiding everyone in how to behave at work as if no one knows how to. I've found reality to be very different, to the extent that, as you'll read in Chapter 11, I regularly challenge how much 'HR' we really need at Mayden. HR policies provide boundaries. They rightly protect employers from employees who are not working well, and protect employees from employers that don't respect them. This is extremely important. Most of us, though, rarely have to resort to an HR policy or employment law to resolve an issue. All those company handbooks we were issued when we started our new job most likely won't have seen the light of day since. We're human, the world is complex, and people sometimes have to be reminded to do the right thing. But that doesn't mean we have to design our whole culture, and overload it with procedures, as if everyone was like the few who experience difficulty. Most of the time most of us don't.

Those for whom this way of working doesn't work may leave by choice or otherwise. No organisation can suit everybody. I've read of companies that have switched to flat organisational structures losing around 15 to 25 per cent of their staff for whom it did not suit. For Mayden, we didn't make an overnight switch to self-management, and the period of time in question was complicated by other factors (including an office move), but an estimate of those who initially struggled with the new way of working and moved on was probably less than 10 per cent.

No-blame culture

Mayden works primarily for our country's state health service. The UK's world-famous NHS is an institution that's nationally treasured. We're privileged to support the front-line staff who serve their patients tirelessly. Because it's part of our public sector, funded by taxpayers, accountability is high. When mistakes are made, heads often roll. Over the years this has resulted in the NHS being more conservative; managers' freedom or willingness to take risks and innovate, particularly at a local level, has been stifled. This is somewhat inevitable – and necessary – in an organisation where patient safety is paramount, but it has translated into management practices. Whatever the latest management restructuring of the NHS brings, it is essentially one big hierarchy, from the secretary of state at the top to the healthcare assistants, hospital porters and administrators at the bottom. The constant pressure exerted from the top feeds down to the front line and is felt most by those in direct caring roles – hardly a recipe for empathic care when the carers need as much empathy as the patients they care for. In the middle sit layer upon layer of commissioner and provider management teams, constantly being reconfigured, whose role, it often seems, is to pass the pressure up and down the hierarchy, alleviating it where they can or adding to it. When things go wrong the most common word we hear is accountability, which in context generally means blame. Why use one syllable when six will do? Contrast this with the Buurtzorg model of community nursing in the Netherlands (see buurtzorg.com), where 10,000 nurses work in 850 self-managing teams, resulting in enviably high client satisfaction ratings within the healthcare sector, while also regularly achieving the accolade of best employer and with lower operating costs. Surely a reason to sit up and take notice?

Facebook once had a motto to 'move fast and break things'. In the 21st century, 'disruption' has become a byword for creativity and innovation on steroids. Successful organisations are tending to be those that break new ground, particularly in technology. For this to happen, Facebook's teams needed to be allowed to move fast and break things without adverse consequences, and they did. Many innovations never saw the light of day. Of those that did, many more never gained traction in the marketplace and got canned. It was evolution in rapid time – the fittest technology survived – and the fear of failure was removed in order to allow the best ideas to flourish. As a company operating in this space, albeit in healthcare, we can't afford to stifle innovation. Although our clinical safety and information governance programmes are substantial, our research and development agenda is equal to them and annually represents around 15 per cent of our turnover. While ensuring we do it safely, we need to be able to try things and make mistakes. When we do, we need to analyse what went wrong, learn from it and make sure it doesn't happen again. What we've never done is apportion blame when that happens. As long as mistakes aren't intentional, or result from repeated failures to learn lessons from past mistakes, there are no reprisals. No one gets sacked.

What are the consequences of this? First, we know that people own up to mistakes even when they would have got away with them and no one would have found out. At company retrospectives, the gatherings in which we reflect on what happened at the end of a project or after a problem had arisen, individuals often queue up to take the blame when something has gone wrong. Retrospectives are designed to be a safe space, and there's something cathartic about being able to say 'I screwed up here'. In fact, at one company staff day at the local racecourse, one employee took the microphone to tell the story of a mistake he was involved with, and inadvertently broadcast it to the whole of the surrounding area via the venue's outside public address system which had been turned to the wrong setting! Second, teammates run towards a colleague who's created a problem rather than flee in the opposite direction. The level of peer support and mutual concern, and the willingness and desire to put something right – even at personal cost late at night or over a weekend – has brought tears to eyes on many occasions.

If you're afraid that you'll be blamed for a mistake that might lead to career-limiting reprisals, and if you sense your peers may even be waiting for you to make an error as you compete with each other for rungs on the hierarchy, you'll naturally adopt the human response of playing safe, keeping your nose clean and your head down... and the world won't come to benefit from your creative brilliance. A no-blame culture was etched into the ethos of Mayden from the beginning. The benefits derived from this simple tenet have been substantial – levels of innovation, openness and an absence of internal politics that are rarely experienced in the corporate world. If employees are not working in fear, that has to be the first step to freeing them to innovate and helping them shine. Paradoxically, the absence of blame, and the culture shift that follows, actually makes the organisation less risky overall. We will explore all these ideas further in Chapter 13.

Everyone should share in the rewards of success

If anyone were to ask me how our way of working could be summarised in a single phrase, it would be this: we want people to behave as if they own the place! Not in the pejorative sense, of course, but rather to have an ownership mindset because it's from this that autonomy, responsibility, community, creativity and risk management naturally appear. When we do own things – such as houses or cars – these things generally follow.

You may have shopped in a John Lewis store at some stage and noticed that there's something different about the quality of interaction and service from the staff compared with similar department stores. It can be subtle, but it's there, and it makes a big difference to how we perceive our shopping experience. Customers haven't shopped at John Lewis for years just because of their historical commitment to being 'never knowingly undersold', but because the service they receive exceeds their expectations and encourages them to return to the store again and again. This quality of service is embedded into the John Lewis culture and it stems from a deeper ethos, the outworking of which is that all John Lewis employees are 'partners'. In other words, they share in the ownership of the company simply by working there, and share in the rewards of success through an annual profit share. That will be helping drive their attention to customer service and satisfaction.

Most organisations hold the view that staff are rewarded for their time and effort through their salaries. Some may add in performance bonuses. It's still rare for employees to hold shares in the company they work for (in the UK there are 15,000 shares schemes out of 5.6 million companies and partnerships – that's just less than 0.3 per cent – see HMRC 2022 and BEIS 2021). Where share schemes do exist, they're often set up for the chosen few at the top of the shop. Indeed, when we initially tried to commission work from a specialist accountant to set up Mayden's share scheme, the contract was declined on the basis that we wanted all staff to be included; they were only used to implementing share schemes for up to half a dozen 'key people'. Employees at Mayden haven't always possessed share options; it's a relatively recent addition to our wider reward strategy, but it didn't seem right to expect people to behave like owners if they actually weren't. It was something we corrected and now all employees are eligible to join the scheme after two years. In all honesty, it's still unclear whether this has made a huge difference to the mindset of most individuals, but it has certainly encouraged a number of good people to stay when they might otherwise have left to pursue other opportunities.

Abundance mindset

This is a trickier concept to explain but is fundamental. It's about behaving as if the success has been achieved and the rewards have arrived, long before this has actually happened. It's an attitude of mind and generosity of spirit that allows us to think big and not be constrained by, well, small-mindedness. Our horizons are far away; we're not looking at the end of our noses. We're focusing on the big picture, not getting bogged down in minutiae that really don't get us anywhere and add no value. It doesn't mean that we all go out and spend lots of money we don't have. Far from it. But we act as if we believe the rewards from our efforts will come. It's about optimism and taking a long-term view. We've all experienced organisations that exhibit an apparent meanness of spirit and we probably also considered that it was counterproductive. Are you stuck using a slow computer because the company can't afford a new one when it's clear you'd be more productive if you could purchase a new machine? Do you have two mice attached to your workstation because only the right button works on one and only the left button works on the other? (I don't know if this example posted on social media is entirely true, but I would not be surprised!). Cost control is important in many settings, but it's often short sighted and the wider, usually negative, implications of austerity, if that's what it is, can be lost. If austerity or meanness is apparent in the underlying ethos of the company, it will be experienced at every turn.

What goes around comes around. It's both experienced and

reflected by employees and the spiral only goes in one direction: downwards. After all, why should someone stay 10 minutes after 5 pm to finish something if they haven't been given a computer that is fit for purpose and has enabled them to finish the work in normal time? We'll talk about our approach to cost control later (essentially, we don't do it, at least not as you might expect), but for now the point has hopefully been made.

It isn't just the impact on employees that matters. The presence or absence of an abundance mindset directly affects our customers' perceptions of us too. Do we have a can-do attitude? Are we willing to go the extra mile? Are we willing to be flexible when it's clear that's what's needed to solve a client problem? Do we let our customers try before they buy rather than tie them into a long-term contract they can't get out of when they discover what they've bought will not help them as they'd thought it would? Do our products or services offer them greater value and benefits than they expected? Do we exceed their expectations? In short, do we act as if the world is full of opportunity and there's more than enough to go round, or do we harbour a perception of scarcity, where my gain is your loss (and vice versa)?

Having an abundance mindset is inextricably linked to taking a long-term view. Often, the choices we make can have far-reaching implications that we don't foresee. While austerity might address costs in the short term, it may prove counterproductive in the longer term. Employees living in an environment of austerity won't be encouraged to stay. Just one person leaving a thriving team for bad reasons can destabilise its productivity significantly, while the costs of recruiting and onboarding their replacement can be substantial. Weighed against the removed benefits that caused the destabilisation in the first place, it rarely works in austerity's favour. Similarly, the commercial world has learned that loss leaders can create future prosperity. Going the extra mile for your customers now – even at the expense of creating a short-term loss – often has long-term benefits that more than justify the investment.

Unfortunately, many sectors, including our public sector, operate on very short-term and sometimes politically driven horizons where even longer-term strategies don't survive more than a year. Constantly chasing short-term results means we're taking a short-term view, and we can entirely miss the bigger picture. Paying the price now in order to achieve a longer-term benefit may often be the better path to take, but is not always available. In any case, it's hard to prove. Consequently, having an abundance mindset is largely an act of faith.

Flexibility

Closely linked to abundance (and trust) is flexibility. It comes from the same mindset. While abundance is a general attitude that's broadcast widely, flexibility focuses more on individuals and how their needs may differ from each other. Some of the examples above could apply equally here but, using our example of the 9 to 5 regime common in many organisations, if we need an employee to occasionally stay late, we should also allow them occasionally to arrive late or to leave early. Flexibility can take many forms because it's about what an individual needs, and we're all different. That said, it makes no sense to micromanage every individual's comings and goings, so adopting some overall guidelines that allow all employees to determine for themselves what's reasonable can be helpful.

Here's an example. The daily commute can be a grind, especially at rush hour. Driving into Bath, where Mayden is based, can literally take three times longer during peak traffic periods than off peak. We haven't ever wanted our employees to spend their time sitting in traffic queues, but historically we've needed them to be in the office together so we can hold those all-important meetings. The problem is compounded by the fact that peak traffic differs depending on which direction you are coming from. From the outset we established core office hours between 10 am and 4 pm and allowed staff to arrive any time up to 10 am and leave any time from 4 pm to suit them, as long as they fulfil their hours. One guideline provides flexibility for myriad individual circumstances. There are lots of ways in which flexibility can be built into the culture of an organisation. Working patterns are the biggest area, and a willingness to consider variations in this regard is key to recruiting and retaining many staff, especially those with children or other carer responsibilities. Flexibility around inclusion and engagement is another. Some staff are perfectly comfortable expressing their views in meetings, while others prefer written communication. Providing options that allow for all preferences will achieve the highest levels of contribution.

Reciprocity

Organisations, however, perform best when there's give and take on both sides. Flexibility that's all one-sided runs the risk of building resentment that can ultimately poison a culture or lead to disengagement or conflict. Ultimately, offering flexibility within an organisational culture only works if there's a willingness to reciprocate. For example, while we try to maintain our working hours within the 8 am to 6 pm window, we do this in the context of running cloud-based software systems that need to be supported 24/7, 365 days a year, not just in the UK but also on the other side of the globe. Occasionally, things go wrong out of hours. If our teams weren't willing to respond to these incidents, no matter how unsociable the hour, our reputation would suffer considerably. Rarely have people had to work through the night, but it has happened. If anything, it could be argued that the company needs staff who are occasionally willing to work extended hours even more than the staff need flexibility from the company. Flexibility and reciprocity are two sides of the same coin.

Data driven

It's amazing, in the 21st century, how many organisations are still driven by HiPPOs – the highest-paid person's opinions, the loudest person in the room, politics (internal or external) or short-term commercial targets, even when the data is screaming at managers to take a different course. At Mayden, we actively encourage our customers to use the data they collect through our software to improve health service efficiency and outcomes for patients. We furnish them with all kinds of analytical tools and dashboards to support this agenda, and we invest just as much resource in helping customers to gain insights from their own data in our systems as we do in helping them to collect the data in the first place. So it would be hypocritical if we didn't run our own organisation in the same way. To that end we gather data on everything that might be useful in helping us measure performance or make sound decisions. This includes a range of quantifiable metrics, but also some softer, subjective temperature checks of how we're doing across all aspects of our organisation. The first question we ask whenever we face a difficult decision: what data do we have and what is it telling us?

These are just a few of the themes that I think define Mayden's ethos. No doubt there are others. Mayden's ethos can probably be summarised as trying to make the company work for the employees and the work they are trying to do for our customers rather than against them. It would be disingenuous to claim that we get it right all the time, or that we're always consistent, but the intent is there. Everything that you'll read in the rest of this book is built on this fundamental belief system about the relationship between the employees and the organisation we all work for. Though mostly unspoken and unseen, it forms the roots from which a way of working has been able to grow, where people are trusted to manage themselves.

Where does ethos come from?

On to the second question I posed earlier. Though ethos can seem intangible at times, it doesn't just happen. It must come from somewhere. Given how enduring and influential I've suggested it can be, it's worth considering its origin. In a small business the source is usually the leadership, most often the founders. The annals of corporate failures are replete with examples of businesses sunk by intransigent founders who were simply unable to shift their mindset, even when morale was at rock bottom, the business was collapsing and they were surrounded by colleagues pleading with them to adopt a different path. If a company's ethos is difficult to shift once it's established then even more so is the ethos of a founder on a mission, whether it's to change the world or simply to make lots of money. Here we uncover a crunch issue: ego, more specifically the inflated or fragile ego of some bosses. In imposing the belief system and attitudes of one individual on the whole organisation, driving or permeating its culture, brand and strategy, an unhealthy ego, if it can't be dislodged, will create problems.

I recognise that much of the ethos I've described at Mayden reflects my personal beliefs and world view, so haven't I done just that? The difference is that this ethos I describe demonstrates that I don't believe I have all the answers. If I believe the company should allow its employees to create for themselves a working environment where they can be fulfilled and productive, with all the flexibility and freedom that comes with it, and that often they may know better than me, as founder I have to step aside and allow it to happen. I have to believe that the company is best served by my ceding control, and I have to do it willingly, not through gritted teeth. It's hard; the 18th-century mill owner, as Bruce Daisley refers to it in *The Joy of Work* (2019), is in many of us bosses. I see it in myself sometimes, even with these beliefs I hold.

I think the seeds of the flat structure were already there. We just didn't know what to call it, we didn't formalise it, it didn't have a name, but it was already: solve your own problems, figure things out, take responsibility for that. If you see a job that needs doing, just dive in. That's pretty much how we approached everything. It was just part of the ethos of the company.

   – Claire, product owner

Conclusion

In an organisational context, ethos – the beliefs we hold about people and work – is injected into the DNA of an organisation from the outset. Once established, it's difficult to shift. As the company and its reputation grows, it attracts talent with similar mindsets who then perpetuate the ethos. It's the acorn from which a whole tree of culture, working arrangements and eventually business constructs, such as product capabilities and brand, evolves – in the case of Mayden, everything you're going to be reading about in the pages that follow. As the founder of Mayden, I've decided to give away power and control to the employees in the belief that the organisation that will evolve from this will be greater than anything I could have designed myself. This will happen as individuals learn to seize their autonomy and use it to collaborate with their colleagues in the pursuit of our purpose and vision. All that raw talent is not completely unfettered – there has to be scaffolding to hold it together, as we will see in later chapters. But in removing the constraints that a rigid management structure often brings, I have seen how individuals flourish, and believe the organisation thrives even more as a result.

   One day it's likely that Mayden will be bought by a bigger fish: that's the eventual destiny of many successful small businesses. It's on that day that Mayden's ethos will face its biggest challenge. If the ethos fails to live up to that challenge, it's possible that everything you'll learn about here might collapse like a house of cards, and that the future organisation you encounter will be unrecognisable from the one described in these pages. It might be better; it might be worse. But that's why we've taken the time to document our journey. It's my fundamental belief that organisations in the future will increasingly be modelled on similar principles to those we have pursued, and that this needs to become the norm and not the exception.

So it's at this point that I cede control of this book about the company I founded to those who have made it happen. The chapters that follow contain their stories and are mostly written by them.

Chapter 4

What has agile got to do with it?

It's all about the people

Rob Cullingford, with Ruth Waterfield and Dave Bould

'Shhhh... I can't hear myself think.' That sentence, repeated often, epitomised the Mayden development team in early 2012 when I (Rob) first arrived. It wasn't that the team was boisterous, unruly or particularly noisy; rather that a few established members of the team preferred to work in silence. Any conversation that broke the silence was met with a frown or a verbal reprimand. As a newcomer to the company, I found it strange to be so aware of how loud my mouse was clicking and that my space bar reverberated around the office like a thunderclap. The regular calls for quiet had helped to create an environment where developers largely planned, architected, problem-solved and coded on their own. People weren't inclined to share ideas, voice opinions or ask questions. It was heads down and get on with your own work. As developers joined the team, they started working individually on separate areas of the system, which further deepened silos of knowledge. Our operations director, Chris E, remembers: 'Tasks were micromanaged. I'd give jobs to individuals, they gained skills in that one area, became specialists, and then were given more of the same work.'

From my perspective, much of the micromanagement was about trying to determine how each individual was progressing with their project, when they'd be available to do the next piece of work and who'd have the knowledge and skills to do it. The result was we had too much work-in-progress for long periods of time, things not getting finished, and some developers with a large backlog of work while others didn't have enough. Trying to let the company's customers know when work might be started or completed was a difficult exercise. Chris E was telling customers they could have reports, but that was followed up with a different kind of conversation in the office with a developer. It went something like this:

Chris E: 'Hey Dave, how are you getting on?'

Dave B: 'Well, I've got three months' worth of reports stacked up already. Do I stop what I'm doing or does this just get tacked on to the end?'

Chris E: 'Can anyone else do this work?'

Dave B: 'Well, no, only I know how to do reports, and actually Rob can't do this work because then letters won't get done, which are also important, and Louis has to do the care pathways.'

The silos were blocking us and stopping other work getting done, and the development team were becoming aware of their organisational limitations. Dave B was the only one who worked on and knew about the reports system, so what happened when he went on holiday? No one else had the specialist knowledge to look after the project while he was away, so it simply stopped. We found ourselves in the position of not quite having the skills coverage or resilience we would have liked. People were also being affected on a personal level, with the lack of variety leading to boredom and, for some, a drop in morale. The team would gather at the start of each day in Chris E's office to run through what we were all working on and how we were progressing. It was essentially the same conversation, every day. Dave B would still be working on reports, Rob on letters, and Louis would be plugging away at the care pathway.

As was common practice in our industry at the time, we accumulated and deployed new features and system updates to our customers every few months. The magnitude and complexity of the changes meant that we would go through lengthy change management processes with our customers, and they weren't benefiting or receiving the value as quickly as we wanted. Some of the team had the desire to improve our software engineering practices but often felt that they didn't have the time, space or the influence to make changes.

You might think I'm painting a pretty poor picture of life at the time in the Mayden development team more than a decade ago. However, the reality was that as the company grew rapidly with the roll-out of the IAPT programme, from a small start-up to a bigger team with many more customers, a talented and dedicated group of people had drifted into a way of working that was starting to hinder their own progression and the delivery of value to our customers. We didn't realise it at the time, but it was also out of step with the underlying ethos Chris M held for the kind of organisation Mayden should be. Some of the less experienced developers didn't have much of a voice. Their opinions and ideas, which were trying to take us in the right direction, sometimes weren't valued as highly as they might have been. They were either not listened to or quickly dismissed by the more established or dominant members of the team.

In stark contrast to the silence while we were at our desks, conversations in the kitchen were excellent and full of life. We'd end up discussing our work at lunchtime: 'I've got this problem; how do I go about solving it? How would you solve it?' We began to wonder why we weren't doing this at our desks. It was in those conversations that I realised we had some brilliant people on the team. I certainly believed something needed to change, and most members of the development team and the wider organisation started to think the same. As the company grew and gained more customers with more demands, the problems that we as a team were aware of came into even sharper focus. We knew change was necessary; we just didn't really know what that change should look like.

Let's give scrum a go

Whenever we met up socially, my good friend Paul Goddard from Agilify would often mention the scrum framework, encouraging me to attend one of his training courses. I had no idea what he was talking about. I didn't know what scrum was and, if I'm honest, I didn't really want to know. I'd always worked in traditional development teams and organisations, or in small consultancies. I hadn't been exposed to scrum or any other agile methodologies in my day-to-day work. However, having worked at Mayden for 10 months and being eager to find a different approach, I finally relented and decided to attend one of Paul's events. I can honestly say that was a lightbulb moment for me. As well as being enjoyable and fun, I could see how the agile values and principles (set out in the Agile Manifesto and the relatively light-touch framework of scrum; see Chapter 1 plus Appendix section A for a summary of both) could be applied to our work at Mayden. It looked as if it could help us to function more effectively as a team and improve our delivery of software. Why hadn't I known about this? Why didn't I listen to Paul sooner?

I returned to work and evangelised about the epiphany I'd had to my fellow developers and the wider organisation. The majority of the developers were sold on the idea, keen to try something different, and the directors could see the benefits that scrum could bring us. Chris M invited Paul to the office for a chat. The directors acted decisively and swiftly by funding the entire development team to go through a training course. It happened so quickly, but perhaps that shows just how ready many people were for change, to try something new and different. Fresh from our training, we formed our first scrum team. My fellow developers chose me to be their scrum master and off we went with our first sprint.

First scrum team, sprint planning session 2013

An immediate impact

Seeing as this is a chapter about agile, you're probably expecting me to spend the rest of it waxing lyrical about how amazing agile is for the delivery of software projects; that overnight we started delivering 'twice the work in half the time' (Sutherland 2014). Well, if you'll permit me, I will do so briefly, as we did see improvements to many of the practical issues we'd been experiencing.

A year after we adopted scrum, Chris E reflected that 'the move to scrum is the single most productive change we've made in Mayden's history'. It wasn't that productivity increased because we were all individually producing more; it was due to the smoother flow of work through the team. Scrum enabled us to work on the highest priority item as a team rather than many different priorities at the same time as individuals. There was no longer too much work in progress before things got finished, which enabled us to deliver value to our customers much sooner and more regularly. We were learning about our capacity and what we were able to achieve in each sprint, which gave a greater degree of predictability for what we could deliver and when to our customers. The two-week cadence chosen for our sprints, and the increased transparency enabled by the scrum framework, meant that we could ask ourselves this: 'What have we produced as a team during these past two weeks and where are we up to with our longer-term goals?' All of this meant that the acute capacity planning problems based around individuals and projects largely disappeared. We also worked hard at improving our resilience as a team. We started problem solving together, using pair and mob programming (software engineering practices where two or more gather around a single computer to design, code and review), which gradually broke down our silos of specialisation as we shared our knowledge and skills with each other.

Scrum really shone a light on the activities we could improve upon. It showed that we weren't as good as we wanted to be at breaking down work into smaller, releasable items, at estimating how much effort would be required and then releasing a feature when it was finished. It would have been easy to blame scrum for highlighting our weaknesses, but it was actually doing its job. Ron Jeffries, one of the signatories of the Agile Manifesto, tweeted: 'Scrum doesn't fix your problems. Scrum shows you your problems. You're supposed to fix the problems.' (@ronjeffries) At times that was tough, but it was about putting that uncomfortable feeling to use and asking ourselves 'How can we get better at these things?' For example, we used the scrum concept of a 'definition of done' to keep ourselves accountable for the quality of work we were producing. It's easy for a developer to simply say 'I've finished', but a common understanding of what 'finished' or 'done' means (tested, peer-reviewed, etc) enabled us to ask each other, 'Does it meet our definition of done?' If the answer was that it hadn't been tested yet, that meant it wasn't done!

As you can see, introducing scrum brought about some much-needed improvements to how we were 'managing the work' and the benefit it brought to our customers. There is a huge body of literature out there that explains and expands on the benefits of adopting agile and using the scrum framework. Take a look at the reading list I've provided (see page 280). However, what I'd like to concentrate on in the rest of this chapter is what I feel is the biggest, most important change brought about by adopting scrum. It was something we didn't plan for, expect or predict, and that was the change in the people and the company culture.

Autonomous teams

Scrum specifies, and agile principles more generally advocate, that teams should be self-managing. What this meant for us was learning as a team how to take responsibility and then be accountable for our decisions relating to our team, our processes and our work. After all, we're the people doing the work, so we're best placed to make decisions about how to organise ourselves to deliver that work. It wasn't an easy process; it was often messy and uncomfortable. Some people didn't need an invitation to share their ideas and opinions. Others found it a struggle, but as they grew in confidence, they shared suggestions about how we could change things for the better. Every single person has a voice and a valued opinion and is able to contribute and effect change, not just managers. This climate where individuals can feel included and have a sense of belonging is one of the biggest legacies created by the adoption of agile ways of working. There were people in the team who'd been really quiet, and who had, seemingly happily, sat in the corner and barely said a word for two years, just working away on their project. Suddenly, they had an opportunity to air their opinion, and the transformation was amazing!

Autonomy doesn't mean individuals doing whatever they like because anything you do will have an impact on your teammates. If you 'go rogue', your teammates are there to hold you to account. A team has collective responsibility for its decisions rather than individuals holding that responsibility. When an idea is shared, people around you can (and have a responsibility to) poke, prod, prompt and collectively shape those thoughts, so that the results are well beyond what you could have achieved alone.

I remember a time when individuals had to run many technical decisions by the technical lead, asking for their approval on each small implementation choice. It was becoming increasingly jarring when many of the development team didn't agree with the decisions the tech lead was making. We realised that having a single person in charge of all technical decisions wasn't working. Over time, the technical lead moved away from development to other areas of the business and the rest of the development team started to figure out how to move forward in a more collaborative way, learning that we work better when we make decisions together rather than relying on a single lead or manager.

Our team at Mayden has been described as 'aggressively social'! In contrast to many software companies, the spaces in which our development teams work are often busy with people talking and working through problems together on whiteboards and pairing up on tasks. We believe that no matter how good someone is at their role,

*it's always better when we work together. The end result
is something that has been built by a group of people who
think differently to each other, leading to a higher-quality
solution, which continues to be improved via multiple
incremental releases. It's given us an incredible reputation
with our customers.*

Dave B, software developer

One of the agile principles is to 'build projects around
motivated individuals. Give them the environment and support
they need, and trust them to get the job done.' (agilemanifesto.
org/principles.html) We weren't given a new environment, but
rather we took the liberty of creating our own environment and
turning ourselves, our workspace and how we worked into what
we wanted it to be, rather than someone else's view of what they
thought it should be.

Holding the space

I use the term 'we' on many occasions in this chapter: 'we want'
or 'we were creating' or 'we started to', as that reflects the nature
of being part of a team and working together; it was and is a
collective effort and no one person was in charge. But how do
you do this in practice? How do you have the conversations
that are needed and decide on what changes to make or which
direction to go in? Over the years, I've often seen that when
you put a group of people together without anyone in charge,
it doesn't take long for one person to step forward and assume
command, even if they don't really want to. They do this because
someone has to take control, otherwise it would be chaos, right?
Not necessarily, though teams do benefit from someone whose
role it is to *facilitate*, to make sure that the interactions between
everyone in the group are what decide the group's actions, rather
than one person's opinion dominating. When we first set off as a
scrum team, this was part of my role as the scrum master, and

it continues to be part of my role to this day. I'm not a manager, I don't tell the team what to do, but I create and hold the space that enables the team. Natural leaders will always emerge in a group, but it's about making sure the conversation highlights more than just the strongest or most experienced voices in the room.

It has been my experience that a team will naturally want to improve, to be more effective at how they work, interact and communicate with each other and the wider organisation. Collectively, however, they are unsure how to go about making the changes needed or state that they're too busy or too stressed to even think about making improvements. This mindset tends to persist when looking to improve is a sporadic exercise and not one that's built into a team's routine. We talk about continuous improvement, but to do this means regularly setting aside time to improve so that it becomes part of the culture of a team. Helping create this culture is also part of my role, advocating for what's sometimes seen as a brave or counterproductive decision to slow a team down in order to create the time and space for them to pause, reflect and explore how they're working. It's about celebrating what's working well and determining what actions to take to become more effective. Scrum prescribes a specific event called a retrospective, which occurs at the end of every sprint, for a team to do exactly that. This routine has become established and valued across the development teams and the wider organisation. Making incremental adjustments, experimenting and testing as you go, can produce powerful and transformative results.

The key ingredient, if any substantive change is going to take place, is trust. Not only does a team need focused time, but you also need to build a safe space where trust levels are high. One of the quickest ways for a team to learn to trust is to be vulnerable with each other, but this can be difficult for some people, especially those from a marginalised group. As a scrum master doing the facilitating and coaching, I've often made myself vulnerable in order to show the team that it's OK to do the same and so encouraging others to bring them into the conversation. Only when trust is established can real issues be fully brought into the open and be dealt with honestly, sharing what's not working or what has gone wrong while knowing that you'll be able to have an open conversation. I'm part of the team so I'm equally responsible for the delivery of work and I share the same experiences day to day, but I also need to be able to take a slightly zoomed-out, more holistic view of the team, in order to help them identify dysfunctions and patterns over time. It's about coaching individuals and the team as a whole by listening and reflecting back to empower the team.

What we work on and why

As previously mentioned, when we first adopted scrum, we worked on the highest priority item, the number of pieces of work in progress was dramatically reduced and we were able to get valuable software in our customers' hands sooner. However, as we grew as an organisation and our number of customers increased, maintaining a simple, clear priority became more difficult. This is where the role of the product owner in scrum is key, someone who is dedicated to maximising the value of the product to customers and determining what we work on and why.

Here, Claire reflects on her emerging role of becoming our product owner:

Having previously worked in customer support, I had a good feel for what our customers needed and wanted, and what frustrated them when using iaptus. As I began producing user stories for the development team – descriptions of problems that need solving – I started questioning our choice of things that were (and weren't) being done, bringing my knowledge of the customers' perspective and how X, Y and Z would be really good for them. I started involving a wider group of stakeholders to figure out what I should prioritise. I wasn't looking for someone to tell me what to do; instead I wanted involvement and input from stakeholders, rather than managers, in order to decide what was relevant and would really give the most value.

It felt as if we were being asked to do everything all the time, so to make sense of it, I wrote down the rough headlines of the current and potential projects on pieces of card and then put them in order, e.g. upgrades to SMS or something to do with the groups feature. This list started off on the back of the door of Chris E's office, as we weren't sure that we wanted everyone to see it; it might seem too much of a commitment, and what if we had to change it? The next step was slowly coaxing it out and putting it on the outside of the door, and then moving it downstairs into a meeting room so that it was visible to everyone.

I planned a game where I got the developers to roughly estimate the 'epics' (large, unrefined chunks of potential work), and then I got them to say roughly how many they think they could do in a year. I kept that estimation a secret, didn't tell Chris M and Chris E, but asked them to play a roadmap game with me. I put out all the cards of potential pieces of work and asked them to put them in a priority order – not at the same level, but strictly one-way priority. Then I looked at my numbers and drew a cut-off line for the first year. Then I asked: 'How about if I told you we could only do this bit for the first year, this the second year? Are you still happy with your priority order?'

'Oh, no, no!' they replied. So some cards were swapped around, until we were happy with a priority for the epics to be working on from a business point of view for the next year, and a rough backlog beyond that. It was a game, but it got us to think differently and come up with something real and tangible to propose – our first attempt at a roadmap. But realising that it was real and not a game brought all sorts of fears and questions: 'We will need more than this; we can't just work on this!' Realistically we couldn't do 20 projects at the same time, so we had to think about what was doable and figure out how to decide what the highest priority really was.

Transparency

With the adoption of scrum, information about who was working on what, when and the progress we were making was much clearer and available to everyone, inside and outside the team. You could see all this information by walking into a team's space and looking at the arrangement of Post-its on their scrum board, just as Claire was trying to do a similar thing with the product roadmap. This was brilliant because it created an environment in which people had a greater awareness and could ask questions or challenge when needed.

However, this transparency had also inadvertently provided the perfect tools for micromanagement. Trusting the process enough to relinquish control took time as directly managing each task and individual was a hard habit to break. It was tempting for people outside the team to subvert the process, especially when they were under pressure. In response, it would have been easy and tempting for us to hide information, but we didn't. Instead, we chose to make things even more transparent in order to force difficult conversations out into the open to precipitate a change in behaviour over time. How did we do this? There was one particular behaviour that we started to label as a 'Secret Squirrel' attempt (named after the 1960s Hanna-Barbera cartoon character).

The interaction and thought process of a Secret Squirrel attempt by someone outside the team (in a position of authority) might look something like this: 'I urgently need this bit of work done, but the sprint is already well under way. It can't wait until the next sprint. If I ask the team, Rob, as scrum master protecting the team, will just say that I could have the work done, but it has to be at the expense of something else already committed to in the sprint. But I can't do that because I want it all! I know: I'll separate the weakest from the pack when the rest of the team isn't looking and get them to do this on the quiet...' In order to bring this type of interaction out into the open, we created a picture of a squirrel that people put on the scrum board if they got cornered by someone asking: 'Can you just do this for me on the quiet?' They also recorded the amount of time they may have spent doing a secret task. If we didn't deliver everything we had committed to, we could clearly show that we'd spent time doing work that wasn't meant to be in our sprint.

Don't moan, do something about it

We were creating a culture where people didn't need to seek permission from above to make changes and could put their own ideas into action. This early precedent set an enduring tone, which was noted by Ruth when she joined as a software developer a number of years later:

> Something that really jumped out at me in the team retrospectives at the end of each sprint was the response to talking about something that I didn't like or voicing a problem. Someone would invariably respond: 'Tell me more... So, what are you going to do about it?' The challenge was that moaning had to lead to action: 'What are you prepared to do to improve it?' It wasn't that the team weren't supportive. You'd quickly find teammates backing you in the conversations and actions that followed as you set about solving the problem. It was the realisation that it's usually in our control to make a change and make a difference.

Another great example of a small number of developers taking things into their own hands to make a necessary change was the introduction of a new release process. Over to Dave B again:

> At the time we started adopting scrum, we were just starting to figure out what working in autonomous teams meant for us. No one was going to tell us how to fix the issues we had with deploys; we were expected and trusted to sort it on our own. As our customer base grew, and the product became more complex in response to their needs, we knew the problem was

only going to get bigger. A few of us in the development team therefore took it upon ourselves to fix the issue. We started to put considerable effort into writing automated tests for the older parts of the system, and all new code had to have automatic tests written for it as part of our development process. It meant that we could find these obscure bugs well before they reached the customer. We introduced steps to ensure that all software was code-reviewed by multiple team members, and quality-tested in accordance with strict guidelines. Very quickly, our deploys became a lot less problematic and our customers gained confidence on deploy days. Our flat structure really helped in this scenario. People with the expertise in deploying software were able to implement changes without waiting for approval from a manager who might not have had that expertise. We were able to quickly try out multiple solutions to solve the problem and continue to iterate on those solutions until we felt the problem was dealt with.

Thinking back, some significant changes were driven by developers from that very first scrum team. Why? Was it a fluke? Right people, right place, right time?

The first scrum team

When the whole team had been on the scrum training course, what excited us about it and why did it resonate? I think what it fired in me was the value it placed on people. I'm a social creature; I like interacting with other people. That's how I learn and get my energy. I've spent my life playing team sports, so I know the value of a team, and I've always been a natural team-builder. A small, cross-functional, self-managing team is the beating heart of scrum, and that's what drew me to it. When we decided to make a go of being a scrum team, we knew we needed to change. We had the commitment, courage and determination to make sure we saw benefits, and used it as an opportunity to change more than just our processes. Agile practices draw your focus to people and interactions, and for us the early questions were: 'What kind of team do we want to be?' and 'How do we want to work together?' We worked hard to remove ego and the idea of 'rock star' developers; none of us is better or more senior than anyone else, though some will have more experience or knowledge to share. We all have a say, all opinions should be welcomed and heard, and there is no such thing as a stupid question. We can all learn from each other. This levelling of the playing field enabled people to step in from the sidelines and gain confidence. We became more comfortable with being ourselves, finding our voices and not being scared to have opinions. I can honestly say that after six months it was as if we'd hired a new group of developers.

We wanted to move from a mindset of 'me' to 'we': thinking of your team and teammates first before thinking about yourself. Not to the extent that people aren't able to progress or that individual differences and preferences are erased, but having the shared belief that the team is greater than the sum of its parts. This didn't suit everyone and those people with the bigger egos struggled and eventually left the company. As a team we wanted to teach, mentor, coach and support each other. We wanted to trust, respect and challenge each other. We wanted to be responsible for, and accountable to, each other. And just as important was our desire to laugh and have fun together. This conscious decision to leave ego at the door and treat each other as equals in the team had a much more significant longer-term impact. The fundamental DNA and personality of that first team – who they really were, what they wanted to be and how they wanted to work – runs through all our scrum teams to this day.

When we started out, we were learning the scrum process and concentrating on whether we were following it properly. Over time it became more about the people and interactions and less about the process itself. I've learned that a lot of it is about gaining experience, and you learn by doing. There are things that you're just going to get wrong. You can read around a subject as much as you like, but when it comes to the personalities in your team, there isn't a book or manual about Ruth or Dave B. They're individuals; they're one-offs; one person can contribute vocally immediately in a group setting, whereas another needs time and space to process in order to bring their best. Even day to day, people can be different; there's nothing that prepares you for a Tuesday morning when someone is feeling down or a Wednesday afternoon when they're feeling angry, and the effect that might have on the people around them. Sometimes it's about learning when difficult conversations with individuals or as a team need to happen. No one wants to have a difficult conversation and most people will try to avoid it, but often some pain now is much easier to deal with than long-term pain because the situation could just get worse if left unattended. Other people in the team could get stifled or disenfranchised and you might get people wanting to leave. Thinking back, if I had the time again, I would have certain open and honest conversations much earlier.

Wider impact of our agile adoption

Over time, a number of teams outside the software development ones have adopted scrum or other agile ways of working. As already mentioned, change can be difficult. Established behaviours, dynamics and processes take time to shift. For some teams in the business, it has been seen as a magic wand to quickly fix an acute problem. Sometimes the baby has been thrown out with the bathwater, and teams have moved on and looked for another solution when scrum didn't immediately give them the results they were expecting. Rather than scrum as a whole, what's perhaps more noticeable are the practices that have emerged from the development teams and have been copied, adjusted and adopted across the business. Daily stand-ups, reviews, retrospectives and working groups can now be seen across the company (sometimes with a different name, e.g. 'Hey @ midday', 'Tea at 3', 'Ketchup', 'Task & Finish groups'). This has come from teams and individuals seeing something that appeals or resonates and asking 'That seems to have helped you with that – do you think it could help us with this?' It's always been very organic and emerged over time as we've constantly discovered more about ourselves and our teams and been allowed to try things – and fail! You could say that Mayden has been agile about its agile adoption, and that experimental and empirical approach can be seen throughout the business.

Why has agile endured?

Using scrum and the adoption of agile practices could have been seen as a passing fad or an experiment that we'd inevitably abandon in favour of the way we were previously working (better the devil you know) or another way of working entirely. However, agility has become embedded within the organisation and underpins much of how the organisation works. Why is this? How has it endured? Being agile doesn't have an end. It's not like building flat-pack furniture, where you might have problems with less-than-clear instructions or missing parts, but once you've overcome those problems and built your furniture you can sit back and admire your handiwork. An organisation and its people are constantly changing and growing, and your agile practices, with their frustrations and sometimes less-than-clear instructions, have to evolve as well. We haven't reached, and will never reach, a point where we think we've nailed this and can sit back to admire our handiwork as we're always reaching for the next adaptation and improvement.

We were most likely to abandon our agile transformation during the early stages before mindsets, behaviours and processes became fully accepted and embedded. It's easy to oversimplify and say that this didn't happen due to the improvements we saw in how we ran projects and delivered value to our customers. The reality is that our agile adoption has endured due to a great deal of courage and steely determination. As the person who campaigned for the organisation to give scrum a try, I wasn't going to let us *play* at scrum half-heartedly. I was committed and sought commitment from everyone in the scrum team and from the wider organisation. As I've already mentioned, there were obstacles and issues to overcome and there still are today, but I had the courage of my convictions that scrum was going to at least help us deliver the changes that we wanted.

It's not uncommon for an individual to be the spark or catalyst for change, but if any momentum continues to rely on that one individual, or if the individual tries to garner support by merely tub-thumping, then any change will be fragile and potentially short lived. Several people within the development team quickly took to our new scrum practices, especially the autonomy that agile prescribes. Not everyone was immediately comfortable with the changes that were being made, but enough people were, and they started to model a different mindset and behaviour. It was this collection of people, rather than the reliance on one champion, that helped to maintain the momentum of change and added to its resilience. When we started to hire new developers and grow the development team, new starters could see how people were conducting themselves, how they were interacting with others, collaborating and taking responsibility for making decisions as a team. Consequently, it was easier for the new starters to identify what was required and expected of them. In turn these people became advocates for our way of working.

One of the powers of taking a coaching approach to much of what we do here at Mayden is that it encourages people to discover their own solutions. When people do this, they tend to be more committed to the solution or course of action that they choose. The directors acted quickly and decisively in getting everyone booked on to a scrum training course, but only after the idea of trying scrum and the decision to start adopting agile practices had come from within the development team. So, changing how we work was not a directorial decision from the top of the business, forced upon an unwilling workforce. It was instead *our* idea and something *we* wanted to pursue; subsequently the passion, determination and commitment to embracing agile was all the stronger and is why it has endured.

I'm sure we can all think of examples where ideas and change initiatives burn brightly for a while within an organisation but then fizzle out and disappear. This can be for myriad reasons, but sometimes it's due to the change being too radical for many, too far removed from how the wider organisation sees itself. In our case, what we discovered was a natural fit between our interpretation of the agile values and principles and the underlying company ethos of high trust and low ego favoured and exhibited by our founder Chris M. I'm not sure everyone explicitly knew of this ethos, and if they did, it had no common language and was difficult to frame. Our implementation of scrum made it tangible and provided a language that many people could understand and engage with, and the ethos was fertile ground for agile practices to grow.

Agile principles have taken root, shaped our culture and given us powerful tools to explore how we work and interact with each other in the absence of managers. Yes, a decision was made by the directors after agile had been in place for a while that the company didn't need (people) managers, but that's very hard to put into practice with a workforce that needs to be or is used to being managed. Through the adoption of scrum, the development team was working in an autonomous way and creating a new culture. We were modelling the behaviours and attitudes needed to thrive in a flatter structure without managers. We were masters of our own destiny and other parts of the company started to take notice. Without realising, we were changing Mayden's way of working.

Scaffolding

Chapter 5

Where did you start?

Building on our values

Alison Sturgess-Durden

In Part 1 we explained how we discovered that if we were to abandon the framework provided by hierarchy, we would still need organisational scaffolding. In Part 2 we will investigate the scaffolding we've been putting in place instead of middle management – those structures, processes, practices and assets that create the order within which a group of peers can operate and engage effectively.

Let's start with where we started – our organisational values.

We all know that every self-respecting organisation should have them, but probably harbour a little bit of doubt about their, well, value. They can feel quite ethereal; it's hard to connect them to the reality of the everyday hustle. At worst, they can be inauthentic and a thinly veiled branding ploy. But I'd be hard pressed to think of four pillars in our organisational scaffolding that carry more of the load than our values. All my years of working in different organisations told me that articulating our organisational values was important. What I didn't appreciate was how desperately the company needed them by 2016, and quite what an immediate, practical and transformational impact they'd have once they were crystallised. Having removed middle management, and with precious few other structures in place at the time, they became the rocks that everyone scrambled to climb on. All our other processes and practices then found their footing in the values. Our values have become our collective behavioural code, fundamentally affecting and guiding how we go about things and, therefore, our culture as well as business decisions. In the absence of line managers as arbiters of what gets done and how, a set of organisational values that are truly lived in practice gives everyone a powerful set of social norms to play by.

My friend's son plays 'Ultimate'. It is better known as Ultimate Frisbee, and I learned from him that it's a sport like no other. There's no referee. The players make their own calls guided by the 'spirit of the game'. According to the World Flying Disc Federation, this 'places the responsibility for fair play on every player'. The rules of play governed by the WFDF go on to say: 'Highly competitive play is encouraged, but should never sacrifice the mutual respect between players, adherence to the agreed-upon rules of the game, or the basic joy of play.' (rules.wfdf.org). How wonderful! Imagine employees in workplaces up and down the land operating in that spirit. In the absence of middle managers as referees, our organisational values constitute Mayden's very own 'spirit of the game'. If something's going wrong at Mayden, or something feels 'off', I can guarantee it's because one of our values is being infringed. They're therefore arguably of even greater importance in a flatter organisation than other organisational forms.

Know, understand, live

So, I'm sure you're wondering what our values are. Here they are:

Forward thinking – *creating a better tomorrow*
Transparency – *seeking insight, sharing knowledge*
Collaboration – *we work best together*
Contribution – *everyone can make a difference*

Mayden's values

Shortly before I had to take three months off work to recover from surgery, we'd had a staff day at which we invited as many employees as were willing to say, to camera, what they valued about working at Mayden. It was 2015. After recovering from the immediate aftermath of surgery and feeling a little bored, I realised I had some uninterrupted thinking time to consider some of the challenges we were facing as we grew and started trying to manage without managers. I looked back at all the vox pops recorded at that staff day, which had by now been transcribed, and drew out some key themes. The result was a draft set of organisational values – the four above. They were presented to the company for review and comment, but immediately seemed to land and received little challenge. We decided to go with them, agreeing to adjust and iterate them if anything started to jar. Years later, they still stand, unamended.

I believe this, and their potency in guiding decisions and behaviour, is because of how they came to light. Just like Harry Potter's wand, we didn't choose our values, they chose us. They emerged from the vox pops about why people worked – and valued working – at Mayden. That in turn had been influenced, we believe at least in part, by the adoption of some of our agile principles. In the story of the first scrum team in the previous chapter, you can see a clear alignment between agile and our four values. Equally, Mayden was probably receptive to agile practices given its resonance with the underlying ethos. Hence the values aligned, and it's hard to discern which gave rise to which, but we found ourselves with the ethos, values and agile approach working symbiotically. The values articulated qualities of the unspoken ethos and the evolving agile approach in a way that would help guide everyone. From this expression of what was important to us, we could build a whole way of working with greater clarity.

Once we had identified our values, we produced graphics for the walls of the office so that they were emblazoned for all to see, and everyone started living by them like true organisational citizens. Harmony prevailed, and no one needed managing any more... Just kidding! If only it were that simple. We did eventually produce wall decals, but that came later – after we'd got used to what the four words actually meant. We realised that we needed to engage everyone in the company with the values for them to become embedded and guide our collective efforts in place of managers. Kirstie Sneyd, who has helped us immensely with coaching across the business (see Chapter 9), counselled us that every person needed to 'know, understand and live' the four values. So, in the summer of 2016, Rob and I embarked on a round of workshops with each team in the business. In the sessions, we asked the following questions about each value:

1. What does that word mean to you?
2. When have you experienced that value in practice at Mayden?
3. Where are we falling short in living that value?

We created a clear, shared definition of each value from the responses to the first question. We crafted a strapline for each, fitting with these definitions and summing up, in a nutshell, what we meant by that value. We chose quotes from inspiring figures that we thought expressed each value's meaning. That's when we ordered the wall graphics – beautiful illustrations of each value and its strapline, as well as those inspiring quotes, placed all around the building. They did, of course, look impressive to our visitors, but mostly they served as a constant reminder of how we wanted to be – and a daily prick to the conscience about where we were continuing to fall short. On some days I found some quotes uncomfortable to walk past. Once or twice I literally had to look away when an uncollaborative meeting or frustrations from someone about their contribution not being recognised left me feeling as if our way of working was at best fragile and at worst a charade.

What we did with the answers to the other two questions we'd asked the teams was arguably more significant. These questions generated hundreds of responses from the workshops about where we did and didn't live our values in practice. The former was heart-warming and regularly dipped into as a source of encouragement and inspiration when times were tough, when all we saw were problems and uncertainties with our way of working; we were able to remember we were getting some things really right, and we had already come a long way. The latter generated an enormous list (or backlog, in agile parlance) of things we needed to improve about how we worked. Indeed, it became known as 'The Mayden Backlog', essentially our agenda for organisational development. We typed up all the suggestions and issues, printed them off and snipped them into individual bits of paper, or 'tickets', one for each comment about our organisational shortcomings. Assuming the posture of humility, on our hands and knees in the smallest meeting room in the building, we got to work grouping and spotting connections between the little bits of paper. What emerged were 12 areas that needed our attention if we were to work effectively, living out our values in practice:

1. strategy and planning

2. learning and development

3. management arrangements

4. innovation/R&D

5. reward

6. autonomy and accountability

7. communication

8. cross-team working

9. product development

10. sharing goals/continuous improvement

11. technical support

12. customer engagement.

Some directly related to ways of working and the need to build the scaffolding (management arrangements, autonomy and accountability), while others were more or less affected by the way we would come to define our way of working.

Not long after, it was time for another staff day, this time at Bath Racecourse. It was now late 2016. The first task of the day was for me to present the aforementioned staff survey results – our worst to date, as we explained earlier. Having laid bare the problems we faced given the scores and narrative comments in the survey, we dedicated the rest of the day to collectively working out how we could live our values better and address the improvements that the hundreds of tickets – and the survey – told us we needed to make.

The morning was spent in groups, reviewing the definitions of each value, then, crucially, personifying them. This involved imagining someone who lived and breathed that value. What would you hear them saying? What would they be thinking? What would you see them doing? Given that our employees are a creative bunch, some entertaining caricatures emerged, along with a (hopefully never-to-be-reprised) song! The caricatures were eventually written up as four 'personas', one for each value. We'll come to these in a moment. As well as serving as practical reminders of how to be at Mayden, they eventually became reference points for providing feedback and even part of the criteria for setting salaries (see Chapter 12). If all of that helped us to 'know' and 'understand' our values, the afternoon of the staff day was all about how we were going to 'live' them. We spent it working on the improvement backlog derived from all those tickets. Giving each breakout group an envelope of tickets from one of the 12 categories, they worked to synthesise the issues and develop 'stories' that would address them. From that day, we started to spin up working groups to design and implement solutions to the stories, much of the outcome of which you'll be reading about here.

That staff day marked the start of our journey of continuously improving our way of working and its grounding on the foundational pillars of our organisational values. Everything we'd worked on to improve how we work had its genesis in a view expressed by someone on one of those tickets about where we were failing to live our values. We had kick-started Mayden's development as a values-driven organisation with a values-driven culture, whatever the management arrangements.

We knew we'd got somewhere when one of our data services team said to me: 'Not the values again – we get it, OK? We know what they are now!' But far from breeding contempt, the familiarity generated by the months of engagement with the values embedded them into everyone's consciousness. Very soon, the values became part of everyday life, explicitly referenced in meetings, as often to garner support for a proposed way forward as to remind others of our code of behaviour. They acquired hashtag status (#collaboration – you get the idea) and, to this day, are still invoked on a daily basis somewhere in the business. We haven't got round to putting up the wall graphics in the new office we moved into a few years ago. Maybe that's because we haven't felt the need to remind everyone of them in that way. They have become Mayden's 'spirit of the game', our code for how to treat one another. We've found that those four values alone make up for layers of people managers – in themselves and in the way they have in turn guided our day-to-day practices.

Let's now look at the four values in turn to see why and how.

Value 1: Forward thinking
'Creating a better tomorrow'

Never believe that a few caring people can't change the world. For, indeed, that's all who ever have. – Margaret Mead (The World Ahead, 2005)

More than any other, this value provides the raison d'être for our chosen way of working. As mentioned in Part 1, the field we work in – digital technologies – is constantly innovating. We have to be creative with ideas, thinking ahead to what could be. Hence forward thinking is a core value, and we needed to develop a way of working that positively encouraged it. Where conventional management structures are designed to control and standardise, more open organisational arrangements create freedom for everyone – unencumbered by the overshadowing opinion of the boss – to try and fail, try again and break through, as our first scrum team soon learned. As part of wanting to get the best from and for our employees, it's the key reason we've adopted this more expansive way of working. Supported by high trust and a no-blame culture that form part of our ethos, the forward thinking value creates the expectation and conditions for innovation to flourish throughout the business. In what follows, we'll look at some of the practices we built on the forward thinking value, such as purpose, strategy and innovation. For now, here's how we personified forward thinking – our expectations of everyone in the business in upholding this value.

Forward thinking: values persona

Brave and bold: Willing to experiment with new ideas and try new ways of doing things; will trial multiple solutions and evaluate the results. Innovative and able to challenge the status quo, questioning current thinking to strive for better ways of working. Uses own initiative, self-starting and takes responsibility for own work.

Questioning: Questions routines, procedures, proposals. Reflects on the past to inform future decisions. Keeps asking questions in a positive and constructive manner.

Looking to the future (visionary): Proactively finds/creates vision, has a vision/looks for a vision/horizon-scanning and takes this into account when making decisions. Understands and works towards Mayden's purpose and strategy. Able to foresee future needs/desires by empathising with the user journey and through close client liaison.

Planning ahead (operationally): Proactively plans and allocates time for tasks. Plans beyond two-week sprint and plans for sprints by deconstructing future work. Connects short-term planning to long-term goals.

Value 2: Transparency
'Seeking insight, sharing knowledge'

Transparency breeds trust, and trust is the foundation of great teamwork. – Joel Gascoigne (2014)

As the strapline suggests, this value has two aspects – furthering understanding and fostering openness. The two are clearly related. Regarding the first, having transparent data about how things are running enables understanding and improvements to be made. As Chris M has already said, we want to be led by data, not opinion, and certainly not just because it's the opinion of someone in a certain position in the hierarchy. The second aspect speaks to openness with information in all its forms and communication around the organisation – the antithesis of the 'information hugging' we heard about earlier. Trust being part of our ethos creates a climate where information can be openly shared without fear of its misuse. Everyone will need open access to information about the organisation if they're to manage their work effectively without a manager funnelling what they need to know. We read earlier how transparency is part and parcel of agile practices because they enable you to inspect, ask questions and adapt. In the next chapter, we'll look at some of our practices for openly sharing information, including our internal communications channels and task management system, Orbit. In the meantime, here's what we expect from everyone when it comes to practising transparency.

Transparency: values persona

Be open with people: Open with others about what they're working on and their successes and failures, and encourages the same in others. Happy to answer questions. Has the courage to surface issues that need to be brought into the open, and does so with sensitivity.

Making use of data: Looks for the truth behind the numbers; shines a light on the data. Inquisitive and reflective. Asks and investigates good questions. Data driven. Not just making information available, but making sure the relevant audience gets the right info. Responsible with the information; follows good processes.

Value 3: Collaboration
'We work best together'

Coming together is a beginning. Keeping together is progress. Working together is success. – Henry Ford

This is the heart of Mayden – people working with people. With the lines between line managers and subordinates removed, the horizontal relationships come into their own. The ability to work well with peers across the business is vital for decision making and execution, and of course it's from collaboration and teamwork that much of the forward thinking and innovation comes. Collaboration is the antithesis of instruction, of 'telling'. With no one in charge, everyone has to manage their relationships with each other, and within Mayden that happens out of a spirit of collaboration, not competition; less chimp, more bee. The context of no blame and high trust supports successful collaboration, as do flexibility and reciprocity – all parts of our ethos.

Collaboration is a hard, not a soft, option. In the next chapter we'll cover some key practices that support it and enable people to work well together, even when things are difficult or there's conflict and no one can pull rank, as Rob and colleagues explained in Chapter 4. Those practices include team coaching, feedback, appreciating each other's unique character and behavioural preferences and knowing how to have difficult conversations within supportive relationships. For now, here are our expectations of everyone in terms of being an effective collaborator.

Collaboration: values persona

Open-minded: Invites and considers others' views and ideas. Involves stakeholders in decisions. Willing to adapt and compromise.

Approachable and respectful of others: People feel comfortable around them and supported by them. Inclusive – actively involves people and doesn't exclude. Patient with others.

A good communicator: Gets their views across effectively. Listens well and understands others' issues and needs. Generous with their time, knowledge, skills and experience.

Creating and maintaining a positive working atmosphere: Supportive when mistakes are made. Celebrates successes. Trusting of others. Not afraid to seek help when required. Willing to surface issues that the team needs to address, even if uncomfortable. Welcomes constructive feedback. Gives honest and effective feedback. Makes good use of tools that support collaboration and effective team working.

Value 4: Contribution
'Everyone can make a difference'

Change will not come if we wait for some other person or some other time. We are the ones we've been waiting for. We are the change that we seek. – Barack Obama

This value reminds us that ultimately we're all here to get work done and make a difference to the customer we work for. It's vital to our way of working, to keeping everyone focused on the desired outcome. In fact, it's probably the part you've been waiting for – how do you get people to do enough of the right work? Without being managed, everyone must still make sure they contribute. We'll look at the systems we put in place to make sure things get done and value is delivered, including very clear work prioritisation, delivery and review arrangements – in our case, often using scrum. In the meantime, here's the expectation we've set regarding everyone's contribution.

Contribution: values persona

A self-starter: Sees a need and uses their initiative to address it. Doesn't wait to be asked. Volunteers to take responsibility for things. Takes ownership of work, seeing it through, making sure it doesn't get dropped until completed or clearly picked up by others. Works well to deadlines, good time management. Determined – pushes things forwards, doesn't give up easily.

Focused on the right things: Works towards common goals. Prioritises time and effort well. Stays well informed about what's going on in the wider business, to have clarity about priorities and developments. Works efficiently and effectively; avoids and challenges time-wasting and diversions.

Making a valuable personal contribution: Makes good use of relevant skills, knowledge and expertise in their role. Committed – willing to go the extra mile, such as in a crisis or with a deadline. Willing and able to do what's needed whenever possible. Contribution to the company wider than their immediate role – involved in improving things across the business. Spends time learning and mastering knowledge and skills to continuously increase contribution.

Enabling the best contribution from others: Recognises strengths and expertise in self and others, then makes sure we play to our strengths. Trusting – allows people to get on with their jobs. Openly acknowledges others' contribution, e.g.

in retros (see Chapter 6), providing feedback. Respects others' contribution, listening and encouraging the sharing of ideas and knowledge. Constructive – willing to talk about issues without 'agenda', challenges thoughtfully, considers others' feelings. Invests in and enables others so they can contribute – gives them opportunities. Aware of others' needs, sharing workload, providing support and advice.

So that is Mayden's very own 'spirit of the game'. As well as providing a normative effect – a guide to expectations and behaviour in the absence of a manager – our four values turned out to be the perfect pillars on which to build the structures and practices of an alternative way of working. So, let's now turn to those and see how.

Chapter 6

Isn't it complete chaos?

Managing the work, not the people

Alison Sturgess-Durden

It's finally time to talk about practicalities. Ethos and values are grand, but managing without managers comes down to the nuts and bolts, the structures, processes and practices. How does a team manage itself? How do decisions get made? How do you know if you're getting value from everyone? The story of our first scrum team in Chapter 4 gives you insight into some of those mechanics. In this and the following chapters we will draw on those experiences to tell you about the organisational arrangements we've put in place to manage the work even though the people aren't managed. Let's start with the part you're probably the most intrigued by, and maybe sceptical about: the idea of 'self-managing' itself.

Self-management

If you don't have managers... everyone needs to manage themselves.

At the epicentre of our way of working is this idea of the individual's ability to be their own manager. If there's no manager to manage you, who else is going to do it? As we pointed out in Chapter 1, the adults we employ manage themselves outside work, so there's a reasonable chance they can manage themselves at work. Do you share that belief? Do you trust your employees enough to stop managing them because you believe they'll still work hard and skilfully on the right things and care about whether they've done a good job? The story of our first scrum team illustrates how you might actually achieve *better* outcomes from doing so if individuals and teams take ownership of their work. But how does self-management work in practice among more than 100 employees?

Autonomy and self-management have been hard concepts for us to grasp on our journey. In the early days, what we heard from some employees was more along the lines of 'I'm autonomous, I can do what I like'. It showed a lack of maturity in our way of working as much as a lack of understanding in the person who said it. We hadn't yet developed the elements of our organisational scaffolding that would provide a constant, natural and necessary check on autonomy, such as our decision-making and challenge processes, and feedback, all of which we will come to shortly.

Dan Pink (2011) identified autonomy as a key driver of motivation and high performance, seemingly in contrast to the business world's default of managing and controlling people or relying on levers such as individual KPIs and performance-related pay to incentivise results (which can lead to unintended consequences, such as chasing the target rather than the right outcome for the customer and business). However, autonomy cannot be a free-for-all. Pink identified two other drivers of motivation and in turn performance: mastery (having the requisite skill) and purpose (guiding the individual's action and direction). When accompanying autonomy, these give employees a sense of direction and skill with which to use their freedom well. David Marquet, in his account of captaining a nuclear submarine, similarly identified competence (skill) and clarity (of purpose)

106

as the conditions under which he could hand control to his crew (see davidmarquet.com/my-story). We're going to look next at the importance of clarity of purpose to our way of working at Mayden, and we look at skills in Chapter 12.

We have further learned that with great autonomy comes even greater responsibility and accountability. First, the people who would typically be lower down in the hierarchy had better take responsibility for the issues they see, or the organisation will be in trouble. As we grew and transitioned from how we were working to how we wanted to work, there was a nervousness among the directors. While they were putting down the ball of responsibility and ownership, people seemed reluctant to step in and pick it up. There was a gap. We will come on to explain how important clear ownership of the work is. Having taken responsibility for delivering their work, everyone must stand accountable for delivering results and value – to the business, to its customers and to each other. Sprint reviews and retrospectives are part of the rhythm of Mayden life, where individuals and teams account for the progress they've made in the last sprint, and give and receive feedback on how they've done. This is from anyone and everyone, not just up and down with the directors. It's not unusual at a typical marketing team sprint review (or 'Show & Tell' as they call them) to have 10 or more colleagues from around the business attending, interested in what has been achieved in the past four weeks. The audience usually includes people from sales, market discovery and the customer features team, all of whom are affected by the work of the marketing team.

Peer pressure is a powerful force. Peer-to-peer connections not depicted on the organisational chart are far more numerous than the vertical links that are between management layers, as the cartoon in Chapter 1 illustrated. Formal hierarchical power will often have less and certainly a different kind of impact to that of peer influence in a network of colleagues, depending on the circumstances (see Herrero 2008). Peer pressure has negative connotations, usually mentioned in the context of teenagers and the poor choices they feel pressured by friends into making. But when those peers are role models and high performers at work, the pressure is a positive one. Without managers, you're left with peer-to-peer working, collaboration, negotiation and influence. Accountability and peer pressure flow in multiple directions (horizontally), not just one (vertically). Coaches, crucially, are there to facilitate and mediate.

Purpose and strategy

If you don't have managers... everyone needs to be clear what the purpose of the business is and the direction it should be heading in.

Our value of forward thinking and level of autonomy require clarity of purpose and direction. At its most basic, what else is management there to do? To make sure employees are working on priorities that will take the business forward. Without management, everyone needs deep insight into where the business needs to go so they can contribute accordingly. Without that, individuals and teams across the organisation cannot make sound decisions about what to do next. Clarity of strategy, however, has presented us with some challenges. We've grown organically in a niche market (psychological therapy services), which kept us busy and deprioritised the need to strategise about other directions we could take. We also wanted to remain agile, with an opportunistic streak, eschewing traditional approaches to business planning. But strategy has come into focus over time as the need to diversify our client base has grown, as well as the desire to provide greater clarity to teams managing their own work.

Our first attempts at developing an explicit strategy were mixed. Nine strategic goals were developed by the three directors in place at the time. Perhaps due to a lack of consultation with the wider business, the goals got caught up in lengthy debates in working groups. What does this goal mean? How will we measure impact? While some goals were eventually achieved, a number floundered, suffering from a lack of ownership. We also struggled to create the bridge between the goals and what was happening day to day: 'If that's the goal, why am I working on this story in this sprint?' Over the past year, we've worked on our strategy once more, but in a far more collaborative way so that everyone has become more intimate with it. We established a strategy working group back when we developed the nine goals. Initially made up of an invited set of people known to the directors as 'strategic thinkers', the membership was immediately called out for being too exclusive. Just like all the other working groups at Mayden, it has become an open forum, allowing much greater collaboration and contribution from across the business. The group is chaired by two people who aren't directors, and anyone can attend. Sometimes there are a handful of us, but at one meeting nearly 50 employees came along. We openly acknowledge the challenges of an emergent versus planned and deliberate strategy. True to our agile ethos, we remain responsive to change while developing a clear enough long-term view that thinks beyond the next sprint and imagines what the future holds (without planning for it too tightly). We've called this approach 'dynamic steering'.

We've now developed a strategy 'stack' made up of our purpose, credo for healthcare (beliefs about the future of healthcare), vision, strategy and objectives and key results (OKRs) for the company, business plan and a set of differentiators (what sets us apart from the competition in our customers' eyes). Round tables have engaged every employee in understanding and contributing to the stack. Supporting strategies (e.g. product and marketing) are being developed in response by cross-team groups. As Chapter 7 will explain, decisions about strategy reside, ultimately, with the directors.

Strategy is the directors' work, just as developing code is the developers' work. The key to success in our strategy, though, has been the level of engagement of the whole company in understanding and challenging the strategy. This in turn enables people to self-manage and be clear about what it is we're trying to achieve in the long term.

Jamie Shaw, business development – an international perspective

My role is to identify possible international export markets. It's the first time I've worked in an agile business. I previously held international sales positions in countries such as China and Malaysia. I assumed my experiences there would be somewhat different to working in the UK, particularly with regard to management and organisational structure. This turned out to be the case. In these other cultures, power distances are strong and hierarchy is prevalent in both business and society. Some argue that a top-down approach is the reason these countries have developed at such a rapid pace; though overly simplistic, there's probably some truth to this. However, development and prosperity can't simply be measured by economic growth; softer factors can be neglected in more authoritarian structures. With this previous experience, I was fascinated by Mayden's flatter management arrangements, particularly in light of the growth the business had experienced over the past decade.

My work on international markets sits within the market discovery team, yet I've noticed the interest and support of those in the wider company whose roles are not necessarily strategic but who would be impacted by any decision. At a strategic level, my work could easily be siloed, yet Mayden's approach to collaboration runs truly deep. It would be all too easy for the directors to identify a high-potential market and as a result 'jump in' without consideration. Mayden's approach enables a deep dive into the pros and cons of such a decision, which makes me wonder: would other companies' high-profile international misjudgements have been avoided with similar decision-making processes and wide involvement?

There is, of course, an irony in me citing my work at a strategic 'level'. While strategic decisions do sit with the director team, Mayden provides the opportunity for all teams to impact the decisions that would traditionally be made by top layers of management. This was evidenced recently with all teams participating in the contribution of an international tender, adjusting their respective sprints to accommodate an extensive piece of work that was completed with immaculate synchronisation.

I've considered what Mayden is exporting – is it simply software or is it something bigger? After all, our values represent our way of working. This gave me cause to revisit my university dissertation, which analysed the management styles adopted by internationalising companies. If Mayden were to expand to more overseas locations, would we hire staff that adopted the home market 'Mayden culture' or one in step with the local management culture? Would the team be able to operate and succeed in an environment similar to Mayden UK, or would it need to be adapted to fit local ways of working? What would this mean for how we promote ourselves in terms of how we work and what we're like to work with? In markets culturally dissimilar to the UK, would this be well received? These are interesting considerations that I hope Mayden will be confronted with in the future. If so, it would enable overseas care services and their patients to benefit from our technology.

Open communication and information sharing

If you don't have managers... everyone must have access to the information they need to manage their work.

Open communication is supported and required by our value of transparency, and is a prerequisite to our way of working. How can people manage their work, themselves and their priorities, make sound decisions and be accountable for their progress without open sharing of information? We have a general rule that, unless something is confidential for commercial or HR reasons, it's openly available to everyone in the company. First and foremost, there's open access to teams' backlogs and roadmaps of work on various boards and via roadmap and sprint planning meetings. Information about whether or not the work in the sprint was completed and the sprint goal achieved is available at open sprint reviews. In fact, we consider any meeting open to all. Instead, you have to justify to yourself and your team that it's worth your time attending, not to the meeting organiser.

Here are other examples of transparency of information at Mayden: Chris M routinely shares the details of our financial position with employees. Orbit, our task and time management system, has no user-based access controls. Any employee can go and look at what tasks other employees have undertaken, how much time it's taken and what clients have been billed. We run fortnightly directors' digest sessions with updates from across the company to answer any questions and invite challenges. In fact, when Chris M hosts, he bills it as 'Challenge Chris'. We run a biannual staff survey in which 26 organisational dimensions are rated by everyone in the business. Scores and a summary of narrative comments are shared at staff days and used to inform the next season of development of our way of working. There's nowhere to hide. As you've already discovered, this was the survey that triggered our work on the practices you're reading about now. Everyone is encouraged to be transparent with each other.

A few years ago, we began using the messaging platform Slack. While there's plenty of direct messaging between individuals and even some private groups (to manage more confidential comms, whether HR or commercially sensitive, or just a private space for teams to share things of relevance to them only), much of the activity on Slack is via open, themed channels that everyone can opt in or out of. Orbit has a library function, and at one point one of our developers created Black Box as a repository for coding-related information and standards. As we grew, a variety of working groups developed resources and helpful tools. There was demand for just 'one place' where you could go to locate key company information. One of our systems team spun up an internal Google site, which caught on, and teams started adding pages. The 'One Place' intranet was born.

The truth is, we're continuing to work out what should be stored where. It's the perennial issue of knowledge management in a knowledge-intensive company, particularly one that has made most of its information accessible. We seem to go above and beyond in sharing information across the business. Maybe that's more our challenge now: we share too much information! As the number of people at Mayden grows (more nodes in our organisational network), the number of connections between those nodes becomes dizzyingly high. A team of four people has a total of six connections between the different pairs out of the four in the team. By the time you have eight team members (the average size of our teams) there are 28 connections between individuals. Imagine how many when you have more than 100 team members! As we scale the business, we know this will be one of our big challenges. It will become less and less practical to involve quite so many in decisions and information-sharing, as it's not possible to maintain that number of connections efficiently. We're learning how to enable everyone to limit broadcasting and expectations of engagement, but for all the right reasons.

Decision making

If you don't have managers... you need a clear protocol for how decisions get made, and by whom.

So, who gets to decide what? The path towards realising a strategy and purpose is paved with countless decisions. People owning the work need to be free to make them, then be accountable for them. This is such a key area that we've dedicated the next chapter to it. Hold that thought...!

Often the decision maker will be the person owning the work in question, so let's look at that next.

Owning and delivering work

If you don't have managers... you need a robust mechanism for prioritising work and delivering value.

This is how we make sure we're all contributing, getting things done. We saw in Chapter 4 how we adopted an agile framework, specifically scrum, as the way we organise the work to be delivered. Scrum provides a codified, lightweight framework for managing backlogs of work. It provides roles, practices and artefacts for organising work and delivering value through self-managing teams as we learned in Chapter 4. It doesn't matter what system you adopt, as long as you have an agreed way for a group of peers, with knowledge of the company's strategy and customers' needs, to prioritise and deliver work on time and to the required standard. In scrum, roadmaps are created that give a medium-term view of what we're going to work on in the product. Sprint planning is the process by which the team prioritises and commits to what's going to get worked on in the next two weeks. Scrum teams are then responsible for working out the best approach and delivering within the timeframe. Sprint reviews call everyone to account at the end of the two weeks as to whether they completed those tasks and the value they've delivered to the customer.

Scrum helps by defining key roles in relation to the work. Product owners are responsible for knowing the customer's needs and 'own' a roadmap of forthcoming product updates that will respond to that. They prioritise what the development teams work on, without coming up with the solution; that's for the development teams to figure out. In the absence of managers, we've found the concept of 'owning' work to be a powerful one that enables us to be clear about who's responsible for what work. This is where the responsibility that has to go with autonomy kicks in. You'll hear people ask: 'Who is *owning* this work?'

For us, this is about clarity over who really is owning what work. Remember the soon-to-be-headless chickens I mentioned in Chapter 1, running around not being very productive because it wasn't clear who was doing what? There really is a significant risk of that. The acceptance of responsibility for anything that needs owning (somebody was) needs to be clear. The alternative is balls being dropped between people (nobody was) or diluted ownership through the pursuit of consensus (everybody was). Neither are great prospects. For each employee, our way of working is all about the products, services, projects and issues (i.e. the work) they take ownership of, not the people and departments they manage. You still have to know who is responsible and accountable for what.

Facilitation

If you don't have managers... you still need facilitators, coaches and mediators.

We have already learned much about team facilitation in Chapter 4. Team coaches and scrum masters 'hold the space' for a self-managing team to manage itself. They facilitate the collaboration and contribution of a group of peers. We have seen the value they bring, as not every team at Mayden has always had a coach. The difference can be stark. We'll consider the role of individual coaching in Chapter 9.

What we've learned is that not only can much be achieved through facilitation – of meetings, individuals, teams, difficult conversations, working groups, etc – but in the absence of management, it's all but essential to this way of working. In fact, it's often even more powerful and effective than management because it empowers while reinforcing responsibility and accountability for your own decisions and actions.

The best way of illustrating this is to let Hannah Cottrill, one of our team coaches and a social media marketer, tell her story:

In lieu of day-to-day people management, having team coaches to help facilitate and hold the space for teams can be crucial. In the marketing team, this began quite organically. We had a lot of projects to deliver and were finding it hard to prioritise our work, maintain healthy working relationships and manage the pressure on our team. We started to adopt agile practices about five years ago, having seen the success that developer teams had in using the scrum methodology. However, since this is a framework traditionally built for developers and tech teams, it didn't neatly fit us, and we had little time or energy to review what it was about scrum that wasn't working. It felt like we were making little headway, and actually things were getting more challenging as our team and the scope of our work grew. We weren't communicating well with our stakeholders in the company about our projects and what we were delivering.

A wonderful colleague agreed to explore team coaching with us. Philippa came in to support us, challenge our assumptions and help us reframe the way we were working and thinking. It helped to have someone outside our team with no agenda or preconceived ideas and who could hold up a mirror to our behaviours. It was hard going, but over the months we made real progress with relationships within the team and, crucially, our processes. We had better visibility of our work and learned to have a shared view of our projects and priorities. We discovered that having strong processes can protect a team from several things, including overloading ourselves by saying 'yes' to too much work. These changes led to feeling more in control of our own work and created a sense of shared ownership, which led to us talking more openly to our stakeholders. This in turn encouraged them to trust us more. In short, we started to build healthier habits.

Seeing the impact that Philippa's coaching had on the team lit a fire in all of us. We could design our team and manage our work the way we wanted! We talked about one of our team becoming team coach; the experience of working with Philippa gave me the confidence to take up the baton when she moved to other projects. Having an existing team member as the team coach shifted the dynamic, but being a more resilient group now, we were up for the challenge. I'll always be grateful to the team for trusting me to give it a go.

As a coach, my main focus is on team wellbeing and trust, as well as maintaining strong processes. Helping a team to work in a healthy and productive way requires good relationships and processes in place. There are three things in particular that, as a coach, I can do to help. First, I show my own vulnerability. I have found that builds trust. How can I expect my teammates to be vulnerable if I'm not willing to be? I regularly share when I'm feeling out of control over work commitments or even overwhelmed, sad or angry in my personal life, which I hope encourages the team to do the same. I'm keen for the team to know they have a safe space where they can talk openly and provide or receive support.

Secondly (and again, I'm very grateful to the team for allowing me this), I try to inject some fun into our work. The projects we do can be intense and detailed with tight timelines and a lot of pressure. Sometimes you need to relieve that pressure with a game, some handstands or chats about terrible reality TV. Despite what some people may think, constantly working isn't always productive and it's certainly not sustainable.

Lastly, I aim to create space for the team to air anything that needs raising. Members of the team may have different views on how best to deliver a piece of work, which is an important and healthy part of a creative team. I can facilitate trickier conversations in a team meeting or through a retrospective session. This ensures there is the time and space to allow everyone in the team the chance to think it through and come to an agreement in a safe space.

I've been team coach for about three-and-a-half years now, alongside my role on social media in the team. Since then, we've grown the team (and continue to grow), have focused on creating an honest and safe environment where each voice counts and had some really difficult discussions that have helped us improve. There have been tears, laughter, we've clammed up, we've overshared, we've fallen out, we've celebrated. But we've always held on to the knowledge that we all share a passion for what we do and all care for each other's welfare. That strength of relationships only comes from constant communication and the opportunity to communicate only comes from making space for it.

Being a peer team coach in a self-managing team was daunting in the beginning. What did I know about any of this stuff? What gave me any right to try? What helped the most was the extra support I got from other scrum masters and coaches around the business. We now have a small support group who share tips, talk about where we're struggling and what we've learned.

Team coaching isn't easy. It can be draining. I've had many moments where I've questioned if I'm doing a good job. Juggling being sensitive to everyone's feelings while still pushing the team to develop is a balancing act that I don't get right every time. Ultimately, I'm there to serve and support the team and that can mean putting your own feelings aside. If you do take on some team coaching, it's amazingly rewarding but be sure to take time to look after yourself occasionally, too.

Feedback

If you don't have managers... instructive feedback needs to flow continuously between colleagues.

The coaches' contribution includes facilitating feedback and even mediating difficult conversations when required – and sometimes it is. Rob in Chapter 4 and Hannah above have both mentioned how a key lesson they learned was not letting issues fester and encouraging the team to address uncomfortable issues early. Line managers can often be a lightning rod for employees' issues and gripes. Rather than manage their own, sometimes strained, relationships with colleagues, employees will commonly go to their manager to complain about them and expect the manager to sort things out. That's not how it works at Mayden. As we will discuss in Chapter 11, occasionally it's appropriate for a line manager to intervene, but often it is possible – and better – that people address issues among themselves, directly. We're all adults after all, and we have to navigate relationships outside work without a manager to run to and do our bidding.

Feedback seems to raise everybody's anxiety levels. There's some interesting neuroscience around that (see the work of David Rock, for example – neuroleadership.com), and plenty of other literature to help with giving and receiving feedback in a positive, constructive way. Suffice to say, feedback is vital. One of our favourite thinkers, Brené Brown, says the number one behaviour and cultural issue that gets in the way of organisations across the world is that 'we avoid tough conversations, including giving honest and productive feedback' (2018). Collaboration is not possible without a free flow of communication about how things are going when working with each other.

> *We recognised as a team the importance of feedback, and were keen to incorporate it more. But when we tried to do this, we found that we were quite uncomfortable about a few things. We soon realised that asking for vague feedback wasn't helpful for either party, but identifying specific topics made us feel vulnerable, as those were the areas we were less confident in.*
>
> *We're a very close team, which can make the idea of difficult conversations challenging, even though we appreciated that they are often necessary to give honest and constructive feedback. Instead, we tended to focus purely on the positives rather than giving balanced feedback, or advice on areas for improvement.*
>
> *We discussed these issues and decided to start having a 'feedforward' session. Feedforward is an approach focused on how we can grow and improve looking ahead, rather than fixating on the past (this is derived from the work of Peter Dowrick – see, for example, Budworth et al. 2015). We bring to our sessions something that we want to improve, and ask the team for their help and advice on how we can do this. This gives us the space to provide real constructive help, without feeling like we're criticising each other.*
>
> **– Hester Gent and Sarah Quintin, software developers**

I think part of our neurosis about feedback is the assumption that it's always negative: 'You need to improve...', 'I wish you wouldn't...' We want to have a culture of feedback where it flows continuously. If you have good people, most of the continuous flow will be positive! I also struggle with the assumption in feedback that the person offering the feedback is right in their opinion and the recipient needs to correct something. As with our challenge process, which you will read about in the next chapter, feedback should start with curiosity – exploring why someone is working in the way they are. You may discover your feedback would have been misplaced. You may also come to learn that it's as much about you as the other person. We simply have different preferences.

The key to successful collaboration is appreciating those differences. We use the colour profiling tool from C-Me (colour-profiling.com) to understand each other's behavioural and communication preferences. There are four basic colours, and we are all a different blend of each. My overall preference is red/blue. The red means I am task focused – I like to get stuff done! The blue means I like to attend to the detail in doing so. (This combination probably explains why I'm so busy all the time...) There aren't many with a red preference at Mayden, while there are plenty with blue (it's a great preference for anyone working with code or data). Another colour is yellow, characterised by the free spirited, who enjoy being spontaneous and sociable. However, the dominant colour preference across the business is green – those who are focused on others and the team, and value harmony. This is a useful disposition for collaboration, but sometimes comes with some reluctance to question or challenge for fear of creating disharmony. We hold our colours lightly as we all flex in and out of our preferences depending on the situation we're in. All types are needed and valued for what they bring. Realising that someone is different, rather than difficult, can unlock tension and frustration. C-me has given us a clearer understanding of how others like to work – that we're all different – and a common language to appreciate those differences. It has been illuminating to understand that we all communicate, and like to be communicated with, in particular ways. We have used these insights to improve our team cohesion and performance.

Feedback is important for individuals and teams alike. We will look at it for individuals when we come on to coaching and individual development and performance in Chapters 9 and 11 later. Here we'll finish by looking at feedback within a team, and specifically during the team retrospective ceremony.

Team retrospectives – Ruth

From my perspective, one of the most powerful tools we have at our disposal that underpins the way we work is the retrospective (or retro). Where possible, the team uses a space away from their normal work environment and distractions, perhaps a cafe, garden or meeting room. The purpose of the retrospective is for the team to have an honest conversation celebrating what went well and acknowledging what didn't go well in the previous sprint. Sharing openly about the processes, actions, interactions and emotions enables the team to come up with changes to trial. This iterative process has a short feedback loop as after two weeks the team checks in to see if the change helped or hindered.

My first experience of a retrospective really stuck with me. It was a pivotal point in understanding the culture of Mayden and what this way of working really looks like in practice. My team was made up of developers of varying experience with strong, diverse characters. What I observed in my first sprint wasn't what you'd normally describe as a perfectly functioning team. Conversations were heated, people talked over each other and it could be difficult for the quieter members of the team to get a word in edgeways. Discussions about implementation options either didn't happen early enough or were emotionally charged. As a new developer, I wondered how I'd be able to integrate.

My outlook completely changed during the retrospective. I can picture it now – we were in the loft room right at the top of the building, sitting around a table. Teammates who'd been sparring were now respectfully listening to each other, recounting their own shortcomings and mistakes, and how others' actions and behaviours had made them feel. The level of honesty genuinely surprised me, but it was brilliant. In that safe space, the level of vulnerability meant that it was possible for learning, empathising, apologising and ultimately for growth and change. I was able to voice my concern about not being able to find a gap to speak when I had ideas and felt listened to, appreciated and that we'd come out with actions to change it. It was amazing that everyone was there to honestly reflect and improve. I realised that if a team is willing to have difficult conversations, be vulnerable with each other and seek to grow to that extent, then so much is possible!

As a scrum master, I've facilitated many retrospectives since then and am still amazed by the power of them to change things for a team. Recently someone in my team remarked: 'That Post-it in the celebration column this sprint was something we talked about a few sprints ago and had actions to improve.' The ability we have as teams to stop, notice the pain points and tensions and do something to change them is what drives our continuous improvement. One aspect I find particularly interesting is the extent to which using analogies and games create space for difficult conversations. Using a format that enables a team to play together and creatively explore their ideas leads to individuals being able to express difficult or challenging insights that they'd feel uncomfortable bluntly saying. One format I've found to be particularly liberating is this: 'Draw the sprint/team if the sprint/team was a (cake, boat, animal...).' Not only is it lots of fun, but it allows each individual to share their perspective and gives them a voice to share what they want to. It can lead to open conversation, led by what the team wants to talk about. You can even draw an elephant in the room if that's what needs talking about.

Structure

If you don't have managers... you can still have an organisational chart!

Yes, we can show you an organisational chart. But no, it's not in the shape of a triangle. You can see it opposite.

So, we have a series of parallel, self-managing teams. Each team covers a fairly traditional business function. Some of these teams are small (until recent growth, one or two were teams of one). So far, so normal. However, what's important to note is that these teams all sit alongside each other. This really is an org chart of *work*, not people, where the people gather around the work. Each team has its work to do, its contribution to make. Each is equally important. If any one team was missing, the others would suffer. None are more important than, or *over*, others. When it comes to their day job of developing strategy and assurance, that includes the director team which you see sitting alongside the other functions. Some of them also make up the membership of other teams – Chris E does sales, so is part of the sales team; I do market research within the market discovery team, but my work is as a team member rather than a team leader. As this is an org chart of where work gets done, you'll also notice that there are no hierarchical groups or meetings coordinating the work of teams. We used to have an executive management team, but it was disbanded for being inherently hierarchical. We replaced it with the open strategy group described earlier. The directors still meet as a team, but are focused on the work they are owning for the business, i.e. strategy and governance, and otherwise contain themselves to the things in their role, as we will see in Chapters 10 and 11.

This all makes cross-team working extremely important, with teams needing to coordinate. Teams organise this among themselves, as you might imagine, including moving where they sit temporarily and developing a shared backlog of work.

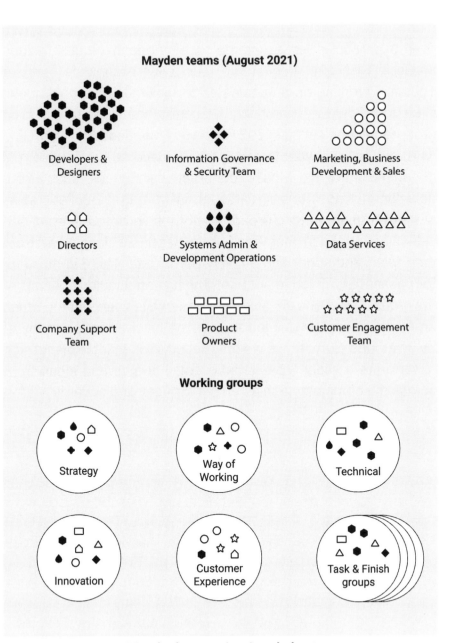

Mayden teams (August 2021)

Developers & Designers

Information Governance & Security Team

Marketing, Business Development & Sales

Directors

Systems Admin & Development Operations

Data Services

Company Support Team

Product Owners

Customer Engagement Team

Working groups

Strategy

Way of Working

Technical

Innovation

Customer Experience

Task & Finish groups

Mayden's organisational chart

Working groups and task & finish groups

We spin up working groups (enduring) and 'task & finish' groups (fixed term) to collaborate cross-company when a need arises over a particular issue. Examples of working groups include strategy, technical architecture, customer experience, and, of course, a working group dedicated to facilitating the continuous evolution of our way of working. A recent example of a task & finish group is the one set up in 2021 to review our place of work policy, with remote and hybrid working having become the new normal during the pandemic. Most of our practices and tools, such as our decision-making process, came about through a collaborative, cross-company working group. All of these groups are open and self-selecting. Each member has to negotiate time away from their team and sprint and actively participate. There is no room for passengers; if you're not contributing you shouldn't be part of the group. Questions are asked if someone is spending too much time away from the day job to become involved in too many of these groups. Sometimes we may set up a round table discussion to facilitate a wider representation of thoughts and ideas from across the company, such as on our strategy and rewards.

Dave B writes:

When making technical decisions, the radius of the effect of the decision needs to be considered. When working on a particular project, the decision makers would usually be the scrum team working on that project. As that grows to multiple teams, scrum teams trust other scrum teams to make the right decisions for the good of the product, and reach out for expertise when they require it. But some decisions are wider reaching and affect our overall technical direction: the overall structure, framework, architecture, coding standards or technology we use. Over time the need to make these decisions well led to the creation of technical working groups.

When we had a single scrum team it was fairly easy to make the wider-reaching technical decisions together. As team members and scrum teams grew in number, we quickly realised that not every team member could be involved in every significant technical decision. In a typical hierarchy, these decisions would usually be made by people with titles such as team leader, principal developer or chief technical officer. As the whole development team is jointly responsible for decisions, we needed a more collaborative way to make those decisions. Working groups are formed around subjects where we identify the need for regular decision making on those subjects.

Our first working group was the database working group, made up of members who were particularly passionate or knowledgeable about database technologies and design. The group advises the rest of the development team on standards, schema design, large upcoming issues we may be heading towards, emerging technologies and whether we should be considering upgrading to them. These decisions will then be communicated to the wider development team. If anyone has any concerns, our challenge process allows any of these decisions to be reconsidered or discussed, but challenge is rare, because most of the experts in that subject area would have been involved or consulted early in the decision-making process. We have a talented development team, and we trust each other to make decisions or seek help from the right people to help make those decisions. Over time, we created more working groups for other areas such as accessibility and front-end development. Some groups dissolve as the need fades, and others are more permanent and integral to support our development team.

As we scaled up the development team further, we realised we were missing a high-level view of where all the software overall was heading. We needed some long-term technical direction. In software development, this would traditionally be the role of a systems architect. It wouldn't make sense to have someone in that role at Mayden in the same way because it would mean one person making all of the overarching technical decisions. In this way, we could end up introducing a hierarchy. Our technical roadmap working group was created to solve this issue. It's made up of delegates from each scrum team who have a keen interest and expertise in big-picture technical thinking. This group is now responsible for delivering a technical vision that caters to our company and product strategies.

With all of this, it seems appropriate to give the final word to something you're probably wondering about as much as autonomy – and that's leadership. Here's another of our directors, Fiona Dawson.

Leadership

Fi Dawson writes:

Etymology, the study of the origin and history of words, fascinates me. The word leader is very old. Unlike more modern English words, it doesn't have a close Latin or Greek derivation; instead, it traces back to the Old English *lædere*, 'one who leads', and its close Indo-European Germanic relative *laidjan* ('to travel'). There's something appropriate to Mayden about thinking of a leader as a traveller, someone on a journey, rather than someone in a position – typically of power. In his book *Reinventing Organizations*, Frederic Laloux (2014) talks about the organisational paradigm where power is currency. Leaders are the embodiment of this, often characterised by displays of strength and grand gestures. In turn, those without power are expected to submit. Mayden is not anti-leadership. Our way of working is not political, bent on overthrowing the corporate oppressor. Equally, it's not leaderless. The idea of a leader as being one on a journey provides an alternative paradigm to power that isn't anarchy. And it's a journey every employee at Mayden is on.

The illustration overleaf summarises how employees, when they were asked what progression looks like at Mayden, understood leadership to be in the business. Far from being leader*less*, everyone is a leader. We are leader*ful*. We ask everyone at Mayden to act as if they own the business. How does this work? First, the formal leaders – the directors – must make room. This isn't an absence of leadership – it's empowerment and generosity. That requires a willingness to give space to both succeed and fail. Trying is respected more than failure is feared.

There are analogies with this type of leadership in the sporting world. A head coach is off the field; they support from the sidelines, having done all the preparation and supported the team ready for that match play moment. Rather than scoring the goal themselves, the coach has empowered and equipped the team to; they then have the autonomy and responsibility to act. At Mayden, ego and charisma are not highly prized. Instead, all individuals are expected to connect with the purpose of the organisation, and leadership emerges from their contribution to it. To paraphrase Clare Graves (2005), having ambition is important; being ambitious is not. This means that leadership is much quieter at Mayden, and could possibly even look as if it isn't there. In actuality, it's the micro interactions and small habits of a multitude of leaders – in their domain, context or network – that takes us along our journey, and, we believe, one of the things that makes our way of working work so well. The Agile Manifesto says: 'Our highest priority is to satisfy the customer through early and continuous delivery of valuable software.' Focus on the customer brings clarity to our leaders. We focus on managing the work, not managing the people. This frees us to focus on what matters, removing other factors such as self-promotion, which can otherwise seep into the work.

What does a good leader do?

Quotes from employees on what good leaders at Mayden do.

Isn't it complete chaos?

This doesn't mean individuals don't have clear roles. We might identify a project manager or a lead from a technical perspective for a particular assignment, but how those people undertake those responsibilities is in line with the principles of being a leader mentioned here. What the roles bring is responsibility and accountability. It's not a green card to act as if you're in charge. The situation may mean those people need to have authority to act and will be expected to use the decision-making process for that, but it will come with challenge and feedback, which are core to our practices. Transparency allows everyone to access the information they need to lead and make decisions. If anyone is just setting off on their leadership journey, smaller project groups such as some of our working groups provide opportunities to gain experience.

Of course, there are times when a director needs to be the leader. Even Laloux acknowledges situations where a 'command and control' approach is needed, including in a crisis, and we've had one or two of those. And sometimes there's a lack of leadership. Perhaps a group of individuals become paralysed by what they've been empowered to achieve. When you identify what's happening here, it's often not a lack of leadership or influence, but that the group have become siloed from divergent views, or they're overlooking one of our key values of contribution, collaboration, transparency or forward thinking. Facilitation and coaching help unblock. We recognise the journey we are all on. Through our leadership approaches, we move towards fulfilling our shared purpose together. Ultimately, we believe that this results in the best possible outcomes for the business.

Dave B writes:

We manage our work; we don't manage each other. We don't have people management, but that doesn't mean we don't have leaders. The difference at Mayden is that nobody is assigned

131

a permanent leadership role; it's earned through how people interact with their co-workers. Naturally, people in some roles have more experience than others. In the development team, we're hiring people who are new to Mayden and often new to software development in general. Gaining influence is therefore an important part of career development at Mayden, in order to get an internal reputation for being effective at solving certain problems, being great at helping those around you by helping each other solve problems or helping your co-workers grow. Leaders at Mayden tend to not only be experienced in their role, but also have the ability to use that experience to help their co-workers and benefit the company as a whole.

Conclusion

That, of course, is not all there is to it. Some of the practices in our scaffolding are so fundamental that we've dedicated a whole chapter to them – practices such as decision making, coaching and governance, among others. Of course, these practices do not work brilliantly all of the time. You might also be thinking some of this sounds familiar – that many of these practices (coaching, feedback, team working, etc) can be found in traditional hierarchies and supported by management. The difference is that we've baked them into our organisational model rather than relying on the benevolence of managers to always empower and coach, for example. Our directors need to step in to make decisions or take corrective action less and less as we grow in maturity in our chosen way of working. One new recruit once explained to me that they'd never have considered working for a company bigger than a handful of people as it would be too bureaucratic, but that Mayden had proved him wrong.

In the following chapters, we will focus on some more of the key planks of our scaffolding, starting with decision making.

Chapter 7

Who gets to decide what?

Decision making and challenge

Philippa Kindon and Ruth Waterfield

Not long after joining Mayden, I (Philippa) attended a staff event that included an awards ceremony: best laugh, best baker... you get the gist. The awards were peer voted and mostly in jest. I was awarded 'decision-making master'. I thought it was a joke, even ironic. I'm terrible at making decisions! I'm a multi-perspective kind of person – I find the pros and cons of different options and can often see things from different angles. This is great for facilitation, coaching, generating new ideas and unpacking possibilities, but not so helpful for decisive action. As it turns out, I didn't receive the award for my decision-making prowess, but for my support around developing our decision-making process. That's the practice Ruth and I will tell you about in this chapter.

Decisions, decisions!

Take a moment to think about decision making in the context of your day-to-day life: at work, at home, on committees, in voluntary groups, on sports teams, at schools and so on. Decisions are made anywhere that people gather with some sense of order or purpose. Who are we? What do we stand for? What do we need or want to do? How shall we do it? How should resources be allocated? What does success look like? Whose turn is it to make the tea? Take one more minute to think. This time, think about *how* decisions are made? *Who* makes them? And what do we do when we disagree with a decision that someone else has made?

Regardless of how you organise – multiple management layers or flat, open or closed, traditional or experimental – knowing who decides what and how they should go about it is important. Like all businesses, we recognise that our success rests in making 'good' decisions. (By 'good', we mean those that result in positive consequences for the customer, the company and staff.) Not only is decision making important because it's everywhere, all the time; it's important because it's fundamental to your business, shaping everything else you do.

The idea of getting something as important as your decision making wrong is scary, isn't it? What if someone makes a decision that loses us an important customer, and no one was able to step in and veto it? What if someone decides to invest in the wrong infrastructure or chooses the wrong supplier? It's interesting how quickly the mind jumps to the awful things that could happen if decision making is devolved. That's why it is usually reserved for the more senior person in a hierarchy. After all, they have the experience, status and accountability to take responsibility. But what about all the things that could be going wrong with top-down decision making that has to go through multiple layers, possibly being miscommunicated at each point? What creative solutions are being held back? What issues are not seen by a decision maker several steps removed up the hierarchy? In other words, if your organisation is founded on trust, be prepared to let others make decisions. You never know, they may make better ones!

There is a distinction between 'decisions' and 'decision making'. A decision is a conclusion drawn that then leads to a course of action, or non-action, whereas decision making is the process that enables a decision to be made. We have designed a framework to safeguard against poor decisions being made in the absence of the traditional hierarchy fulfilling this role. The 'who', the 'how', and the 'when' all need careful thought. And as we said in Chapter 6, there is no autonomy without accountability – in this case, to make decisions. As such, decision making is a critical practice and often a conscious and deliberate process within flatter organisations. We don't want to try and replicate what you can learn from existing resources (some of which we have listed in the References at the end of the book). Instead, we want to help bring to life what it really feels like to implement more open, devolved or decentralised decision making and try to make it work well. Our decision-making process grants the authority to make decisions that goes with autonomy, but builds in the responsibility and accountability of the decision maker that has to accompany this level of freedom.

Our decision-making process

Our 'orange hands' poster (see below) for making and challenging decisions was one of the first practices we developed when we started working on our way of working. It was developed by our management arrangements working group and was our take on the 'advice process' (as covered in *Reinventing Organisations*, Laloux 2014). Also inspired by David Marquet (2016) and mentioned earlier, it pinpointed the need for competence and clarity if there is to be greater autonomy in decision making. The steps are designed as a broad guide, taking the form of seven questions that any employee can use to coach themselves through making a good decision. They bring home the reality of ownership and responsibility.

While we describe them as 'steps', they are not always applicable to every decision, and they don't necessarily have to be taken in the order laid out. We've grappled many times with whether we call it a process, a protocol, a framework, or something else!

Making decisions at Mayden

Is this my decision to make?

Competence: Do I have the skills and experience to make the decision?

Clarity: Do I understand the context and have the information to make this decision?

Consultation: Have I involved those with knowledge in this area and those who will be affected by this decision?

Consequence: Am I prepared to take responsibility for the communication, outcome and consequences of this decision?

Cash: Have I considered the financial implications of this decision?

Customer: How does my decision impact customers (mine, my team's, Mayden's)?

Clinical safety: Does your decision have clinical safety implications?

What if I disagree with another team or individual's decision?

Context: Ask questions, listen to the answers and uncover assumptions.

Common ground: Focus on working together towards the company's best interests, rather than creating debate.

Clarify: Use evidence, examples and context to clarify your reasons for this challenge.

Consider your approach: Discuss face-to-face, don't let it get personal and consider inviting a mediator.

The decision-making process at Mayden (2018)

This emerging process was used when the iaptus developers decided a fundamental shift was needed to modernise the way we structure and write our code. Roy Lloyd, one of the developers involved, explains:

> There was a growing realisation among the developer team that the iaptus codebase was not growing in a sustainable way. We had adapted the system to support our growing customer community over time and we planned to offer new functionality and features to add value to the product, helping our customers serve their patients better. However, the code base was getting old in terms of the practices that had been used to put it together and the technology it relied on, which had been right at the time. There hadn't been a clear shared architectural vision, so over time each developer had sought to improve in the way they thought best, resulting in 'spaghetti-fication': a piece of spaghetti isn't just in one neat place on your plate, it's throughout your entire meal, and we saw that our code was becoming tangled! Adding features and making sure our code updates were testable and reliable was becoming increasingly difficult, time consuming and frustrating for developers and product owners. We were having to slow down and work was taking more time and effort, so it was affecting our delivery capacity and so our customers were impacted too.
>
> We took on development of a new feature in early 2017 – 'bulk actions' to enable an action that might be applied to one patient to be applied to many at the same time, e.g. sending SMS messages or letters. We realised that if we tried to build this in the way that the system was written previously it would be very tricky. We therefore took the opportunity to start to modernise the way we structured our application.

We will use Roy's example throughout this chapter to illustrate how the seven steps of our decision-making process are applied in practice, so let's get started.

Step 1: Competence

Do I have the skills and experience to make this decision?

The first step in our decision-making process is to identify the decision maker. When an organisation steps away from traditional hierarchy, how do you figure out who decides what? Who decides who decides? We found this 'catch-22' takes some unpacking. If you're the person, or people, feeling the pain or spotting the need for a decision to be made (as some of the developers were in Roy's example above), you're well placed to be involved in that decision, and probably to make it. Agreeing that decisions need to be made by whoever is closest to the issues helped us move forward with self-managing, but as it was rolled out across the business, a 'fear of freedom' took hold (see Fromm 2001). Nowhere was this more keenly felt than in taking responsibility for decisions. Employees were unsure what they were allowed to decide for themselves and uncertain of the consequences if their decisions turned out to be poor.

It's amazing how far into decision making you can get without knowing who's actually making the decision. Sometimes a group close to it needs to discuss, and collectively agree upon, the nominated decision maker/s. But most of the time the decision maker is self-appointed. This is a bit recursive and probably sounds more complicated than it really is: in most scenarios, by asking the right questions, the person closest is quite clear and the experience and expertise needed is a good match with that person. When we considered autonomy in Chapter 6, we saw how it needs to be accompanied by competency and clarity, by mastery and purpose. So, if you're contemplating being the decision maker, the first step is about competency: 'Do I have the skills and experience to make this decision?'

As we go on to outline in Chapter 10, the directors' role means that some decisions are still reserved for them and them only as they are the ones with the skills, expertise, oversight and authority, such as setting the company-wide strategy. But even they must follow the decision-making process and ask themselves if they are best placed to be the decision maker. In the main, however, decision makers are found throughout the organisation and decision-making is devolved.

Returning to the example of the decision to modernise the code base, here are some more thoughts from Roy as to who the decision makers were and what competency was needed from them:

> The small team of developers I was in at the time (The Sherbs) began exploring options for implementing the new feature, as is normal practice for a development team picking up a project. Making the connection between this project and the earlier conversations about the need for modernisation of the code base, we realised there was a connection to the wider development team. We thought it might involve choosing the approach, tools and libraries that we (the wider development team) would be using going forward. Those with knowledge of industry best practice and previous experiences of ways of structuring code and using frameworks were important voices in the conversation to enable us to decide the way forward. This meant that the iaptus developer team as a whole was recognised as the decision maker. It felt like we made the decision together, reaching enough of an agreement to move forward.

Step 2: Clarity

Do I understand the context and have the information I need to make this decision?

We aim to be data driven. Our transparency value requires access to and analysis of relevant data to inform decisions. Fortunately, it also ensures that decision makers, wherever they are in the business, have the information they need. Clarity of the business's purpose and strategy is particularly important in making decisions, so they are aligned with the direction of travel.

Returning to our example, here's what Roy had to say about how those involved worked towards achieving clarity:

> We started by putting together a list of different code libraries, frameworks and approaches that we could take, both from what we already knew from past experience and others that we found. We collated the information in a document that enabled us to compare and then share the results of our research on these different options as we explored them.
>
> We investigated each one in increasing depth as we narrowed down the options, questioning and testing from different angles, then to be weighed up and prioritised:
>
> - Is it a well-used, well-maintained, proven library with good support from a team or community? We want something that is going to be kept up to date with good security practices.
>
> - Do we already have the skills to use and maintain this, or will we need to put a training plan in place?
>
> - Would it negatively impact existing functionality or performance for users?
>
> - What benefits will it give us now and flexibility for the future?

Step 3: Consultation

Have I involved those with knowledge in this area and those who will be affected by the decision?

Whether close to the decision or not, anyone in the organisation may have fresh insight or wisdom. Sometimes this can mean reaching for external sources that could be relevant. Also, we need to think broadly about who might be impacted by the decision, who might be set to benefit and who might be negatively affected. According to our process, it's about considering how to involve the right people at the right time.

So, let's hear from Roy about consultation:

This wasn't a decision to make and enforce on everyone else, because it would change the way we all wrote code going forward. In addition, given the conversations, training and accumulated wisdom on how we might go about 'de-spaghettifying' the codebase, it was important for it to be an open developer team conversation. The documents detailing the context and information on the different options were shared and widely commented on, and conversations were initiated to include those with specific insight to share.

We then moved on to voting on the various options, I remember walking round the rooms in our office in Widcombe with sheets of paper, collecting ballots. At that time there was the idea of reaching a consensus; over the years, I think this is one of the key areas where our decision making has matured, but at the time we went with voting. The results helped us narrow down our options, and over a few rounds we whittled them down to the last few options, which we explored in a bit more depth. Ultimately the team chose the one to try based on the results of the vote. This wasn't a consensus as some still disagreed with the decision, but once the decision was made everyone got behind it and supported the implementation.

As they were stakeholders, we kept the directors and product owners in the loop because the choice we made and the time we were spending investigating impacted them and potentially delivery of projects. Ultimately the decision for how we were going to approach structuring our code was down to the developers, and we were trusted to get on with it.

Step 4: Consequences

Am I prepared to take responsibility for the communication, outcome and consequences of this decision?

As we have said, with great autonomy comes great responsibility and accountability. This step is an opportunity for the decision maker to check their sense of ownership and willingness to be accountable for it. This is also a question that drives the value of transparency around decision making. It means thinking about what will happen if the impact of the decision doesn't go well or work out as hoped. As with all businesses, the consequences of decisions can range from fairly inconsequential to complex and critical. In our case, we pay particular attention to understanding the implications for information governance (IG), as covered in Chapter 13, and clinical safety, alongside meeting commitments to our customers and the overall success of the business. Clinical safety is identified as a specific factor to consider in the decision-making guidelines and is described later in this chapter.

Having the right policies in place, adhering to the correct frameworks and reaching out for professional advice are all tools available to support the decision maker. Ultimately, the decision maker has to ask: 'Am I prepared to take responsibility for that?' This isn't, however, about having someone to take the blame, as our no-blame culture testifies. Rather it is about making sure someone is going to see a decision, and its follow-up, to a conclusion, and if it doesn't work out, be willing to go back to the drawing board and think again.

So, how did Roy and his colleagues weigh up some of the consequences of their decision?

At one point we were seriously considering two framework libraries, one that was lighter and more flexible and another that had more functionality but was more prescriptive in the way you would need to write code, so prompted strong opinions among our developers and in the wider industry. We weighed up the possibility of choosing the more open framework leading to us having to design and implement more functionality ourselves, as opposed to a framework that did more upfront but didn't have buy-in from across the development team. We knew that whichever framework was chosen it would not be everyone's cup of tea, but it was more important to have enough buy-in to make it work.

The final steps and questions that follow are all about the next level of thoroughness, making sure the decision maker has looked at things from every angle.

Step 5: Cash

Have I fully considered any potential financial implications of my decision?

In this step, the decision maker needs to ask themselves: 'Is there a cost and have I done the due diligence to ensure it's the best price, quote, product, etc?' The decision maker will consider the company's approach to expenditure described in Chapter 8.

In Roy's example, this played out as follows:

When building the bulk actions feature it was important to consider cost implications, so we looked to compare the cost of building it in the way we had been writing code previously and implementing it in a new way. Given the reduced risk and complexity brought by using a framework and that it would enable us to write well-structured, maintainable code that is easy to write automated tests for, we estimated that the cost of the project would not be significantly different by doing it in the new way. In addition, the cost of future developments would likely be reduced by the structural improvements we were proposing.

143

Step 6: Customer

How does my decision impact customers (mine, my team's, Mayden's)?

You will recall from Chapter 1 that the main reason we work the way we do is because we believe it helps us to deliver value more effectively to our customers. It helps us to achieve better customer service by ensuring those closest to the customer have the autonomy and authority to make decisions efficiently. It also helps us innovate rapidly and adapt our product to fit with the needs and demands of our customers, again by making sure the decision makers are the ones closest to the information that informs us of the changes needed.

We recognise that customers can be anyone to whom you are delivering value – the user of your product or service, whether they are paying customers or another team within the company. Regardless of whether we are thinking about an internal or external customer, there are lots of different ways a customer might be involved in decisions made at Mayden. For example, sometimes decisions need to be made directly related to a customer need or request. In these circumstances, decisions are made with the customer. Consultation with the customer is baked into the process and explicit prompts and reminders to think about the potential impact on the customer are not needed. Sometimes, however, it's not that clear cut.

There are circumstances when decisions need to be made that are not directly in response to a customer need or request. In these circumstances a prompt or reminder to consider the implications for the customer can be helpful. This is because it may not be obvious, or the decision maker may not realise their decision could impact the customer. By paying direct attention to what could impact the customer, even with the decisions that aren't being made directly *with* the customer, all decisions are still very much made with the customer in mind. All this means that, ultimately, our customers are at the heart of our decision making, and this is arguably the most important factor to take into account.

While the decision making guidelines ask the decision maker to consider the impact on the customer, more often than not a decision is being made *because* we are proactively seeking a solution that benefits the customer, as demonstrated in the next stage of the decision making by Roy and team:

> We realised that using a framework would mean we could implement this feature better, and by better we mean well-structured, testable code that could be developed in a timely way while still being confident in it. We'd be able to meet what we needed to do for the customer and the complexity of the legacy code would be reduced. It was clear this wasn't just a technical decision; our focus was on delivering this for the user. We asked ourselves: 'What is the best way of achieving these things for the quality of the product and what we want to deliver for the user?'
>
> The decision to change the way we write code also had the potential to make our future developments more reliable and sustainable and enable us to react sooner, with less effort and with more confidence to what our customers and Mayden need from the product. Ultimately our focus wasn't on choosing a new framework to use in our code – it was delivering a high-quality feature for the user.

Given that our customers serve patients, Step 7 must follow and is equally important.

Step 7: Clinical safety

Does my decision have clinical safety implications?

This is crucial to Mayden, given the field we work in. Decisions that might have clinical safety implications are regularly discussed with our clinical safety officer. We make this a specific step in the process to help decision makers focus on whether there could be clinical safety implications of a decision they are making.

Ultimately, the decision to modernise the code was all about making improvements for the customer so that they can serve their patients even better:

> We knew we needed to write the new feature in a way that was easy to test (some ways of structuring code are easier to write robust tests for than others). The new bulk actions feature would be building upon an existing feature (sending SMS messages to patients) and we needed to be confident that the changes we were making to this sensitive area would be safe for our customers' interactions with patients.

So those are the steps a decision maker should go through. Although this may feel like a drawn-out process, we make decisions every day and often go through these steps automatically. But when decisions are complex it helps to pause, break things down into these steps and take the proper time needed to achieve good decisions. In the case of Roy's example, the outcome of the decision is described here:

> The developers chose a particular framework and started using it, one that gave us what we needed for that project, and in the longer term to keep delivering great features to our customers. It achieved buy-in across the team at the time, and generated lots of ongoing conversations as we made more implementation choices.

What if I disagree with a decision?

But what if someone makes a decision you disagree with because you believe it presents a risk, is wrong or you just don't like it? To address this, we devised a challenge process as a guide to effectively disagreeing with a decision that has been made or is in the process of being made. Like the decision-making process, the challenge process was devised by the management arrangements working group in early 2017, and was designed to help people work through disagreement or difference of opinion, and work together to reach a helpful solution.

As with decision making, the challenge process is a guide for effective action. It's intentionally designed to provide guidelines rather than rules in recognition that every situation is different, and guidelines provide plenty of scope for adjustment and adaptation for different circumstances. Having commonly understood principles is a way to support everyone to challenge decisions in a healthy and constructive way.

The key points of the challenge process are as follows:

+ **Context:** Ask questions, listen to the answers and uncover assumptions.

+ **Common ground:** Focus on working together toward the company's best interests rather than creating debate.

+ **Clarify:** Use evidence, examples and context to clarify your reason for the challenge.

+ **Consider your approach:** Discuss face to face, don't let it get personal and consider inviting a mediator.

This simple set of guidelines can be surprisingly difficult to follow, especially when one feels strongly that a poor decision has been made. It takes a great deal of awareness and steely resolve from both parties to keep the company's best interests at heart (rather than trying to 'win'). One way we support achieving high levels of awareness is to encourage the use of tried and tested tools such as the Ladder of Inference and transactional analysis (see Argyris 1982 and Berne 1968). These tools help us to understand our internal thought processes and slow us down in the moment so we can have dialogue based on considered responses rather than knee-jerk reactions.

The Ladder of Inference is a mental model that points to the steps we take or 'the ladder we climb in our heads' when we are working out how to respond in any given situation. The model suggests that at lightning speed we go from the observable data around us to selecting small portions of that data, to giving that data meaning based on past experience (assumption), to drawing conclusions and taking action based on our interpretation of the data we selected. This can help us to understand the filters we're applying to a situation based on previous experience, and therefore the conclusions to which we're jumping rather than really hearing the information in the present moment. Transactional analysis can help us to understand which 'ego state' we are in at any given moment, such as 'parent', 'adult' or 'child'.

This helps us to understand what emotional state could be driving our behaviours and responses, which could override the facts of the matter in any given situation, when what we often need is a balance of emotion and logical thinking. Tools such as these are introduced to all our employees via 'toolbox talks' (see Chapter 12) and through coaching (see Chapter 9). Having these tools at our fingertips can help us bring constructive and self-aware challenges, and be self-reflective about whether we are really acting in the best interests of the company.

Here's Pat to tell us how slowing yourself down in the moment can help when it comes to challenging decisions:

There was a project to replace part of the system and the developers were looking at a different way of doing something... I went into it and there were bits I knew I didn't like from what I'd already seen. I was very aware that was because they were different from what I'm used to and it's a different way of doing something that I don't know about because I've not done it.

Rather than doing what I used to do and just stomping my feet and being very grumpy, I said to myself: 'No, digest, think, just find one positive to start with and then you'll find some more.' That for me was one of the big things, was being able to do that, be involved but find positives as well. If there's something you don't like, why is it you don't like it? What is it that's making you not like something? Then actually explaining that. Don't always look to the past as to the reasons but also look to the future for what might happen in that situation, knowing that you can make a small adjustment down the line.

Having an explicit process helps people to think through what effective communication looks like, which can be especially important when differences of opinion need to be considered, as Pat goes on to say here:

You can challenge things, but you can't just say 'No, I don't like it' – that's not good enough, you have to have a reason and you have to be able to explain that reason to people and be open for your opinion to be challenged. Having a differing opinion is OK; you don't have to agree with everything. What you do need to do is understand where those disagreements are and why your opinion might not be the one that is upheld. Understanding the whys is so important to it.

Questions that seek to understand and invite sharing of information create an atmosphere of collaboration rather than confrontation. They keep us curious and open. For example, instead of asking a challenging question such as 'Why can't this other date work?' (which can lead to a defensive response), opening with a more open and powerful question such as 'What led you to suggest this date? Can you tell me more about other dates you considered?' can completely change the nature of the interaction.

It's also not easy when even the company's best interests can be subject to debate; it can look different from different perspectives. This is when our strategy and purpose are put to the test. For example, some years ago we were asked to provide iaptus to a potential customer in an overseas market. One of the directors was thinking of going ahead but several teams in the business felt there were some significant risks attached to providing our software in the country and mounted a challenge. The teams felt that the scope of the decision and its potential impact for the business were greater than that perceived by the decision maker. They challenged that the decision-making process hadn't been followed – all those with wisdom and knowledge and likely to be affected felt they hadn't been adequately consulted – and as a result that the decision maker lacked clarity as they didn't have all the information needed to make the decision.

The group asked for the background as to where the lead had come from, all the factors that had been taken into account by the decision maker (context). Shared documents were generated to capture the facts and impact on teams (common ground, clarify). Finally, a meeting was held where everyone's views were heard, the opportunity discussed openly, and the decision to provide iaptus in that particular country at that particular time was turned around. A successful challenge had played out.

What of the person having their decision challenged? By engaging with the challengers on these terms, they have an obligation to consider the challenge, but they don't have to be persuaded. If they decide to stick with their decision, they continue to be accountable for it, being willing to think again depending on how things go. And what of our challengers at this point? Well, if their challenge isn't sustained, that's the time to get behind the decision and the decision maker, even if they still disagree. This is vital to keep things moving forward. I'll now hand over to Ruth to go through some of the lessons we have learned so far.

Lessons learned

In the few years following the launch of our decision-making process, a number of habits emerged that diverged from the steps described. Even though the orange hands posters were all over our offices, over time they, and therefore the process, became overlooked. Here are some important pitfalls we learned to correct and improve.

It's not about consensus, but rather, the right people at the right time

Our culture is built upon the value we place on collaboration, involving and listening carefully to all parties involved, believing that everyone at Mayden has perspective, ideas and insight to contribute. However, the pursuit of exploring all options then building consensus can seem unhealthily attractive. The trap easily fallen into is that the alternative to top-down decision making is keeping the discussion open until everyone agrees. This can be time consuming, inefficient and problematic: a decision that everyone agrees with may not be the right decision. As George S. Patton said: 'If everyone is thinking alike, then somebody isn't thinking.'

While waiting for consensus is rarely the best approach, we have found there is a relationship between good decision making and getting buy-in. According to one old proverb, 'If you want to go fast, go alone; if you want to go far, go together.' While our decision-making process identified that being a decision maker is about having the skills and experience, we've learned that an equally important factor is being able (and willing) to take responsibility for the consequences of that decision. In practice, one person rarely shoulders the full responsibility of a decision on their own, so the decision maker is rarely just one person; it's more often a small group of people, or at least sufficient buy-in is needed from those who need to implement or adhere to the decision.

We've learned the importance of identifying and communicating who the decision maker is (or are) so that it's clear how to direct a question or challenge (we've also learned the importance of distinguishing between the two). The decision maker needs to feel ownership and responsibility for seeing through a decision and its consequences. In a larger group this sense of ownership and responsibility can be too dispersed or watered down, leading to the 'everyone/no one' problem outlined in Chapter 6.

One context in which I have found this to be problematic is in the bi-weekly meeting for all iaptus developers. Over the years, it has taken on various guises, but the basic premise is that developers bring topics that may affect everyone to an open discussion. Someone might bring a question or suggestion about code standards or the use of automated testing tools. There will then be some discussion from those who have thoughts or opinions, but it can quickly reach a stalemate with no clear agreed decision or action. When someone brings their question to a room of more than 20 people looking to them to form a consensus on the answer, it's likely that you will only hear from the few voices who are confident enough, have knowledge in the area and care enough about the issue to speak up. Sensing both the frustration and ineffectiveness of this forum and approach, one developer with the support of his team proposed cancelling it. They suggested instead that anyone wanting to bring a topic could instead post it in the Slack channel, phrasing it as a proposal – i.e. intent to make a decision – and then invite challenge. This way the individual with the question is able to take ownership of making the decision and only those with interest and/or knowledge need to engage in discussion.

As we expand as a business, we're learning to involve just enough people and trust each other more to get on and make decisions without asking everyone what they think first. We're also learning to do so at the right time. Involving too many people too early when there isn't much clarity can open too many options and waste people's time, but missing key information held by individuals costs time too. In some of the decisions that led to the latest revamp of the decision-making process, a source of tension was individuals and teams feeling they'd become involved or were consulted too late in the process. In relation to deciding whether to take on a new customer in a new overseas market, this was problematic because important information was missed and led to more confrontational meetings that would've been easier conversations to have earlier on.

Consultation looks different depending on the circumstances, consequences and scope of a decision. It's even more important to consider who you need input from, whether they are directly affected, indirectly involved or a source of wisdom. Will broadcasting the information followed by ad-hoc conversations or a survey engage them, or is more active consultation appropriate? Would a round table or one-to-ones, seeking out individuals or groups, work better? The goal is to get the right people involved in the decision making at the right time by making information transparent and sharing clear timescales so that you know how to get involved if you have a piece of the puzzle.

The role of confidence, courage and ownership of consequences

We've noticed that confidence plays a big part, as do levels of trust. Even in a no-blame culture you need courage to take on the responsibility for making a decision, going through the process and accepting the consequences. When confidence and trust are high, and the no-blame culture is authentically felt, decision-making is robust and individuals feel supported, even when opinions differ.

Knowing colleagues will be supportive and there will be no negative repercussions from directors gives people the confidence to make and scrutinise decisions, ensuring we are continually striving for the best possible outcome or progress towards our goals. Any challenge the individual may receive will be from others who are working equally hard to solve the current problem.

— **Jen Talbot, analyst**

Conclusion

What no text can tell you is exactly what it's going to feel like in your organisation as you figure out how to put devolved decision making into practice. For us, we have sometimes felt stuck and a bit frustrated. There have also been breakthrough moments. It has been hugely rewarding for so many people throughout the organisation to be empowered to 'own' decisions and has led to good decisions being made where those who need to carry out the actions have been invested from the beginning.

I love our decision-making process. Once that existed, so many problems were solved by saying: 'Did you follow the decision-making process?' And usually there was only a problem when they went and said no. 'OK, go back. Read that. Follow it; come get me.' It helped so much. It just adds to our communication, adds to the collaboration, to the transparency and to the forward thinking. It literally hits all of our pillars in one go, in a seven-step process. The seven steps. I love it. It's one of my favourite things that has ever been done at Mayden.

— **Claire, product owner**

Chapter 8

What about cost control?

Managing our resources

Chris May

Not long ago, a LinkedIn post appeared in my feed proposing the radical idea that companies should not set expenditure budgets. It provoked quite a discussion but left me bemused. Mayden has never set budgets for expenditure, and it has never been a problem. The managing director of the consultancy company where I worked before founding Mayden sowed the seed for this. His philosophy was to focus on the income, and the expenditure would take care of itself. I worked there for six years, and it never failed. If income fell, we curbed expenditure. But as long as income held up in line with targets, the levels of expenditure just seemed to magically stay in line. Turnover, gross profit and net profit simply climbed in unison. Admittedly, this probably wouldn't work in complex businesses with lots of capital equipment, stock and consumables or with complex supply chains, so the challenge outlined here is primarily directed at service companies, which today form the greater part of the UK economy.

In many organisations, managing a budget is one of the most taxing tasks of a departmental manager. The work doesn't start at the beginning of the financial year. Before that, a huge exercise is normally undertaken to set an overall expenditure budget and then subdivide it into smaller budgets categorised by expenditure type and business area. An overall financial plan for the year spawns staffing budgets, marketing budgets, IT cost envelopes, budgets for training and development, professional services, building costs, utilities and so on. In larger organisations, the top-down approach is often run in parallel with a bottom-up exercise in which cost centre managers estimate their expenditure needs and put together their version of what they'd like their budget to look like and feed it up through the hierarchy.

Very rarely do these two approaches meet in the middle. The bottom-up budgets fall short of the top-down budgets even less often. Consequently, these two exercises almost always result in an aggregation of bottom-up budgets exceeding the overall budget, at which point a process of negotiation and challenge begins until a compromise is reached, and the budget is finalised and etched in stone. Typically, this whole process will need to start three to six months before the beginning of the financial year and consumes a vast amount of time and resources. Budget holders then begin managing their allocated budgets from the start of the year. From that point onwards, it's simply a process of making sure expenditure, month by month, doesn't exceed the individual lines on the budget statement. Since nothing is ever likely to happen that causes this process to be derailed, the managers can work confidently, assured that the budget has accurately predicted and allowed for all the eventualities that the year will bring.

Yeah, right.

If all the time and resources spent planning and managing budgets were actually focused on improving products and services, or on providing a better customer experience, could it be that this effort might result in more income? Maybe more than enough to compensate for, or wipe out, a budget deficit? And if we're not managing people *or* money in the way in which we are accustomed, what more can we do for our customers and our sales with all that saved time? That, in a nutshell, is the hypothesis we chose to test at Mayden pretty much from inception. Let's look at how we did it and how well it worked.

How Mayden manages expenditure

The philosophy we chose to adopt is quite simple:

+ Set an income target and a bunch of financial ratios.
+ Instruct the staff to spend whatever they need to get the job done.
+ Monitor the ratios at regular intervals.
+ Initiate mitigating actions if things get out of line.

More specifically, Mayden aims to grow sales at a steady 15 per cent per annum, which is equivalent to doubling in size every five years. So, each annual sales target is generally 15 per cent higher than the year before (there are exceptions – usually when we've won additional one-off grant funding – but the 15 per cent principle generally applies). Why 15 per cent specifically? Because that seems to be the level at which the company can grow comfortably, attracting, recruiting and onboarding additional staff, converting sales, maintaining customer service levels, all while achieving a healthy work/life balance. It seems to work, so we've taken the view that if it ain't broke...

Next, we set financial ratios that also seem to maintain a healthy business dynamic. These will be different for every organisation, but for Mayden, keeping recurring revenue growth higher than non-recurring revenue growth, maintaining gross and net profit margins, ensuring staff costs are around 50 per cent of expected turnover, and setting a target for financial turnover per whole time equivalent (WTE) all combine to create

157

the right balance. No budgets, just a handful of metrics that can be produced and monitored quite easily.

In line with our values, this is all made transparent to everyone in the company. They know what the revenue target is, as well as the ratios being monitored, and they then promptly forget about it. As long as everything stays in step, the only instruction they are required to follow is to spend whatever they reasonably need to spend (left to their own judgement, not defined for them) to get the job done. And they do. Everyone, no matter their role, experience or tenure, has permission to spend money if they need to. If someone wants to spend a lot of money (again, not defined) then they can check in with colleagues or directors before initiating the spend. Or simply follow the decision-making protocol (explained in the previous chapter). Some feel confident in spending more money than others; some see it as a challenge to spend as little as possible! There are no other rules, other than to follow the decision-making and challenge process outlined in the previous chapter.

In truth, it surprised me that, given the power and responsibility and no budget, people generally spend less than might have been expected. I would characterise this as acting as if they were spending their own money. For example, when away on business trips, staff generally spend less on hotels than I would expect. At a London conference that many of us attended a few years ago, one team elected to book a hotel just outside London and commute each morning because overall the cost was much cheaper than staying near the venue, even though that's where the rest of us were.

Pat, an account manager, outlines here how this plays out in practice:

Even when you go on a customer visit, if you want to take some biscuits, tea, coffee, milk, that's OK (NHS staff often have to bring their own, so we like to take our own as well as some for them). Nights away are expected as is the need to pay for things on the company credit card. There isn't a cap set on that; it's to use your best judgement. And because of that, people don't abuse it. If anything, we probably underdo ourselves at times – we do things detrimental to ourselves because we want to give the best value to either the client or the company. That autonomy, to be able to spend money and not have to worry about whether you should be able to do it or not, just allows you to make changes and do those little things that make a difference to the customer.

Checks and balances

Each week, as the director covering finance, I'm presented with a list of planned payments to review where our money's going. It's too late to stop it – the money has already been committed – but it provides a simple 'appropriateness check' and only takes 15 minutes. If the decision-making process has been followed, there shouldn't be anything surprising on the list. And there rarely is. Each financial period (currently quarterly for Mayden, but we'll soon be moving to monthly) we check in on the finances and review where the ratios are. If the ratios are within the envelope set, no action is required. If any of the ratios have deviated from the plan, then we seek to understand why, and whether decisive action needs to be taken. We also look at each expenditure line in the accounts against the long-term trend; if we've maintained the steady growth we were aiming for, then the expenditure should generally climb in step. If some expenditure lines are overshooting the trend in one particular period, this is quite often offset by underspends elsewhere, so even then mitigation isn't needed. For example, increases in the use of external contractors mostly goes hand in hand with lower staff costs; we may have looked for resources externally because we weren't able to recruit for a vacancy. The beauty of this approach is that it creates a simple PDSA (Plan-Do-Study-Act) cycle (see deming.org/explore/pdsa), using a small number of simple metrics, which aligns philosophically with our agile way of working. No huge financial planning exercise; no budgets; no budget management.

What I'm also committed to is regularly and openly sharing the company's financial results with the whole business. I do this at one of our 'all hands' fortnightly meetings or a staff day. Not only is this transparency in keeping with our values, but it helps to improve the financial literacy of everyone involved and is part of the feedback loop on progress towards our strategic and financial goals.

Does it work?

So far, so good. In 20 years, we've only once had to ask our employees to curb expenditure – and that wasn't even due to employees overspending. When we bought our new offices, there was a potential three-month gap between paying the property tax and reclaiming it, creating a temporary but sizable cash flow pressure. Employees responded, expenditure fell, and we sailed through the cash crunch unscathed. In terms of the ratios, our staffing costs – targeted at 50 per cent of turnover – have varied between 47 and 53 per cent. Turnover per WTE – a key metric – has ranged from £60,000 to £85,000 (although this target is purposely designed to climb as the company grows). Both of these have impacted on profits that have similarly fluctuated. So, we've never hit any of the targets precisely, but over many years a less successful year has been offset by a good year and vice versa. It's virtually impossible to hit a range of targets like this on the nose, but it appears, for Mayden at least, not to matter within a reasonably widespread range.

How does Mayden's approach compare with other organisations?

Thus far, there hasn't been a great deal of interest in running organisations without budgets, but a Beyond Budgeting movement has been in existence for more than 20 years (as old as Mayden, even though our paths have never crossed). Beyond Budgeting (bbrt.org) has gained significant traction over this time; it too is based on agile financial management and has set out some useful principles to follow. Equinor (formerly Statoil), Handelsbanken and Norwegian IT company Miles are all organisations that have moved 'beyond budgeting' to create their own agile cost management systems. They each do it in a different way. If you're interested in exploring this further, the Corporate Rebels website is a good place to start (as it is for much of what we discuss in this book).

Moving forward

Just because something has worked for 20 years doesn't mean it will work for the next 20. Yet there's no immediate reason to change course. I do wonder what would happen if we were to make a significant investment in breaking a new market, though. Would we really throw money at it without some sort of cost control? I can't imagine we would, but I do expect we would, in true agile style, try to fail fast to limit any losses. We wouldn't want to keep investing in a project that clearly wasn't working. Prior to that, it may be appropriate for us to set some budgets – not to limit expenditure but rather to drive it. Actually, Mayden already has one budget – for training and development. This isn't in place to ensure we don't overspend; rather the opposite, so that employees use it all up and support their development. There's generally an issue with under, not over, spending here. It's possible that other target spending budgets may emerge, for example in marketing to make sure we spend enough on campaigns and events to attract new customers. But for the foreseeable future they'll continue to be in the minority and directed at those areas we believe will drive the business forward.

Time

Closely linked to cost control is the issue of time and how it's used. In service industries that's where most of the expenditure goes. Here again, Mayden's approach is different.

In the month that I wrote this chapter, I learned that:

+ Twelve per cent of our clients took up one third of our customer support resource.

+ The amount of marketing effort we have put into developing a new overseas market is nowhere near what we had planned.

+ A system upgrade in our main data centre had been completed ahead of schedule and had only required two engineers and not the three we had estimated.

+ We have so far this year dedicated one sixth of our expenditure to research and development.

+ An unexpected bug required two developers three days to fix, which meant we were unable to complete our planned work.

+ Our sickness/absence levels were less than half those seen the year before when a winter bug swept round the office.

+ A quarter of the staff were not on track to use up their annual leave during the current year due to the pandemic.

+ Six members of the team were working hours that the company considered to be inconsistent with a healthy work/life balance.

I'm sure you'll agree that all of these metrics are useful when it comes to understanding and managing a healthy business. But the fact that I know these things is not the point; it is *how* I know them. In a book that seeks to explore many innovative and different ways of working, I'm predicting that this section may be one of the most contentious. And that's because, when we're asked to give seminars and workshops on our culture and management arrangements, this is the aspect that causes some consternation. In fact, when one leading advocate of the UK's 'reinventing organisations' movement heard about this, he swore that not only would he never work for our company, but he also wouldn't even turn up for the interview!

What do we do that's so distasteful? We monitor how we spend our time. Accounting for time is nothing new. Agencies, consultancies and professionals who charge by the hour do it routinely. They have to, otherwise they wouldn't be able to send out accurate invoices. Most of these types of organisations even have chargeable hours targets and continually monitor progress against them. Usually, though, the non-chargeable element of work is ignored; it's not of interest. This is surprising to me. In an organisation that primarily charges for services rather than goods, staffing costs typically represent around two thirds of total expenditure (and is certainly true of all the organisations I have worked for). These same organisations usually run sophisticated financial and accounting systems in which every transaction the business makes is recorded in detail, from purchasing an office building to buying a sandwich on a business trip. Yet these expenses only represent one third of the total.

What about the other two thirds? What is that being spent on?
On people.
On people?
Yes. We buy their skills and experience.
Oh, right. Using what currency?
Pounds sterling, usually.

That's your currency. What's theirs?

Time.

Bingo. You pay them for their time.

Yes.

So how does that time get spent?

You get the point. We monitor one third of expenditure in minute detail and largely ignore the primary two thirds. In an organisation of 100 people, that amounts to around 170,000 working hours each year. Think what you could achieve with that amount of time and then ask if the organisation as a whole is achieving the equivalent. Is the time being spent wisely? Is it adding value to the business? Is it furthering the organisation's strategy? Are those skills and experiences being utilised optimally? These are the key questions; monitoring how we spend our time for its own sake is meaningless if we don't then compare it in some way to the value added and contrast it with how that time might have been better spent.

But there are other questions we might want to ask. Are all our clients receiving their fair share of the support they are paying for? Do we have the right balance between maintaining our products and new product development? Are we devoting enough of our time to R&D? Is our marketing execution effort helping to deliver our commercial plan? All of these questions have partial answers that involve understanding where we are spending our time. For a data--driven organisation intent on using insights to drive the business forward, it's crucial that we understand where those 1,700 hours per full-time employee per year are actually spent.

So, what's the problem? In a word: trust.

Asking people to account for their time, to clock in and out, to complete timesheets, at first appears to be at odds with an enlightened, self-managing organisation. New starters sometimes express the view that completing timesheets is counter to the culture they thought they were joining. After all, how is behaving like Big Brother consistent with requiring people to be their own boss? Doesn't it show a lack of trust in individuals? And doesn't that fly in the face of everything we believe in and are trying to achieve? Essentially, does it bring into question the underlying ethos we so boldly stated in Chapter 3?

Well, yes and no.

I say 'yes', because clearly, in the wrong hands, the information could be used for individual surveillance purposes and would be countercultural. But, of course, that isn't the organisation we're trying to create, and if we've succeeded then it shouldn't be an issue. In our case, we couldn't really excel at any of our four core values if we didn't track how we spend our time. I would even go as far as to say that not tracking time is selling short the whole 'reinventing organisations' movement. After all, if an organisation truly is flat, then who's actually doing the monitoring? Who is Big Brother? Surely a fear of being watched is a clear indication that the desired culture change has not been achieved.

For the avoidance of doubt, we don't require our staff to clock in and out, we don't monitor their activity directly and we don't require them to have subcutaneous trackers implanted. But we do ask them to account for their time. For most, this is not achieved by filling in timesheets directly, but is captured as a by-product of completing tasks and adding actions to our internal management system, Orbit. These tasks are created by individuals and placed on task boards set up by those same individuals to plan and execute their roles. Teams and individuals are completely free to organise their work however they wish. Remember, we are managing the work, not the people.

The data is then freely available and used by individuals, teams and the directors to help them understand how they spend their time, and to challenge themselves and each other as to whether they're spending that resource in the best way. More often it's used by teams to analyse how time is being spent collectively, and to seek insight into all the types of questions that were posed at the start of this chapter.

At Mayden, buying people's time comes with a price tag of several million pounds. For the use of this time to be completely opaque would be countercultural to an organisation that professes to be data driven, seeking insights from the information at its disposal, notwithstanding that we also profess to do this for our clients. This transparency applies across the organisation and to every individual. It's not a caveat to everything we claim to have achieved; it's part of our DNA.

What's important is that the data is used. There's little point collecting all of the data and then not doing anything with it, and once time tracking becomes part of the DNA, there's a danger that the data just gets collected for no obvious reason. There's a cost – in time – to collecting all of this data, so it needs to be seen to be worthwhile. It's therefore important not only to analyse the data but also to surface those insights so that employees can see the benefits of their labour, especially those employees who struggle to integrate time capture into their daily routines and inevitably end up having to catch up.

Data quality can also be an issue. To encourage employees to capture how they spend their time, we allow them to do so in whatever way makes most sense to them or suits them best. This can create a very mixed picture with some employees capturing their activities in minute detail and in real time while others add the minimum necessary to tick the box and do so retrospectively. So, this isn't a nut we've managed to crack perfectly – yet – but the data we have still provides an immense contribution to our understanding of how we work.

That said, tracking and analysing how time is spent is not a prerequisite to developing an autonomous management structure. It's not for everyone. But if transparency is a core value, and we really mean it, then building a complete picture of how we work – who and what benefits from all those hours we put in – must be a key component of our culture.

Chapter 9

Aren't coaches just managers by another name?

From manager to coach (and why I couldn't go back)

Michele Rees-Jones

'Mayden won't have managers anymore.' It was 2016 and this one sentence was about to change my entire career. Managing teams of people was my bread and butter, and I'd carved out a fulfilling career managing fundraising and marketing teams. I loved the people element of my job, but it was always within the traditional framework of bureaucratic management structures, most often based on seniority within a hierarchy. No matter which organisation I worked for, every year saw the (excruciatingly onerous) round of appraisals, pay reviews and occasionally unpleasant staff disciplinaries. Mayden had always been a bit different in that these formalities were more relaxed, but I was still a manager with a team of people. The culture was different to previous organisations I'd worked in, but the management arrangements were largely the same.

In November 2015, I headed, for the second time, into the world of baby groups and nappies, fully expecting to return to my role as line manager within Mayden's marketing team at the end of maternity leave. I stayed in the loop while I was away from the office and, during a catch-up with our directors, heard about a new way of working that would change the way we operated as a business: 'flat structure'. Every team would become self-managing, inspired by agile principles, responsible for agreeing priorities, setting goals and outcomes and coordinating projects without being told what to do by a manager, team leader or supervisor. To help facilitate this, coaching was to be introduced for teams and individuals where managers would previously have taken on that role. If it worked, there would simply be no need for managers. It sounded really progressive. And yet, I was a manager – and one of those managers at Mayden to boot!

Fast-forward five years, and a member of the Mayden team described their experience of coaching as 'life changing'. That's a pretty affirming statement about one of the key changes Mayden made – from management to coaching – and it's one we're proud of. It was certainly life changing for me as I transitioned from manager to coach, mirroring the transition of the whole organisation. This chapter isn't intended to be a sales pitch for coaching – there's plenty of material out there if you want to scrutinise it. The truth is, companies have employed the services of coaches for decades, and for good reason. Coaching has become a clear trend in the business world. It's an empowering way to engage employees in their development and careers. What's important to us is how central it is to our way of working, filling several important gaps when choosing something other than traditional line management. When we decided to try out peer-to-peer coaching as part of our way of working, it made a profound difference. Our intention in this chapter is to offer some insights from our journey – things that really made a difference to us – that you might find helpful in deciding whether to introduce coaching within your organisation.

The reason for coaching

If coaching is on your organisation's radar, before reading any further, just take a few moments to consider the following questions:

1. What is your motivation for introducing coaching?
2. What changes do you want to see by introducing coaching?

Our motivation was simple yet significant. When Mayden started to seriously consider moving away from traditional hierarchy to a much flatter structure, we quickly learned that you can't just remove managers and expect everyone to crack on, empowered and invigorated by their new freedoms. You need to think about the impact that could have on teams and individuals. We gave serious thought to how that management vacuum would be filled. If you don't have managers orchestrating a group of people to deliver work, we soon learned that you need something, and for us that something was coaches, facilitators and mediators. You may find that at first some of your people will find the transition to a new way of working challenging. Making the required mindset shift from being managed to self-managing can mean that people need support to find their way (this has been our experience to some extent). After all, most managers don't simply set the work – they're often also facilitators, mediators, the ones who give feedback, decide the promotions and how an individual progresses, and act as informal careers advisors and problem-solvers. They may be seen as the senior staff who have climbed the ladder and have control over pay rises and the ability of others to rise up the ranks, or tell an employee what training they should do next. They can be sponges for frustration and resentment from above and below in the hierarchy, and can be a buffer against which others can absolve themselves of responsibility or accountability. Take out your managers and where does that leave the people who have come to expect all of this from them?

In a self-managing model, many of these responsibilities are given back to teams and the individuals within them to manage for themselves. That's a significant change – and for some, a pretty disconcerting one. How could they be supported in managing their own contribution, their decision making and personal progression? We've already heard about team coaching – in the development teams in Chapter 4 and from Hannah in the marketing team in Chapter 6. A key part of the scrum master's role is coaching their teams to be high-functioning, productive, ever-improving units. Given that every team is made up of individuals, the question then followed: how do we support the *individual* to thrive within their team and maximise their potential? If *team* coaching through scrum could be part of the scaffolding, then *individual* coaching could be too. This is where our team of internal coaches comes in, along with my role as the owner of our individual coaching programme. If everyone is expected to manage themselves, we believe this has to mean offering coaching to *every* Mayden employee who wants it rather than a privilege extended to just the 'top talent' or the senior leadership team, as is so often the case in many companies. Right from the outset we accepted that an appropriate level of investment would be needed. We were satisfied that coaching had enough potential and credibility within the company to try rolling it out. Our answer to the first question I posed was clear. Now it was time to try putting it into practice.

Getting coaching off the ground

We were clear that we were not simply replacing management with management-by-proxy. There was definitely a risk as we left a management gap that coaching could become a euphemism for management. Coaches were most definitely not going to be there to do appraisals, review people's performance or judge anyone on their contributions or productivity. We wanted to support our people to contribute well, confidently, creatively and collaboratively within our new structure. While we felt as though our collective management style often reflected coaching practice, none of us really knew how to go about being coaches.

The first step was to find colleagues who'd be willing to become coaches. We put out a call for volunteers to come forward to do some foundational coaching training and were delighted when a small group stepped up. It's important to remember that none of them were going to be full-time coaches – each had a day job, from developers to marketers to product owners – and would be required to negotiate time out of their team sprints to work in a coaching capacity. We expected that some flexibility would be needed within teams to support this initiative, and sure enough our teams responded positively.

The next step was to commission an experienced and credentialed coach to deliver the training for us. The new coaches spent a day learning the fundamental principles and practices of coaching with Kirstie Sneyd, a professional coach whom we first met in Chapter 5 in relation to her work with us on our values. Refresher training was scheduled for six months later, and the two coaching team leads were able to work with her on a one-to-one basis in a coach-mentor capacity. In addition to the training, Kirstie helped us to figure out some of the things that we might want to implement in order to practise with credibility. This included getting to know the world of coaching a little bit better, networking at International Coaching Federation (ICF) events and extending our network of coaches outside the business. Coaching consists of a vast and varied tapestry of approaches and models. Getting some fundamental training was a necessary first step, but we were keen to explore other methods and techniques too. One of the coach trainees (Philippa) remembers asking the coach trainer after the refresher training: 'How do you think Mayden is doing with this coaching programme?' She cautioned: 'Well, you've only got to the tip of the iceberg.' Five years on, it's clear what she meant but we have continued to build our expertise. During the past year we have commissioned leadership and team coach Will James to help the coaching team take our coaching practice to the next level of professional competence.

At this point you may be wondering why we didn't just pay external coaches to deliver our coaching sessions as well as our training. It's true that buying in coaching would be an expensive enterprise, but this wasn't the reason why we decided to train up our own people. We wanted to make sure that coaching was available to anyone within the business whenever they needed it. By upskilling a team of internal coaches, we were able to achieve this quickly and cost-effectively. But it spoke to the way we work more broadly too. This was an opportunity for some colleagues to expand their skill sets in an area that was interesting to them, but would also deliver a benefit to the business. It enabled a coaching culture to permeate the business. By embedding coaching skills in our own coaches, the coaching team, as well as those they are coaching, take a coaching approach out of their one-to-ones and into everyday work and engagements with each other. As a result, if you get stuck on something at Mayden you are likely to be asked a powerful question to help you get unstuck rather than just being given an answer or advice.

Once we had some foundational training under our belts, we were able to start coaching our colleagues. They could choose up to three coaches from the team with whom they felt they could develop a constructive coaching relationship. Then, depending on their capacity, we'd pair them up with one from that shortlist. We've found that this does result in some coaches being requested more frequently, but we often broker the new partnerships while taking individuals' capacity into account. Depending on the number of coachees they have, this means that some coaches gain experience faster than others, but we tackle that by ensuring that we all engage in the same training and share our learning and skills with the wider team. Early on in our coaching venture, we organised a 'coaching cream tea' event where colleagues could meet the coaching team and figure out who they would like to try working with. It was like a coaching version of speed dating, and some have been paired in a coaching partnership ever since!

How coaching works

From the outset, we knew that it was important for people to choose a coach with whom they could have an open and trusting conversation. Confidentiality is particularly important when setting up an internal coaching programme, especially in a reasonably small company where everyone knows everyone else. We knew it was likely that coachees would want to explore conflicts and challenges that were happening within their own teams. We suggested (and still do) that coachees should choose coaches from outside their teams or business areas. As a consequence, we have coaching partnerships between individuals from every different part of the business, and so far this has worked effectively. It has also resulted in some fantastic additional benefits, as colleagues who wouldn't usually have the opportunity to work together are able to. Coaching is a great leveller. The skills of a coach aren't necessarily based on experience or background and therefore sometimes less experienced colleagues find themselves coaching those with more experience, even directors. This is definitely not the norm in most organisations, but it works effectively for us and reaffirms that we're walking our flat structure talk.

Our coaching philosophy has always remained the same – sessions are offered to the individual to give them the headspace to work on any challenges, goals or ambitions that they want to focus on. For good reason, coaching at Mayden isn't mandatory. It's not helpful to assume that everyone will *want* to work with a coach, as coaching requires the individual to engage in open dialogue. People value different ways of accessing support. Therefore, in line with our company ethos of self-management, coaching is optional. It's important to understand that coaching will only be impactful if the individual wants to engage in it. Some may prefer to work with a mentor; some may need to speak to a director; some may prefer to work things through directly with their teams. That's all OK, as our coaching programme is part of the broader support that the company makes available.

Right from the beginning we felt it was important to offer clarity around what a coach was there to do and what fell outside their remit. We drafted some expectations and principles that our coaches and coachees discuss in their first session. This clearly sets out what the expectations of the partnership are on both sides. Crucially, this contracting makes it clear that the content of coaching sessions is completely confidential – unless the coachee shares something that suggests the coachee is putting themselves, a colleague or the business at risk. Then we have a responsibility to escalate it. These red lines are a major part of the coaching contract. We have a clear protocol, agreed with our HR team, for when an issue raised in coaching needs to be referred. It's to protect both coach and coachee as Mayden employees, as well as the business. We understand that this is essential to an internal coaching programme such as this.

Even without crossing one of the red lines, the 'what happens on tour, stays on tour' mindset may sound as if it conflicts with our company value of transparency, but it's critical for building trust and an effective rapport between coachee and coach. Expecting someone to manage themselves is huge. They're going to need a safe space to figure things out. The confidential coaching relationship allows them to work on issues that may be holding back their contribution without the inhibiting fear that a manager is going to hear all about it.

Once a partnership is up and running, we allow the individuals involved to set the terms. No coaching relationship needs to be permanent, and we strive for flexibility to suit the individual coach and coachee. Some of our coachees have worked with the same coach for five years and counting, but we also actively encourage our coachees to try working with other coaches to experience different styles and techniques. We offer taster sessions, and an introduction to coaching has become a key part of our induction programme for new starters. Introducing coaching at the induction stage has definitely increased uptake as many of our new employees expect and want to work with a coach right from the start. Our coaches and coachees are free to agree on the frequency and duration of their sessions, and it's up to the coachee what they discuss in their sessions.

As colleagues, we have the freedom to suggest that a colleague may want to discuss something with a coach, but nobody has a say in what the coachee actually works on with their coach. This is possible because, as we'll learn in Chapter 12, each individual at Mayden is responsible for their own development and progression. Often, colleagues use their coaching sessions to discuss the feedback they've received with a view to working out how to improve and progress; to assess their own performance, set their own goals, to understand their professional identity at Mayden, work on blind spots or tackle things they've identified as wanting to improve, such as confidence, self-esteem, developing expertise and so on. They will use coaching to work out how to better contribute to the company, unblock obstacles and reflect on decisions they need to make. Sometimes coachees come to sessions with no plan for what they want to discuss. These are often the richest sessions. Issues surface that the coachee wasn't even conscious were bothering them. We've gone a step further by allowing the coaching setting to flex for each individual depending on what suits them best, so our coaches offer walking coaching, coaching in cafes, remote coaching by video, as well as the odd coaching session on the swings in the nearby park (never underestimate the power of play in unlocking our creativity). Not surprisingly, most sessions take place on a walk or over a coffee.

The coach's perspective

So, how is the experience for the coach? It was while sitting in a pub for a maternity leave catch-up with Ali SD, my line manager and director at Mayden, that I heard that career-changing sentence with which I started this chapter. It wasn't immediately obvious to me what this meant. Where would the support for our teams come from if we didn't have managers? What did this mean for me? My brain was racing: 'What about my job...? Coaching... What exactly is that? And what about my team? And... and... and...' I was suddenly overwhelmed with questions about my role, my place in the company, my career – my very identity. Like so many of my peers, I'd grown up conditioned to strive for accomplishment. From GCSEs to A-levels, from a degree to a good job with ranks to climb and salary increases to pursue – it was all laid out before me as naturally as putting one foot in front of the other. If I wasn't going to be a manager anymore, what did that mean for my professional status? As it turned out, it didn't mean much. Over the next few weeks, I realised that I'd never needed 'status' but had conflated achievement and purpose with status; what I needed was purpose and meaning in my role. When I reflected on my previous career choices it was clear that social purpose had been key to my choices so far – first in international aid, then in the NHS and then at Mayden, which is an entirely purpose-driven business. This wasn't a promotion, but it was a clear recognition of my skill and ability to help people get the best out of themselves, as well as being a fantastic opportunity to take my own development in a really positive direction. I realised this was an opportunity that actually played to my core strengths.

Back to the pub... Ali SD went on to explain that some of the programme was already under way – a group of internal coaches would support their colleagues to navigate our new way of working and help them to find their own solutions without resorting to managerial direction. The programme was being piloted among our software developers and the next step was to roll it out to the rest of Mayden. I agreed that, on my return, I'd leave my manager hat behind to train as a coach with the cohort of internal coaches, and encourage colleagues to participate in our fledgling programme.

Five years later, here I am – a professionally certified coach, loving my role at Mayden, and no longer a line manager grinding through the annual cycle of 'people management'. I couldn't go back. I've been genuinely surprised by what I've learned about the positive power of coaching and how it can impact people and company dynamics, as well as by how much I've enjoyed shedding my 'manager' label and embracing a new identity. Introducing coaching was a brave step for Mayden, and indeed for me and it has been liberating.

Seeing the impact on those being coached has been equally satisfying. Coachee (and more recently newly trained coach) Ali Bisping, PA, shares her own experience of coaching and how it has been transformative in her world:

> As soon as the programme was announced at Mayden, I signed up to work with a coach. I remember being nervous – what would we talk about? How would this work? What could I discuss? I didn't know my coach that well – was that an advantage or disadvantage? Of course, there were guidelines which helped me to understand that I could take various areas of my life to our sessions for discussion. It required me to be open minded and ready to be challenged. I'm not shy about sharing the main topic I've taken to my sessions. This is because coaching has helped me to move forward in such an impactful way, and I'm proud of the progress I've made.

By the time I started working with my coach, I'd been with Mayden for quite a few years. All of our work meetings were open, and we were all encouraged to contribute, and we still are. The only issue was I didn't feel comfortable doing so in front of a group. I was afraid of not knowing enough, of wasting people's time. This wasn't only related to my work life. I was often told that outwardly I appeared confident, but for various reasons my self-esteem was low. My coach and I discussed my fears: what would it feel like if I were to speak up? What was the worst that could happen? What had happened in the past that made me feel this way? The team I'd been working with knew not to push me too hard, but sometimes they'd gently ask me towards the end of the meeting if there was something I wanted to say. I appreciated that approach, but I was starting to feel as if I needed and wanted to share my opinion. I started small. I remember that my coach happened to be in that first meeting when I spoke up. I looked at her and received a beaming smile of encouragement. At my next session, we discussed how I'd felt. The overwhelming feeling was relief that I'd survived! I knew then that I had to practise, and so, with encouragement, I'd speak out a little more and then a little more – and my confidence grew. I still don't like speaking up, but in spite of that I do.

To emphasise how far I've come, I'd like to share the following. I recently found myself in a meeting challenging something that was being said – in other words, not only did I speak up, I disagreed. I was able to say something rather than keeping quiet. That felt liberating. I was in a safe space to do so – and I hope I'll be able to build on that if I ever find myself in a less safe space.

The opportunity to work with a coach and being given the headspace to work on my own goals and challenges has been great. It's a great way of making you think for yourself, of challenging yourself, of trying to think of your own solutions, but with the support of someone listening to you and asking constructive but probing questions. I've benefited from this experience so much that I've now trained to become a coach myself. I want to be able to help and support others, to help them grow. I'm thankful for the opportunity Mayden has given me and grateful to my coach for being at my side.

We've also taken care to make sure that those who, for whatever reason, don't want to participate in coaching sessions don't get left behind. We're working to embed coaching as a core part of our organisational fabric. To help achieve this, in past years we have offered company-wide 'coaching conversations' training that colleagues can participate in for half a day. During these sessions we shared the fundamentals of coaching – foundational techniques such as active listening and how to ask more powerful questions – so that we're all equipped to coach in day-to-day situations, with our teams, in meetings, and not just in a coaching one-to-one. We're aiming to roll this out more regularly in the future. The team of coaches work together to maintain standards and share learning. Getting a coaching programme off the ground takes commitment from the business and needs to be taken seriously as a fundamental part of *how* the business operates. Ultimately, it's an investment in your company's best asset – its people and their futures.

Measuring impact and success

I would invite you now to think again about how you answered the questions at the start of this chapter (if indeed you were able to answer them at this time).

1. What is your motivation behind introducing coaching?
2. What changes do you want to see by introducing coaching?

We've already explored some of the possible motivations for introducing coaching in the first place. However, what about the actual changes you want to see as a result of introducing coaching? How will you know if coaching is helping your organisation to effect change? If you've made an investment in your own coaching programme, or are planning to, you'll expect a return on investment (ROI). ROI in coaching is not usually purely financial or something that you can clearly identify on your bottom line. Pinning down exactly what constitutes ROI in coaching can be different for every organisation, so you might want to consider what a reasonable ROI looks like to you. This might include an evident step change in colleagues' behaviours and mindset that your organisation values and wants to amplify; an increase in employees' confidence and better decision making; clearer and more creative thinking; an increase in people's productivity and their wellbeing, and so on. Once you have clarity on this then you're on the way to developing metrics to test and iterate how much coaching impacts your indicators of ROI. You may find it challenging to identify a tangible impact on your bottom line, but the non-financial return will be evident in what coaching can enable your people to do and how they're developing and progressing. We haven't perfected this yet, but we're working on it.

Feedback from our staff tells us that coaching is a positive enabler of personal development and supports behaviours that enable them to be more impactful in their roles. By running annual coaching surveys we're able to review what's working well within our programme, where we're effecting change and what we need to do next to ensure we flex and grow our programme according to what colleagues tell us they need. We also encourage our coaches to seek feedback from their coachees about their practice and how much it's benefiting them. Much of this is anecdotal feedback but we make sure we review it and build it into our coaching team development.

Getting out of the blocks

Reflecting on our own experience, this checklist may help you to plan some first steps to get a coaching programme up and running. It certainly helped us to get going and to keep the momentum up, but how you organise your programme will depend entirely on what your organisation wants to achieve.

1. Assure yourself that you have the capacity within the organisation to enable coaching to happen effectively. If you don't have capacity, you'll need to think creatively about how to find it.

2. Plan how you'll communicate from the outset about what coaching is and what it isn't so that everyone is clear about what to expect. Coaching isn't management or mentoring, yet without clarity people's perceptions of what it is can become blurred.

3. Gather together trainee coaches keen to get on board. You might decide to start small and then expand your numbers depending on uptake. Think about the make-up of your fledgling team – is it representative of and accessible to the people who are going to be working with them?

4. Find a credentialed coach (a coach who has achieved a level of professional competence with a recognised body such as the International Coaching Federation or Institute of Leadership and Management) who can train your team in the fundamentals of coaching theory and practice, so your programme is credible and working to a good standard from the outset.

5. Consider writing a vision statement that supports your fledgling coaching programme and makes your objectives clear.

6. Decide how you will measure the impact and success of your programme based on what is important to your organisation.

Figuring out how to navigate Mayden's way of working isn't always easy, and people experience it differently. Coaching is a fantastic tool for supporting people with their progression and development, but it isn't always the answer that people are looking for, or necessarily what someone needs at that moment. We recognise that a one-size-fits-all approach isn't a sensible way to operate. For various reasons, not everyone is so keen to focus on growth and development, and that's OK. Some of our colleagues simply want to do what they're trained for and to focus on doing that to the absolute best of their ability. We recognise them and appreciate them for this too.

We make coaching available to everyone because we believe everyone can benefit from it. Coaching is an integral part of the scaffolding that helps our people along on their Mayden journeys, should they ever want or need it. You may discover that it could be an impactful part of your organisational scaffolding too, even if you just want to start with a pilot. You have nothing to lose and so much to gain!

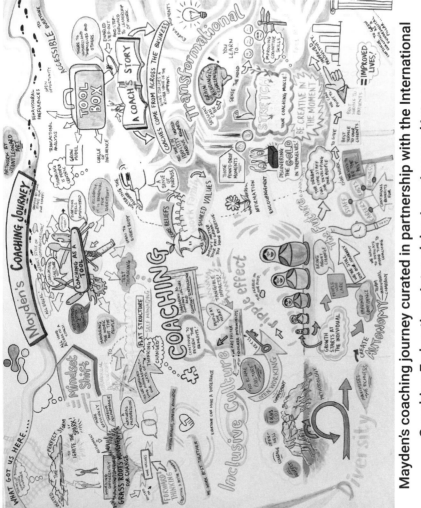

Mayden's coaching journey curated in partnership with the International Coaching Federation. Artwork by JennyLeonardArt.com

Chapter 10

Why do you still have directors?

Getting out of the way

Alison Sturgess-Durden

Let's be clear, all this talk of flat organisations is something of a misnomer. We're flat-*ter* than most, but there's still some hierarchy. As you've already spotted, we have four directors, and between them they line-manage all the other employees. Worse than that, three of the four directors are line-managed by the other one – our founder, Chris M. Yep, that's three organisational layers right there – Chris M, the other directors, everyone else. Not many, but it's not flat, is it? Busted! To be honest, as a company nearing 120 people, I think if we'd established a traditional hierarchy as we grew, we might only have one or two additional layers of middle management. So, is this all a charade? Or is there something different about our directors within the hierarchy?

We're trying to satisfy two related requirements with our organisational arrangements: our preference for how we work with each other to achieve our purpose, and our legal responsibilities. With the first, we've explained how our approach fits our beliefs about humans at work and the kind of work we need doing. We're managing the work rather than managing the people because we believe most people can manage themselves. They desire, and can be trusted with, a great deal of autonomy. We're also working this way because we believe it to be the most effective way to support innovation, sound decision making and achieving value for our customers – in short, our purpose. Which brings us to our legal requirements.

Mayden is legally constituted as a private limited company in the United Kingdom (Mayden House Ltd, Company Number 04005808). Governed by the Companies Act 2006, limited companies must have at least one director. Among the seven legal duties of any director laid down in the act, there's one about needing to act in a way 'most likely to promote the success of the company', having regard for such things as the long-term future of the business, employees, suppliers, customers, impact on the community and environment, reputation and members. Directors are further expected to exercise 'reasonable care, skill and diligence'. That's a pretty high watermark for the directors sponsoring these unusual organisational arrangements. It's the ultimate safeguard and sense check on whether or not we've lost the plot. The business must, at all times, be managed *well*. Our way of working needs to be able to (possibly, quite literally) stand up in court. If something happened to our data or a member of staff, would we be able to testify that we'd exercised appropriate management control? Of course, we want to run our company professionally, and be recognised as doing so by external stakeholders. Indeed, we have external accreditation, such as ISO27001, the international standard for information security and governance, so vital to the service we provide our customers.

We must manage the company effectively. We've just chosen to do so by retaining only as much hierarchy as is needed for that. That's because we believe too much hierarchy can actually get in the way of effective working, decision making and even risk management. The directors are different from all the other employees, having statutory responsibility for the activities of the business. All other employees are under contract with the company via their contractual terms of employment. The directors are the countersignatories to those terms on behalf of the company. There is, therefore, a contractual relationship between the company, represented by its directors, and all other staff. This creates a 'power gradient', as David Marquet (2020) puts it, between the board of directors and all other employees. Our objective, as Marquet advocates, is to keep that power gradient as shallow as possible. The role the director plays in holding that office is the key.

The role of the director

Mayden's four directors make up the company's board. We don't (yet) have non-executive directors, so we're currently in the position where our board and our director team are one and the same. That, and our way of working, heightens our awareness of the roles we four play and when we play them. The problem with being a director at Mayden is, well, you're a director. Let me tell you, being a director in a flat organisation is a tricky business – something of an occupational hazard! In the minds of the employees, you're a walking reminder, at all kinds of conscious and subconscious levels, of the very thing that you're claiming to be avoiding: hierarchy. You're in charge, but you're trying not to be. You're the boss, but you're not to be bossy. You're legally liable for the business, but have decided to hand over a great deal of power and control.

The peril of being in a formal leadership position is that as soon as you express a view, it becomes amplified. Why? Because it's you, the leader, the one with at least positional power, who hires, fires and sets salaries, who has said it. It's the highest-paid person's opinion (HiPPO). Before you know it, a thought you mentioned in passing has been taken as instruction and acted upon. No one gets fired for doing what the boss said, right? The double bind with Mayden's way of working is that any residual HiPPO mentality that anyone in the company carries exists alongside equal but opposite anti-HiPPO ideals: 'She's telling us what to do [when she wasn't, actually]. I thought we had a flat structure. She needs to stop managing us!' On a number of occasions, I've felt like the only person in the room *not* entitled to an opinion. This can get even more interesting on the rare occasion when a genuine instruction needs to be given by a director, such as in an emergency or something significant is really going off track. One director was approached by a colleague after a conversation with their teammate, who said: 'I heard that you told [x] that they needed to do [y]. That sounded like an order, so I told them that they needn't worry, that's not how we do things here; it would have just been a *suggestion.*'

The research presented in Liz Wiseman and Greg McKeown's highly recommended book, *Multipliers* (2010), identifies leadership behaviours that can multiply or diminish the performance of those being led. These are useful to any leader, but I've found them to be especially practical as a director of a flat organisation. Wiseman explains that, to allow their people to bring all they have and more, a leader needs to create space. This can be by saying as little as possible (for example, in meetings), clearly labelling their opinions (soft or hard), avoiding being the one that makes decisions (let others make them whenever possible) and getting out of the way (not getting overly involved in details and solutions). I've learned to be much clearer in expressing my intentions: soft ('Just a thought, could we...'; 'It's just one person's opinion, but I wondered...'; 'I'm saying this as a contributor to this team, not as a director'); and, sparingly, hard ('I think we should...'; and sometimes, 'I am the decision maker on this, and I've decided...'). I'm explicit about which hat I'm wearing when I speak – director or team member, and our decision-making process helps make sure that directors are not making all the decisions.

Just as much, I've found that employees need to remove the 'director' filter that they may have placed between my mouth and their ears. It's easy to respond in a Pavlovian fashion to something a director says. It's why we're so intentional about our challenge process. Directors can and should be challenged too. They may have experience and skill that has got them to the office of director, but they are at the tip of the 'iceberg of ignorance', and may not have the best knowledge or perspective on the decision. After expressing an opinion, I often ask for my views to be challenged. Equally, the director needs to be able to question and challenge, and for that to elicit a proportionate response, not become amplified.

I recall a particularly tetchy episode when I discovered one team was aggrieved with me at what they took as critical comments I'd made in a document. I read and re-read my comments, even shared them with a colleague not involved in the situation, and was stumped as to why they'd caused such offence. In fact, it was me on the receiving end of SHOUTY COMMENTS in capital letters in the document from one of the team. When we found an opportunity to talk it through, it became apparent that my comments appeared to be passing through a filter. It's fair to say that the filter had been created in part by the team's past experience of my impatience. While I've adapted within Mayden's way of working, dialling down my red preference (for swift action, then frustration if it doesn't come quickly enough for my liking; you can read an explanation of the colour profiling system we use in Chapter 6), memories were long, and this team I'd worked with for years still remembered that tone from me. It appeared to be that having passed through the filter (of an impatient, critical director), my questions and suggestions had acquired an edge and a volume that had not been intentionally transmitted. (This example also illustrates the importance of a couple of features of our challenge process: face-to-face over written communication, and avoiding climbing the Ladder of Inference mentioned in Chapter 8 before openly exploring the issues.)

With a core belief in everyone's ability to manage themselves and their work, we've created many checks and balances to make sure the directors can govern effectively (our legal duty) while not having undue influence on the best work and judgement of those closest to the issues. These checks, including our decision-making and challenge process, are especially important given you can't get away from the fact that directors at Mayden continue to have ultimate responsibility. Who isn't going to be careful and compliant with the person holding your contract of employment and setting your salary? We therefore knew we needed to go further – to formalise the degree of restraint required from our directors in how the work is managed and how people work with one another. We gave our directors a four-part role as follows:

1. Set direction.
2. Set expectations.
3. Get out of the way.
4. Seek assurance.

Let's explore each in turn.

Set direction

Every team and individual at Mayden has a day job – the work they 'own', are responsible for, have decision-making authority over and are accountable to everyone else for. For the marketing team, that includes our brand and product campaigns that generate sales leads; for the account management team, that includes supporting our customers; for the software developers, that includes deploying features. The directors' day job is setting direction – our purpose, vision and strategy. Much of the time, the director team is like any other; we also have a day job to deliver for the company, and it's not managing everyone else to do what they're meant to be doing. It's managing the part of the work that falls to us – long-term thinking and overall priority-setting. The directors' primary role is to set overall direction and priorities for the business so that everyone else knows and can manage things from there. And, of course, we set direction after much consultation across the company.

Set expectations

Directors also have a role in defining broad expectations of how everyone should work in pursuit of that direction and purpose. These expectations are summed up in our organisational values. Setting expectations includes defining the value that needs to be delivered from everyone's endeavours, yet stopping short of determining *how* it should be delivered. That's up to teams and individuals. Suffice to say, making this part of a director's role ensures that delivering value, and upholding our values, is front and centre. But it also keeps the directors focused on outcomes rather than micromanaging what the teams should do day to day.

Get out of the way

So, having set direction and expectations, the director's job is to get out of the way. Chris M frequently refers to himself as 'Chief Interferer' – it's a joke, but also a self-deprecating and honest recognition of how disruptive and disempowering having a director involved in the detail can be when they slip into it. If a director is hanging around, checking what's going on, expressing opinions, even getting drawn into making decisions, it's not long before everyone else starts to sit back to make room for the HiPPO. How can others step up unless you leave the space for them? If you trust your employees, and the best results come from letting people manage their work and themselves, you'll just be in the way and have undue influence. The directors should be getting on with their own day job – setting strategy and making the decisions only they can make. If you don't step away, you're not really handing over responsibility and authority to others. Remember, those people are accountable for what they go on to do, which brings us to the fourth role.

Seek assurance

That doesn't mean you sit there hoping for the best! Having set the direction and expectations, it's your job as director to assure yourself that the value you asked for is being delivered in line with the company's strategy and ways of working. After all, those who have been given the responsibility and authority to deliver are accountable for the results. That's why we have processes such as sprint reviews where everyone reports on their progress, and where directors ask awkward and challenging questions about what the business and the customer are getting from the past two weeks' worth of investment and effort. Note that the assurance is focused on the team, not individual, level. The directors are assuring the outcome, not appraising the people. The focus is on the performance and outcomes of the overall operation.

This also means that we focus our time on monitoring company-level performance metrics, not individuals' performance against personal objectives. When we meet as a board, we're in 'assure' mode. We park the day-to-day business of the director team and focus on key company results and risk management. Indeed, while everyone else is getting on and managing the work, one of the major functions of the director is managing whole-business risk. We have a well-established company risk register, which is reviewed on a regular basis. At every board meeting, each director is required to state the three main risks they believe the business is exposed to. This is anything from cyber threats to our ability to recruit technical expertise. At each weekly directors' meeting we pick off two risks from the register to review in detail. This keeps the risk register live and updated.

Chris M will discuss our governance regime more in Chapter 13, so I will stop here for now. The final part of the directors' assurance role is to deal with issues across the business that need to be escalated if they're going awry or would simply benefit from more support and the expertise that the directors have. This might be during an emergency when something in our software needs urgent attention. The directors' involvement might be anything from coordinating our response if it's a major issue to ordering takeaway for the team working long hours to deploy the fix.

This four-part role holds the keys to how you can direct without being dictatorial. With self-managing teams, it's not your job to tell everyone what to do. It's your job to clarify for the teams the overall direction we need to go in, the value that needs to be delivered and how we expect everyone to work together; to hold them to account for those deliverables, then get out of the way and let them get on and find the best approach, knowing you're there for support and advice if needed. The table at the end of the Introduction summarises these differences from conventional management arrangements.

Line manager

There's one more role the directors, and only the directors, at Mayden carry out – line manager. What shouldn't surprise you is that, while we still retain a line management function, the role is very much in the background, a backstop when all other alternatives have been exhausted. We don't talk about it as the fifth role of the director. Rather, we talk about 'residual' line manager duties. We'll explore this remaining role in more depth as we turn to all matters HR in our next chapter.

Taryn writes:

Throughout my education and career so far, I've been fortunate enough to have had excellent leadership role models. I've had some great line managers who were more on the coach end of the scale than micromanaging end. So, the way the directors worked at Mayden felt quite natural. When I first arrived, I felt encouraged and empowered but also unsure. I decided I had nothing to lose and jumped in, boots and all. It was brilliant, it was messy and I'm sure at times I was an annoying young pup. There I was, challenging much more experienced staff members and a director on what I thought was a better idea and why! But they believed in me; they cared about what I had to say and listened to my ideas. I wasn't going to be punished or laughed at for being wrong or too simplistic. They made me feel as if I had something to bring regardless of my experience. What I appreciated most was that they saw me as a whole person, not just an administrator.

Don't get me wrong – it wasn't all sunshine and roses, I didn't always get it right, and my South African 'say it like it is' style didn't always help. I often misread others' intentions, and in my eagerness I stepped on some toes. But it was inspiring to see how much the directors were willing to let go and empower others to run with the business. I didn't always appreciate what was going on and how tough it must have been for them. I didn't always respect the path and opportunity they'd created. Sometimes the way I navigated this openness was rather disrespectful, and I'm sorry about that.

Reflecting on that time, I can see the value in being really clear about the director's four-part role. It helped me to check: am I clear on the direction of this piece of work? Do I understand the expectations? Now that I'm clear, I can put in a boundary and be strong about where I start to take ownership. There were times when I did bump heads with Ali SD, really wanting to establish the space of ownership and make sure she got out of the way. We had to learn how to work together and find what was needed in both directions to give me the confidence to get on with the job and Ali the assurance that I was considering all the angles. There were times when I felt Ali was too involved and other times when she wasn't involved enough. We were working out our roles and responsibilities in this new way of working.

'Get out of the way' may sound strong, but it has been necessary for staff to really understand the shift, take ownership and, if need be, help them have challenging conversations when they felt a director was getting in the way. We were all unlearning hierarchical habits and learning and designing a different approach. I had no prior examples of how to do this, so I will be forever grateful to the directors for creating the space and opportunity to work this way, for seeing a better way of doing management and for letting go and trusting us all.

Chapter 11

What about all the HR?

Creating a workplace where employees thrive

Alison Sturgess-Durden

You may recall from the opening chapter that one of the first questions I'm usually asked when I talk about our way of working is: 'But what about the [poor performer/slacker/bully – delete as appropriate].' If your recruitment is sound and you don't have terrible luck, most of your employees should be competent, trustworthy and hardworking. So why build a way of working around the handful you are concerned about, as if everyone would underperform if not managed? Indeed, as Chris M argued earlier, the more autonomy you give people, the more you might find that they respond to your trust and the expectation placed on them. With all the other practices in our scaffolding in place, we've found that there's relatively little traditional people – or line – management left to do. Yet employment is a serious matter. Employer and employee need to honour contractual commitments laid out in the standard main terms of employment, and the employer to uphold their duty of care and wider employment law. And, yes, poor performance occasionally needs to be managed at Mayden. In this chapter, we're going to focus on core aspects of employment practice, including line management, the role of the HR function, recruitment, wellbeing and individual performance.

What's left of line management

In the last chapter, I explained how the four directors, and only the directors, retain 'residual' line manager duties at Mayden. That's after seeing how the traditional line manager role managing *work* and *people* has mostly been replaced by all of our other organisational arrangements. Our agile practices were effectively taking care of the work management. Coaching, feedback and the rest of what we'd put in place to enable self-managing teams and individuals were taking care of much of the people management and personal development that line managers would ordinarily support. Turn back to the table in the Introduction for the summary of what replaces each aspect of the traditional line manager function at Mayden. With so much of the conventional line manager function fulfilled by other organisational processes, the line manager role had, over time, been diminished to something covering some formalities or a final escalation point when necessary.

By 2020, the duties that remained for the line manager at Mayden covered the following seven areas:

Residual line manager role for the directors to undertake by 2020:

1. **Recruitment** – second interviews and approving job offers.

2. **Probation for new starters** – monitoring performance, undertaking the probation review.

3. **Employment terms** – setting standard main terms of employment, including individual variations (e.g. flexible working requests). Setting any other internal HR policies and procedures.

4. **Rewards and benefits** – setting individual salaries, bonuses and the company's benefits package.

5. **General check-ins** – regular one-to-ones with direct reports.

6. **Pastoral care** – support individuals in times of need, such as in the event of a bereavement.

7. **Individual performance issues** – active management of more significant performance concerns (informally and, where necessary, formally) if not resolved by the individual themselves or within teams, or issues which teams are not expected to manage themselves (e.g. high levels of sickness absence).

Even with this much-reduced role, we began to sense that if we took on too many more staff, our existing line management arrangements wouldn't scale. We had 90 employees by this point, and four directors/line managers. One director had more than 40 direct reports. Even great, self-managing employees change their hours, have babies, take time off and get sick. We still didn't have an in-house HR manager, though we made good use of an external HR advisor when needed. We had a dedicated HR officer managing payroll, letters of variation and coordinating recruitment, supporting employees at times of need, among many other tasks. Despite this, a much-reduced line manager burden, and relatively few HR issues, just the growing number of employees meant the directors were becoming increasingly stretched.

You may also detect in the seven residual duties above some lingering inconsistencies with our professed way of working. If we trust our teams to choose the best people to work with them, why does a director need to do interviews? If a new starter's team knows first hand how the newbie is performing, why isn't the team engaged with probation? If people are accountable to each other for their work and they have supportive teams, feedback, coaches and open access to a wide range of personal and professional support, why do employees still need regular one-to-one check-ins with their line manager? Given the number of direct reports, these check-ins were also the most time-consuming aspect for the directors. We admitted to ourselves that we weren't really pushing through with self-management if our line-managing directors still retained even this much responsibility towards individual employees. We wondered if challenging things further might hold some answers to our scaling issue.

We organised a series of round tables to which everyone was invited. The conversation confirmed the contradictions. We learned that employees:

+ fundamentally stood by the flat structure and self-managing principle, but were reassured by the escalation point that a line manager provided.

+ thought line managers should retain certain responsibilities, such as salary setting. Most people said these should *not* be devolved to be peer-set or self-set, often a hallmark of this way of working in other businesses.

+ the line manager role should be further diminished, yet they wanted more time with their line manager!

It was clear that we were still probing the edge of our collective comfort with, and belief in, self-management. And it felt self-perpetuating – we wondered if people still wanted to maintain such a regular relationship with their director because they retained so much responsibility for hiring, firing and salaries. Yet this couldn't scale if we continued to grow without more hierarchy and line managers. How on earth would we resolve this?

Through the company-wide conversation, we identified further adjustments to the seven residual duties. These were designed to promote even greater self-management by individuals and teams, and further diminish what's left for line managers to do. We agreed the following:

1. **Recruitment** – directors would no longer necessarily sit on interview panels (though they could, and still often do), but would still sign off on job offers after assuring themselves of the team's process and conclusions. More HR support would be provided to teams to safeguard good practice.

2. **Probation** – to be shared between the new starter's team and the line manager, who retains some involvement due to the contractual implications of passing or failing probation.

3. **Contractual employment terms** – peer panels would be convened to come up with recommendations for the directors to consider. This is what we did when we reviewed our 'place of work' policy when the office reopened after the Covid-19 pandemic. Directors still decide when terms should change, after appropriate consultation.

4. **Rewards and benefits** – directors still set salaries, but more comprehensive peer feedback should be gathered to inform decisions.

5. **General check-ins** – encourage self-management of work and of self, given our working arrangements and a wider range of support available to individuals. Be mindful of the director role in relation to work and the line manager role in relation to employment, depending on the reason for the one-to-one.

6. **Pastoral care** – line manager to continue to provide support; HR team able to support too.

7. **Escalation point** – more guidance from HR to teams in resolving issues earlier, and to line managers when escalation is required.

We agreed that teams could make this further shift at their own pace, but it has started. Since then, I've acquired five new direct reports whom I didn't meet until they started. I've been delighted with the choices the teams have made. I also sense a shift in ownership. I remember many years ago a new recruit who didn't work out. At the time, teams had less involvement in recruitment than they do now. As we began to deal with some performance issues, I was struck by how many of the team made a point of reminding me they had not been involved in recruiting the individual. I see teams now fully owning and being extremely careful in their selection process, then making sure their pick works out with excellent induction, training, coaching and support.

The HR team

You might think that all of this ability of teams to self-manage might mean the end not only of line management, but also the need for an HR function. It's not uncommon to hear of flat organisations claiming to have no HR department. We have an HR team now. I don't know how its size compares to other SMEs, so I'm not going to claim it's smaller. In fact, there may be a paradox compared with the headlines that with less line management, teams and individuals might actually need more access to HR guidance to take care of their own issues without recourse to the line manager. What's important is the positioning of the HR team as a source of advice and support.

Our information governance team are respected for their expertise. Anyone can consult them for advice, including the directors, and people follow it. Mayden's HR team have a similar position in the business – there to provide specialist advice, support and coaching to any individual or team in managing their own employment or addressing issues with teammates, minimising the need to escalate to a director in their line manager capacity.

HR policies and procedures

Just as with HR departments, it appears fashionable in companies practising similar ways of working to claim to have no employment policies or procedures. Haven't other workplaces managed to boil their staff handbooks down to a singular 'no asshole rule' (Sutton 2007), or even the 'no rules rule' (Hastings & Meyer 2020)? I'm mindful that these are often in other territories such as the USA where employment laws are quite different. Nevertheless, we're more pragmatic and less headline grabbing. As well as standard main terms of employment (our employment contracts) covering salary, hours and place of work among other terms, we have a conventional set of employment policies and procedures. Much like any other employer, these cover things such as annual leave, sickness absence and capability. But just as with any other part of the business that needs to set out procedures, we continuously strive to keep these to a minimum.

Wherever possible, these procedures incorporate authorisation points at individual or team level, enabling self-approval or team approval within company-wide guidelines. For example, annual leave is subject to peer-based approvals within teams. There's no line manager authorisation. The team knows best when someone really can't be away, or too many are trying to be away at the same time. It'll be the team that suffers if the work can't be covered.

The conundrum is that while being kept to a minimum, our policies need to provide enough clarity to guide someone to self-manage. Guidelines need to be sufficient to promote consistency and fairness without going too far so as to become unnecessarily prescriptive, though this may be appealing as it is clear. Individuals and teams are expected to manage themselves within the guidelines and policies. Our recent review of where people can work following the reopening of the office after the pandemic is a case in point of the conundrum. After much consultation, we proposed a 'place of work' policy containing a guideline about where someone can work. We could have come up with an arbitrary number of days a week each person has to be in the office – probably two or three. That's where many employers seem to have landed. While that might be nice and clear for everyone, it is arbitrary, and a deal struck between employer and employee. It leaves the team and the work out of the pact. It's a policy unrelated to the needs of the business, team or customer on any particular day. Because of the nature of the project you're working on with others, you might need to be in the office with colleagues. At other times, it will not matter, or you may benefit from being at home as you need to avoid distractions. What would happen if someone had already done their requisite number of days in the office one week, and refused to come in for that whiteboarding session on Friday?

Instead, we clarified what must be preserved wherever people work (such as our values, customer service and team relationships). A guideline we're trialling is to be led by the work and be where you need to be for others, most importantly the customer. Having done that, bear in mind that if you're coming in 'much less than half of the time you're working' you'll probably struggle to uphold those other things that need to be preserved (values, etc). We've had two responses to this from our employees: (1) can you be more specific? and (2) if we're self-managing, why do we even need a guideline? And that just about sums up what it's like here! Yes, there's autonomy, but it's vital to provide some boundaries around it. Those boundaries should be broad, kept to a minimum, enough to provide a level playing field and fairness across employees while enabling self-management. The responses also show that people will always be at different levels of comfort with autonomy and guidelines, as will the organisation as a whole. Over time it will evolve, just as our continuing adjustment of the scope of the line manager role is evolving. We're nearing the end of the trial. Most are saying it's generally working. Others are questioning the guideline, whether it's the right one at the right level of specificity. We will review, and no doubt iterate if necessary.

Recruitment and selection

An obvious place to start with this way of working is to find good people in the first place – people who are great at what they do and can also manage themselves and thrive in our working environment. But I have a philosophical issue with selecting for 'fit' with our way of working. That might sound strange, but what I'm thinking is this: can our way of working offer much benefit to working life in wider society if there's only a certain type of person who'll work well within it who we need to try and find? In Chapter 2, Chris M speculated that the way of working could work for most people as most can be trusted and are capable of managing themselves. Furthermore, what would it mean for diversity in a workplace like ours if the way of working only suits a certain kind of employee?

If we believe most people could work effectively in a self-managing environment, what do we select for during recruitment, then? The year after we started formulating our way of working, with growth driving the need to continuously recruit, we engaged the business psychologist, Caroline Gourlay (carolinegourlay.co.uk). At the time, some of our existing employees were thriving in our culture while others were struggling and becoming quite a negative influence. With our culture becoming increasingly distinctive, we asked Caroline what we needed to learn about our star performers to help us find more of them.

While discussing Mayden's culture and purpose with Caroline in preparation for her work, a lightbulb moment came. With divergent thinking so crucial to the way we problem-solve and innovate, we realised that if we selected for a set of preferred ('star') characteristics or competencies, this could unintentionally result in a homogenous team of people that fit a Mayden 'type'. If our recruitment had a shift in focus towards selecting *out* candidates who really wouldn't work well with us, rather than selecting *in* a certain preferred type, we were much more likely to safeguard diversity. We were excited by the concept of turning traditional selection ideas on their head.

Caroline's work with us bore this out. She held a series of focus groups with our technical teams (the largest portion of the business at that point, and more advanced in our way of working than other areas of the business due to the rollout of self-managing scrum teams) as well as those who worked closely with them, including our account managers. Asking them to describe three different types of colleagues – star performers, negative influencers and the steady ones who fell in the middle – Caroline drew out the similarities and differences between each group. There clearly wasn't enough data to claim any statistical significance; nevertheless some patterns emerged that intrigued us. First, we noticed similarities between the stars and some of the negative influencers. Among other things, both were often natural leaders, having considerable influence on their peers. The technical skills of both were admired, they were passionate about their work and they clearly articulated their views. Second, we noticed what was distinctive about the negative influencers compared to *everyone else* (star or steady) – things like not asking for help when stuck, not joining in discussions and shirking responsibility. Both of these observations supported our idea that recruitment needed to be about spotting and avoiding the negative influencers as much as anything.

Of course, most employers will be trying to avoid responsibility-shirking, moaning and overbearing candidates, so this wasn't particularly radical. But Caroline's work identified many positive attributes in those who, in our experience, had had a net negative impact at Mayden, so they are not always obvious. But our focus groups identified two particular, although quite different, issues with the negative influencers that set them apart from everyone else: their desire for status and authority or their need for a significant amount of structure and guidance; in other words, to be the boss or to need a boss.

Regarding the first, the findings underlined that it would be a difference in *values* (such as collaboration over individual achievement and personal ambition) that would help us differentiate between candidates. We noticed how some of the patterns of behaviour identified in the negative influencer mapped to, and were the antithesis of, the values personas we had previously developed (outlined in Chapter 5). Regarding the second, we recognised the possibility of being able to support individuals to work more independently with coaching as well as sufficient organisational scaffolding in place of the structure provided by a day-to-day line manager.

We also recognise that some behaviours associated with negative influencers may be more a behavioural preference than anything necessarily sinister. Does preferring to work alone or being reticent to speak up in meetings really present a problem if it's because someone is more introverted, or has a tendency to process information better internally rather than externally, or is simply shy or lacking in confidence, rather than because they wish to hug information or disengage from the team? We were challenged about where the organisation needed to adapt to different styles of working, rather than expecting the individual to always fit in. For example, we have developed ways for people to contribute to group problem-solving without always having to speak in front of lots of people. All in all, we learned to be careful before concluding a candidate was likely to be a negative influencer.

Armed with these insights, our recruitment process, supported by a set of probing interview questions that Caroline developed for us, has proceeded to carefully uncover underlying values and patterns of behaviour that may give us cause for concern so they can be probed further.

Mayden's way of working isn't for everyone. This will not be a 'fault' with the company or the individual, but some people just prefer to manage people or be managed. This can sometimes make it harder to recruit new employees. The success of our culture relies heavily on the people within it, so it can become quite disruptive if we hire someone who does not thrive in a flat management structure. From experience, this is typically because the individual finds it difficult to work day to day without a management figure to refer to for decisions and direction, or the person is used to being the management figure and struggles with decisions being made as a team. In order to maintain the balance, we spend a lot of time carefully getting to know and assessing candidates, and we do not hire people in a rush.

– Dawn, product owner

Induction

Taryn writes:

A thorough induction gets everyone off to a solid start, including a detailed introduction to how we work. For many, our way of working will be a big shift from how new recruits have worked in previous jobs. We recognise that it will take some time for them to get their head around how we work, let alone learn the particular role they were recruited to fill. It's crucial that they get off to a strong start to avoid disorientation. An active grounding in the principles and our organisational practices begins on day one. Coaching is also offered from the start, creating a reflective space for a new starter to process their early experiences and the adjustment they're going through. Having been with us for a few months, we love to ask our new starters how they would describe our way of working. To give you an idea, here are a few of the comments:

+ 'Shared work.'
+ 'Responsible to self and others.'
+ 'Genuinely listened to, actively listened to.'
+ 'Involved in other things beyond role.'

We've created Mayden Village as a visual map to provide early orientation around the business and our way of working. We started to visualise the employee journey from the day they came on board. It began as a path, which then became a road, and finally evolved into a village with many streets! There's a well-known phrase that 'it takes a village to raise a child'. Well, we believe it takes a village to support a new employee. For new starters, the focus is on 'Welcome Way', which provides foundational information any new starter might need from their first day through the first three months. Beyond 'Welcome Way' are a series of buildings that serve as signposts to key elements of our way of working, such as the 'Agile Arcade', where you can find more information around our agile practices, or the 'Coaching Cathedral'. The village is a fun and engaging way to become orientated and discover what support is available to you.

(See overleaf for an illustration of the Mayden Village.)

Evaluation

So, you've been hired and inducted. You've already found out you won't be meeting regularly with your line manager after you've passed probation – and, surprise surprise, when it comes to performance reviews once you've passed probation, there's no appraisal system! There are values personas and a clear work programme giving you a good general idea of the contribution you're expected to make, but otherwise you're simply expected to manage yourself. No one will set your personal performance objectives, let alone check if you've met them. From here, how do you know what's expected of you, whether you're on the right track or improvement is needed?

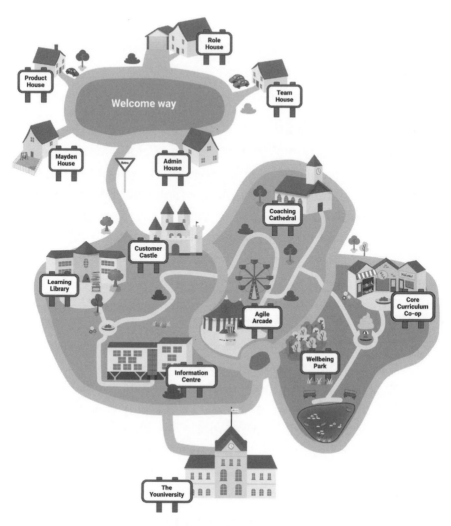

The Mayden Village

We used to do annual appraisals. They were a huge time commitment at 'that time of year' even when we were a small company and had a handful of middle managers. We eventually dropped them, but it wasn't just for logistical reasons. It simply didn't align with our emerging way of working. It's usually teammates and other colleagues more than line managers who know the most about an employee's performance – and even more so in a self-managing team, as our development teams had become by then. Just like the probation review meeting, why were people going into an appraisal with a line manager they didn't work with every day to receive second-hand information about their performance? How bizarre! Also, everyone benefits from much more regular feedback – continuous, even, in the flow of the work itself, in real time. We've therefore endeavoured to create a feedback culture rather than an appraisal system.

Appraisals have two broad purposes: (1) to give feedback and agree where performance improvement and personal development should focus and (2) to inform salary reviews. We'll cover how we do the latter in the next chapter. In terms of the former, we believe peer-to-peer feedback from the people you're working with day in, day out, should be the primary source of feedback. Furthermore, decoupling feedback from salary setting means the feedback can be freely given, motivated by nothing other than the desire to work well and support personal growth. Of course, there's a link, as we'll come to explore, and it's an important one. But first and foremost, people need the most useful and relevant feedback they can get, which in turn will support their performance and then their progress, and ultimately from there, their earnings. We wanted to focus on the first step, confident that the rest would follow.

Marta Pleszynska, one of our software developers, writes:

> We empower everyone to seek feedback for themselves and use it to grow personally and professionally. Seeking feedback can take many forms: one-to-one conversations, sending around a survey inviting feedback about your contribution and how well you're fulfilling the values personas and team retrospectives. Feedback works best when people are seeking it out (creating pull), hence we create a culture of openness and honesty.

Marta took the initiative and created her own personal feedback survey; it is based on the Mayden values and our salary setting criteria (see next chapter) and gave respondents access to her colour profile, so they could feed back in this context. About how the feedback she received became instructive in helping her develop, Marta writes:

One thing people fed back to me was about communication. It became clear that the information I was trying to convey in conversations or meetings was often not understood or misunderstood. I took a couple of communication courses after learning that. I also took another psychological profiling tool to better understand myself and what I need from conversations. Communication works both ways, so I worked on understanding others as well as giving them a better chance to understand me. I started to receive positive feedback about the changes I'd made soon after this. But the feedback that stuck with me the most was: 'You don't have weaknesses! I think you just need to use your strengths at appropriate times!' For example, people told me they appreciated my attention to detail and being willing to say when something doesn't feel right. However, I sometimes did this at the wrong times (probably still do at times!). I decided to put effort into strengthening my skills and learning to use them at appropriate times when they would bring the most value. Also, I realised there seems to be some misconception about progression and growth. People often think that it only means gaining new skills or taking on new responsibilities. However, I learned that it is also about recognising what you are good at, knowing what people appreciate in you, making sure not to lose that and using that skill regularly and more effectively.

Soliciting feedback directly from teammates and colleagues who were there in the moment, Marta was able to gain deeper insight than may have been funnelled and filtered through a company appraisal system.

We have a page on our intranet, One Place, dedicated to

tools and techniques for giving and receiving feedback. It's a core skill, and team and individual coaches are there to facilitate the flow of feedback and reflection on it. With the gift of clear, relevant and timely feedback, you have what you need in order to know what to keep doing and where to improve – to manage yourself and your own progression. This is the topic of our next chapter. But first of all, let's cover what happens when things are not going well.

Poor performance

We all have times when we're not doing as well as we might, but some employees can start to struggle more generally with their performance. Self-managing teams are expected to address their own issues, including supporting a colleague who's struggling to contribute effectively. The scrum master or team coach has a vital role at such times, facilitating the team to have the necessary and sometimes difficult conversations, including sharing constructive feedback. When that's not enough, or the issue is something that we don't expect teams to deal with (such as a more serious capability issue or sickness absences), our approach is fairly standard. Issues are escalated to the line manager, who is supported by the HR team. They're dealt with informally where possible, but if they remain unresolved, we pursue a more formal remedy. We have capability, disciplinary, grievance and other core HR policies just like other employers. We don't have to revert to them frequently, but they are there for when they are needed to protect the business and its employees. Employment law and good practice are embedded in our approach.

What has been hard to get right sometimes is deciding when an issue should be escalated to the line manager. When has the team done all it can? We have painful examples of both too slow an escalation (and the drag that can be caused to a team's productivity as they try to navigate low levels of contribution or a disruptive individual) and too quick an escalation (and how undermining of trust that can be within the team that the individual is in). As Chris E reflects, there's the risk that when the line manager gets involved it feels like 'a sledgehammer to crack a nut' – in another organisation, a middle manager or team leader, rather than a company director, would have those conversations. Of course, that director isn't a number of levels above the individual at Mayden as they would be in a hierarchy. They're just one step (and often one desk) away. Nevertheless, they are directors, and the familiarity may not mitigate the impression Chris E describes. Again, the HR team is key, as a first point of contact and sense check, and then the team usually continues to work in partnership with the line manager in addressing individual issues.

Employee wellbeing

The motivational signpost on a running trail near my house reads: 'The start of a happy life is health.' One could say the same about the start of happy work. Being in good physical and mental shape is a prerequisite to healthy work performance. I imagine employees are also more inclined to look after the business that's looking after them, which is part of the reciprocity in our ethos. We work in mental healthcare. We're well aware of the burden of poor mental health in society – we literally have the data on it, holding in our data centre millions of records of patients with common mental health conditions. Working in this field makes our awareness and commitment to employee health and wellbeing even greater. As well as a range of health benefits for employees, for several years we've offered access to free mental health services and had in-house mental health first aiders. Their role is to be a point of contact for any employee who's experiencing a mental health issue or emotional distress.

Martin Davies, product owner, writes:

Only a short time into the first Covid-19 lockdown, there was a rising tide of concern and anxiety among those in employment about the future of their jobs and of the companies they worked for. Being in the business of providing technology that supported the remote delivery of mental health services was, sadly, the right kind of business to be in at this time. Nevertheless, many colleagues shared concerns about job security as Covid-19 turned our world upside down. Indeed, a number of our own employees had to be furloughed in order to care for their children due to school closures, and some family members experienced redundancy. The team of directors reacted swiftly. A range of helpful measures was announced, including short-term interest-free loans and extended leave for those needing it. What stood out was their genuine concern for colleagues and the desire to assist as best they could, given the commercial constraints that any business would be under.

One other thing that has been important to us from the start has been our offices. When we're working, we typically spend about eight hours a day in the office. If we're going to spend that many waking hours in one place, it should be an inspiring, happy and productive environment for everyone. This doesn't mean space that's luxurious or expensive. Our first two offices were in converted annexes of rural country houses. In both we were surrounded by countryside and wildlife. At the second, every day we would watch a kingfisher sporting Mayden brand colours diving for its lunch in the large pond outside. Despite all of this, neither was expensive. But our requirement for more software developers eventually led us to central Bath. City offices are not usually as inspiring, but Bath is famous for its grand Georgian streets, and we discovered an end-of-crescent residence full of heritage features with a large garden. Formerly a family home, it became our home – some people even wore slippers when they were at work.

Further growth saw us move on yet again. The Old Dairy is open plan and has a much more industrial feel with lots of pipes and exposed brickwork. It has a great atmosphere – when we're in it. During the pandemic our office became an empty shell. The buildings need the people as much as the people need the buildings. There's a symbiosis here. Remote working during the pandemic taught us that people appreciate flexibility, and we've managed to work effectively due to the strength of our routine work processes. However, we also learned there's often no substitute for being in a room together and the office is naturally the easiest place to do so. Face-to-face works best for some of the things that are most important to us – collaboration, innovation and sustaining our relationships and culture. We'll therefore continue to need an office, and one that's flexible and conducive to face-to-face interaction in all its forms, as well as somewhere we're happy spending our waking hours.

Now let's turn to another area of concern for individuals concerning their employment – how to progress when there are no hierarchical ladders to climb.

Chapter 12

How do you get promoted?

Personal development and progression

**Michele Rees-Jones, Dave Bould
and Alison Sturgess-Durden**

From the minute you start work as a school leaver or graduate, you're expected to strive for the next step on the ladder to career success, power, wealth and recognition. In his story at the start of this book, Chris M talks about how it's something to do with chimpanzees rather than bees. Some people achieve promotion through professional qualifications while others find satisfaction in the status and financial rewards that a more senior post can bring. If you've read this book from the beginning, you might guess what's coming next. Here at Mayden, progression isn't all about getting promoted up defined rungs on the ladder. But this has definitely been a challenging part of our way of working to design – how does progression happen and get recognised? However tuned in to our values and mindset our people are, it's entirely reasonable that they should want to progress and receive internal and external recognition for it. Yet there are no clear-cut paths, and our employees experience progression in myriad ways. We encourage self-management right across the business; this applies to individuals' progression journeys too.

Grow, not climb

Hierarchies are made up of defined jobs or posts, stacked on top of each other. There are, therefore, a finite number of them. However good you are, in order to progress in a recognisable way, you're waiting for a vacancy to open up above you that you might apply to move into, or you have to go elsewhere to find one. Those posts are aligned with how responsibility for different parts of the organisation have been divided up. While this will in turn be linked to the work that needs doing, it is an approximation. The work itself will be ever changing, depending on the demands on and in the business, especially in an advancing field such as technology. Such a rigid structure just doesn't seem like an optimal way to arrange work, let alone individual people and their career paths. And of course, in a hierarchy those fixed posts are defined by the people the post holder is managing as much as the work they are responsible for.

At Mayden, we wanted to create a system as responsive to the dynamic, growing and constantly changing nature of the people working within it as to the changing needs of the business and the customers we serve. We also wanted progression to be built on growing ownership of work, not management of people. At any one time, an employee will be fulfilling a number of roles and responsibilities; they will be owning different work projects, programmes and tasks. Some responsibilities will be core, such as account management or software development. Some will be supplementary or even temporary (owning a one-off project, facilitating a working group). One of our campaign owners in the marketing team also chairs our strategy group, another our customer experience working group. Every individual has opportunities to acquire new roles and responsibilities for the work, and shed old ones when it seems like the right time, either because the needs of the business have changed or the individual is progressing. Someone in our marketing team once let her team know she planned to hand over a particular responsibility for some routine work to someone else. She'd held the responsibility for many years and, as a result, now gained little challenge or interest from it; she'd progressed. But it proved to be an exciting new opportunity for the individual she came to hand it on to. It was a win/win. Both individuals progressed as a result of this transfer of ownership.

If this idea of ever-evolving portfolios of roles versus fixed posts describes the ends of a spectrum, in practice most people at Mayden experience something between the two. Most occupy one of our core roles such as product owner or data engineer. We advertise these roles when we have vacancies, and sometimes an employee will apply for a core role change as an internal applicant as well as us receiving external applications. If they're successful, it will lead to a change in their core role, just like moving to a new post in a conventional organisation. Recently, for example, one of our account managers successfully applied for a role as a campaign marketer and moved to the marketing team. But within a core role, there's scope to gain and shed responsibilities for different types of work to suit the team, business and individual aspirations. It's hard to think of two of our product, feature or campaign owners who are in identical jobs. Each has developed specialisms or taken on other roles in response to the needs of the business, personal interests or aspirations, whether that's in sales, client on-boarding, customer experience or company strategy. We find the concept of 'T Shaped' people helpful – creating resilience with enough people sharing core skills (the crossbar of the T) while having a variety of specialisms where individuals have gone deeper into an area of work (the downstroke of the T) (Bodell 2020).

In more traditional organisations, developers are assigned titles such as 'senior developer' or 'junior front-end developer'. For someone to climb a career ladder in a company with pre-defined levels like this, the employee would need to meet certain criteria to qualify for the next grade and achieve a promotion. These criteria would be defined according to the role, such as when a developer starts producing better code, taking on more complex work or managing junior developers. This creates a fairly standard, predetermined progression path. We've found that giving employees the freedom to grow according to the areas in which they excel and are most interested, and where there's business need, has allowed them to grow in a range of sometimes unexpected directions. Some developers have emerged as natural facilitators taking on scrum master duties, while others become experts in certain areas of our tech stack. There isn't a limited number of job roles or pre-defined levels of seniority available for promotion, which means there's considerable flexibility and scope for everyone to progress in their own unique way. In that sense, it offers more not less opportunity for progression. It also supports progression by providing more increments in someone's personal trajectory. In a hierarchy, those next steps can be significant leaps – one day you're a developer, the next you're the team manager, a wholly different role with significantly different responsibilities. Our iterative process of gaining and shedding responsibility for work over time means individuals are on a more flexible, personalised progression path than the traditional climb up the hierarchical career ladder. One coach we spoke to summed it up like this: that people here 'grow, not climb'.

Find your path

However, this more organic approach to growth in responsibilities is less clear cut than applying for the next job on the ladder. And the expectation, as ever, is that the individual will 'own' and manage their progression for themselves, not look to a manager to navigate it for them. Mayden's responsibility is to provide the opportunities (fresh work challenges arising from a growing business) and tools (training, coaching, feedback, etc) to support progression. It's up to the individual to make the most of those and manage their personal development. Here are a few of the quotes we received from staff when they completed a survey about progression:

> 'You have to figure it out for yourself. It's amazing, as there's so much opportunity. It's more personalised, but you have to think about it yourself.'

> 'No one is going to do it for you, and it's not going to look like anyone else's journey.'

> 'You can progress in a way that makes sense for you at Mayden. Take it in your own hands and make it what you want.'

Two of our software developers conducted the research to clarify how progression worked at Mayden with a view to providing better guidance and structure to everyone. The pair spent a number of months talking to colleagues about their personal experiences. They identified seven main ways in which progression was achieved:

+ gain work-based experience
+ improve role-specific skills – training, development
+ develop core skills (collaboration, feedback, etc)
+ take on new responsibilities (ownership)
+ help others to grow
+ build personal influence among peers
+ exhibit leadership in different situations.

But the prospect of developing a career without a predetermined path can be daunting, and some individuals have become stuck, confused or frustrated when it hasn't simply been about applying for a core role vacancy that fits their progression path. Employees can work with a coach to figure out their personal development aspirations, but they may not be completely clear what constitutes a sidestep or an equivalent to a forward leap in career terms, nor know what opportunities are available, or would be best, for developing in that direction. With a growing number of employees, and more and more work opportunities as the company grows, this may need further scaffolding going forwards (see our final chapter).

Ultimately, we have directors, so can employees aspire to that? Three have already trodden that path; all our directors are homegrown. With such an open approach to progression and flexible opportunities for all, Chris M was challenged on how far the philosophy went. The question put to him was: could anyone become a director at Mayden? The answer is yes, as long as anyone demonstrates the required attributes to bring value to the board. We don't have four directors because Mayden needs four. There aren't a fixed number of seats around the boardroom table.

Sarah Q, software developer, writes:

I've been a developer for about 20 years, most of that time working for organisations that were very much rooted in the hierarchical model of working. I was used to multi-layered organisation charts, big decisions trickling down and prescriptive job specs and career paths. In order to progress you had to 'climb the ladder'. For developers in such places, there are two main options for progression: management (stepping away from a technical role), or by climbing pre-defined technical 'rungs' (junior, senior, principal developer).

I love writing code, so I decided to take the technical route, but eventually I felt I'd reached a point where I needed to change who I was in order to progress even further into technical seniority. I was perhaps not assertive enough; I thought I had to be more bullish among others who were more extroverted and 'alpha', but I couldn't quite find my voice. I worked with lots of great people, but those who spoke the loudest always seemed to dominate, even if their views were in the minority.

The 'ladder' seemed to fit those people best. I started to change direction, but it resulted in me writing less code while attending more and more meetings. I was progressing again, but I just wasn't enjoying it.

When I came across an advert for developer positions at Mayden, I was immediately drawn to the company's ethos. Something just clicked and the spark reignited. Joining the company has been career changing for me, life changing even! I don't think I have ever grown so much in such a short space of time – not just technically, but in my confidence and enthusiasm for what I do. It took me time at first to break out of the old hierarchical thinking habits and to tackle the imposter syndrome, but the feedback culture and coaching really helped. I have the freedom, responsibility and trust to shape my own career – it's liberating.

I've been able to look at my strengths and passions and grow my responsibilities without having to give up my love of coding by having to follow a traditional managerial path. I feel valued not just for my experience, but also for my whole self – for the things that make me unique, rather than trying to fit a predetermined job spec. Not only have I finally been able to find my voice, I've also found that it's stronger than I realised. I'm now exploring how I can use that voice to help support others early on in their careers, to hopefully help them find as much enjoyment and enthusiasm for being a developer as I still do.

Learning and development

Fitting with individual ownership of personalised development and progression paths, everyone decides where their training efforts and training budgets are best spent. Each individual has a personal budget to purchase training materials, courses, subscriptions or tickets to conferences. There's also a central 'company pot' providing further resources that can be applied for. How to spend the personal allowance is completely up to each individual, based on training goals that they set for themselves, often after coaching. The company pot exists for funding training that might be tied more immediately to company needs rather than individual growth, but it's also available for topping up individual budgets for training that's beyond the limit of a personal budget, or for funding group training. Anyone can put in a request to use some of it, and anyone can challenge someone else's request to use the pot. In service of complete transparency, everyone's training spend is published.

We also regularly hold lunchtime talks where employees can share knowledge based on the skills they have. These skills could be relevant to the day-to-day business of Mayden or something completely different, and our lunches have ranged from sharing new code programming languages to tips on how to professionally apply make-up (yes, really – we employed someone who had a career in artistic make-up before joining Mayden so we thought it would be fun to learn more of her skills) and everything in between. It all helps to create a culture of constant learning and curiosity. What better conditions for growth, progression and innovation?

Coralie Major, ETL developer, writes:

Just a couple of years ago, our office was a grand Georgian townhouse. The biggest meeting room happened to be right next to the main kitchen, and together these rooms formed a natural hub for colleagues to meet and chat over the kettle (or our rather impressive array of coffee machines). We'd regularly migrate to the enormous table in the meeting room to eat, often with colleagues I didn't usually get to chat with. From time to time, someone would stream a video on the TV and we'd spend our lunch break hearing about something that may have been helpful to our work or that was simply of interest. Fast-forward a year or so, and I noticed that these interesting videos and learning opportunities had become few and far between. I realised the reason for this was that we'd moved to our new premises in a different part of town, where the kitchen/dining set-up didn't lend itself to larger gatherings. People were dispersing and eating elsewhere in the building.

During this time, I'd been mulling over the idea that I'd love to have a greater understanding of the mental health conditions that our customers deal with on a daily basis. I believed that, by increasing our understanding of the problems that their patients were experiencing, we might be able to build better software. Reflecting on those old lunch breaks, it seemed to me that this learning could be delivered as a series of 'lunchtime talks' which people could bring their lunch to, making it easier for them to find the time to come along.

Now, two years on, 27 talks have been delivered across a wide range of subjects, from personal struggles with mental health to career progression at Mayden. We've also welcomed external speakers who've been so passionate about their subject that they've come to speak to us free of charge, as well as our own colleagues who've shared their learning from training courses or research that they're interested in or knowledgeable about.

Our lunchtime talks are beneficial in many ways. We share new information with colleagues, strengthen relationships with people outside Mayden, provide a safe space for employees to practise their presentation skills, and perhaps most importantly, our talks bring everyone from across the company together in a learning environment where discussions have led to new ideas or simply better understanding and empathy.

Core curriculum

Our way of working places considerable expectations on every individual. Without a line manager, they have to be able to manage themselves and a raft of horizontal relationships around the business – to communicate, listen, question, challenge, influence, negotiate, encourage, be open minded not defensive, and be aware of their emotions and surroundings. We realised, with the best will in the world, that all of us needed some help with these personal skills and that they were particularly vital to success, and therefore progression, within the business. We set about providing training and development in them for everyone. A passionate group of colleagues who had undertaken various forms of training over the years identified the skills and tools that had really supported them to grow and develop in our way of working – the skills you need to manage yourself. These include things such as transactional analysis (Berne 1968), how to give and receive feedback, the Drama Triangle (Karpman 1968), coaching conversations, imposter syndrome, the Five Dysfunctions of a Team (Lencioni 2002), divergent and convergent thinking – the list could go on and is constantly evolving. And so Mayden's 'core curriculum' was born, offering everyone the tools and skills to manage themselves, their relationships with others and their work.

Job titles

Humans like to apply labels. They act as cognitive shortcuts that help us filter an overwhelming set of data. 'Meet Sue, she's the managing director.' OK, I've got it. She's the one in charge, so I have to pay attention to things she says and respond quickly to her emails. 'Meet Carol, she's our receptionist.' OK, she might be able to help me with a taxi. This is easy and ordered, but completely misses who Sue and Carol really are and what they fully bring, especially in an organisation like Mayden where everyone has the opportunity to grow their role and influence throughout the business.

The person who has always made a huge impression on our customers and other visitors to the office is Dave Rogers. I can't even tell you what Dave R's job title would be if he had one, but he basically makes sure the office is in a fit state to work in and often plays a front-of-house role, welcoming our visitors with his deep and genuine interest in them. This is in addition to being a coach and a mental health first aider. We think 'Dave R' will do as a job title, or more specifically, 'Cool Dave', as he became fondly known soon after joining us.

While finding the issue of progression a hard nut to crack, we've put the question of job titles in the 'too difficult' box for now. This might be because it feels like it may create more problems than leaving it. As a result, we have a mixed, and maybe unsatisfactory, approach. Contracts of employment by law do not have to state a job title, only a basic explanation of the role. In contracts and email footers alike, some of our employees have a job title, while others don't, and just refer to where they work, e.g. marketing. At one point, four people in our account management team were going by four different titles while doing approximately the same job. In general, people use the job title that relates to their core role – data analyst, account manager, etc. Where possible, we use scrum role titles as a common vocabulary. Hence, a while back, our marketing leads chose to rename themselves 'campaign owners' in line with scrum roles. To advertise opportunities at Mayden, we have to give the role a job title as an approximation of the type of opportunity it is, in order to attract people with relevant skills and experience. Job titles just don't get used within the business; instead, people are aware of your responsibilities and the team you're in. People know you for the value you bring, through the deployment of your skills, experience and interests, which in turn lead to your achievements, reputation, respect and influence, not your job title.

As a shortcut, job titles are important for reflecting status and career progression. We realise that, by not being big on job titles, we're not supporting people in demonstrating their achievements outside the organisation. Outside Mayden, titles convey expertise, seniority and progress, whether talking to customers, networking at a conference, telling the world about yourself on LinkedIn or on your CV. But we feel that *internally* job titles have the potential to be divisive. There's the politicking that comes from job title 'bingo' when additional adjectives are added to the core role title to qualify seniority or expertise – when do you say you're 'senior', or a 'front-end software developer' or even a 'senior front-end developer'?

At Mayden, there are more than 30 people with the job title of software developer. Some have been developers for a few months, while others have been here for more than 10 years. We decided early on not to reference each developer's level of experience in a job title in order to avoid a skills-based hierarchy and to encourage everyone to have a voice whatever their experience level. This works really well. There are no egos, everyone listens to each other's ideas, regardless of who it's coming from, and less experienced developers are happy to challenge ideas coming from more experienced developers.

The problem is 'software developer' doesn't describe what each person does day to day, and their responsibilities. It's a catch-all for anyone who works in the software team. In reality, daily tasks and responsibilities differ between developers. A new, inexperienced developer is most likely going to be learning the ropes, trying to get their head around the code base and getting a lot of support in doing that from their teammates. As you look at more experienced developers, they are able to work more independently, exhibit leadership skills, mentor other developers and start to specialise in technical areas.

This system generally works well inside Mayden. You get to learn who people are and what they can achieve based on their actions and knowledge, not what their title is. It does get a bit confusing for people joining the company, though. It can be difficult to know who to go to for help, but they learn quickly. However, job titles are important in the world outside Mayden. They provide a common language that describes your responsibilities and daily tasks with a couple of words. They help other people to understand your skill set and how you might be able to contribute.

As Dave B says: 'I have previously felt a bit uncomfortable giving my role title to a room full of senior professionals from other companies, who are less experienced than me yet have all these fancy titles! There has been a regular barrier to get over where describing your skill set becomes a conversation rather than simply being able to say your title. Day to day at work this wouldn't bother me, as people understand each other's contributions. But in an outside setting you can feel as if you won't be taken seriously unless you have the job title that helps others understand your responsibilities.'

Ultimately, there's an unwritten agreement that anyone can call themselves anything outside Mayden to show the world where they've got to and what they do, as long as it's commensurate with the reality of their current contribution in the business. They will soon face challenges from co-workers if they call themselves something they're not on LinkedIn. We know. It has happened.

Salary setting

All this flexibility and opportunity have created another conundrum – salary setting. There is, of course, a relationship between progression and salary. The more you contribute, the more you should be rewarded and paid. It would be simple enough to have a set of fixed roles that you could price according to the duties and benchmarks in the labour market, but everyone is in uniquely different roles, even if their core role is similar. How can salaries be set in a way that's commensurate with each unique contribution while being fair and consistent with others in different roles? It's apples and pears. We saw the need to bust some myths around salaries. Here are some key principles:

+ The relationship between progression and salary is not fine grained – you don't get a salary bump every time you acquire a new skill or deepen your existing ones. Performance can also go up and down over time, while salary only goes up. Salary changes periodically; progression is more continuous.

+ Salary can increase ahead of progression (when you step into a new role and before you've fully developed into it) or in recognition of it (once it's clear that your contribution has consistently exceeded what your current salary recognises).

+ Salary is affected by external labour market forces as well as internal comparisons, and is also about affordability to the business.

+ Salary has to boil down myriad factors to a single number. It will never be perfect. If everyone in the same role was paid the same, that would be imperfect too as not everyone will be performing that role in the exact same way.

The next challenge was how to assess when a salary change might be due. The paradox we faced was that peers know best how someone's contribution has changed over time and how they're doing, but we consistently got the message that peers didn't want to be implicated in decisions about how much money someone gets to take home. While the company was small, Chris M would conduct an informal triangulation exercise, asking many people about each other's contribution. When we had a staff of about 20, it was reasonable for him to get a good gauge this way. But as we grew, people saw the flaws in the approach of one person, and a director at that, collating and evaluating all that feedback by themselves. The other directors became involved over time, and yet our way of working suggested the directors couldn't have a complete view of each individual's contribution.

You'll likely have heard of setting salaries in other flat organisations – it's one of those headline-grabbing aspects of the approach. We undertook a comprehensive review of our rewards and benefits package a few years ago and investigated all the different approaches adopted by companies like ours. Some convene panels of peers to do the benchmarking and salary setting. Some go all out and allow individuals to set their own salaries. Complete transparency around who's paid what often goes hand in hand with such approaches. We once tried to run a peer evaluation survey to garner more comprehensive feedback to inform individual bonuses at the end of one financial year. Interestingly, it confirmed the directors' evaluation of individuals (their assessment was pretty close to that of peers in terms of how people were doing). But the exercise went down like a lead balloon. In fact, one team boycotted it altogether! At our more recent round tables about the shift in line management, the message continued to be received that salary setting should remain in the hands of the directors, even though they didn't have complete visibility of each individual. Our most recent rewards and benefits survey once again confirmed that there was little appetite for comprehensive peer evaluation. How to proceed?

We're still working on it. It's one of the areas in which we could be criticised for being too conventional. We feel challenged by the fact that, if salary isn't transparent, there's an elephant in the room about all the other wonderful things we do, and isn't trust a vital part of our foundational ethos? We'll continue to wrestle with this for some time to come, but maybe it will help to show that working in this way doesn't have to be so radical that it puts you off. You can remain conventional in areas where you feel that's where the organisation is currently at. It isn't all or nothing. The managing director of another software firm known to us decided to grow his company with less hierarchy. His opening move was to make salaries transparent. He's a brave man. You don't have to be that brave!

For now, the four directors manage to maintain a clear enough view of each individual to be able to reasonably set salaries. The directors are more aware of people's contributions than they may be given credit for, partly because they're just one step removed, not multiple layers of hierarchy away. They see contributions in sprint reviews, meet with teams, have one-to-ones, receive unsolicited positive and negative feedback about colleagues, receive nominations for commendation and ad hoc gifts, and generally pay attention. They actively seek feedback from peers. Given the coarse-grained relationship of salary and progression, we believe that's been accurate enough in terms of paying people fairly compared to each other within the business. But we recognise we may need to get more comprehensive in collating peer feedback as we continue to grow in number.

While we haven't made salaries transparent, what we have done is to make transparent the criteria (see Appendix section C) that the directors use when setting salaries. You won't be surprised to learn that our values personas, roles and influence feature heavily in these criteria.

Conclusion

There's little that's set in stone about progression at Mayden. We all experience it differently. It's helpful to come back to the 'grow, not climb' philosophy, meaning that individuals can explore where they make their best contributions and take incremental steps in pursuit of that. They don't have to wait for the person above them on the ladder to win a promotion or leave in order to take meaningful steps in their own development.

We ask everyone to self-manage, and progression is really no different. We want our people to take the initiative, to work with the freedom we have to 'go off piste' if it's beneficial; we want people to enjoy the flexibility that comes with 'roles not posts', and people can take smaller steps forward rather than having to wait for a big role change to present itself. The challenge for us is supporting people to make those steps. We have got the scaffolding fundamentals already in place to support our way of working – coaching, the core curriculum, mentoring, reward and recognition criteria and so on. What we need to do now, as we scale, is clearly pull all of those things together into a framework that provides consistency of experience across the board and offers clarity about the process to anyone that is keen to progress.

But we also have success stories that have their roots in Mayden's approach to progression over traditional promotion. From Michele, a marketeer who took a career-changing detour into leading our coaching programme, to Cool Dave who doesn't have anything even close to a job title but can be found fixing a tap one moment and coaching a colleague the next, to Claire who joined us as our receptionist and is now product owner for our flagship product iaptus, to Martin D, product owner and sales team member who started helping with an office refit, became product owner for bacpac and then went via marketing to sales – every one of them has experienced the highs and lows of their own journey but they have all progressed in ways that are meaningful to them as well as encouraging them to put their skills to the best use within the business.

Chapter 13

Who's to blame when things go wrong?

Managing risk and delivering value

Chris May

In Chapter 3, I mentioned 'no blame' as one of the founding tenets of our ethos. Our no-blame culture was in place long before we decided to adopt agile or explore new ways of working. But over time it has become a cornerstone of a much bigger governance and performance regime, where *governance* focuses on *minimising risk* to both the customer and the organisation, while *performance* focuses on *maximising value* to the same. I will return to both of these later, but it's important to first demonstrate how 'no blame' plays out in practice.

Our no-blame culture

I am pleased to have this opportunity to share my first encounter with the no-blame culture. I was a newbie, just a couple weeks after arriving at Mayden. It was the daily stand-up, and the team was going through our Orbit sprint board. I was still learning how to use Orbit boards and made a mistake. I ended up deleting the current team sprint board *(oops!). Immediately my team realised that the sprint board had gone, and for a moment I thought I might have to pack my bag and bid farewell. I gathered all my courage and admitted I was the mastermind behind the disappearing Orbit board (trust me, I was shaking). The response? 'Don't worry, we can survive this.' To my surprise, all the members of my team (angels!) began examining their timesheets and messages to find what tasks were on the board, and within an hour the entire board was reconstructed from scratch. **My team didn't blame me.** Rather they identified the root cause and raised an action to develop a sprint board history feature within the Orbit application. I love my team and Mayden for its values, and the team spirit we have here. PS: I have now learned how to use Orbit. :-D.*

– Snigdha Swain, data scientist

Snigdha's testimony is just one of many submitted for this book, which in turn are just a sample of those that could have been included. Ultimately, a culture stands and falls on how it responds in adversity. In the 21 years that Mayden has been in existence, no one has ever been reprimanded for making an isolated, unintentional mistake. Challenged, yes – there's a difference – but never penalised.

We recently gave everybody the opportunity to take part in a 'no-blame culture' survey. To the question 'What does our no-blame culture mean to you?', the responses were substantially aligned, agreeing that it involved:

'Being able to try an alternative approach without fear of blame if a negative outcome occurs.'

'Knowing that the consequences to individuals of making an unintentional mistake will not reflect badly on them.'

'Confidence that teammates will run towards a problem rather than away from it.'

'Constructively focusing on resolving the problem before trying to ascertain how the problem occurred in the first place.'

'Subsequently conducting an open review to understand the root cause of the issue – which is rarely the individual in any case – rather than apportioning blame.'

'Learning from mistakes and putting in place solutions to ensure that the problem can't recur.'

Respondents also cited the confidence boost provided by the no-blame culture, and that it made them feel both valued and secure. I've witnessed how working without fear of censure appears to increase innovation and creativity, freeing team members to play with ideas that might not otherwise see the light of day, safe in the knowledge that the team will have their back if something goes wrong. But even more importantly, I fundamentally believe it has the opposite effect to the one you're probably worrying about. I believe it *lowers* the risk to the organisation. If individuals aren't scared to be open about their mistakes – the alternative being to cover them up – then the organisation can address them and reduce its overall risk profile. The alternative – accumulating skeletons in the cupboard – will raise the level of risk and the organisation won't even be aware it's happening.

But what if it *is* someone's fault?

There have been events over the years which led to significant problems. In each case it was reassuring that people focused on the problem rather than the person who caused it. However, our no-blame culture doesn't equate to no personal responsibility. In each case there was a review of the incident, and a correction of individual actions is often part of the mitigation. We can't allow our no-blame culture to be abused, either openly or through complacency.

Most importantly, our no-blame stance encourages people to raise the alarm as soon as something happens, even if they're the one at fault. This means problems can be dealt with more quickly and efficiently. It contributes to a more trusting culture where employees aren't afraid of being made 'the fall guy' when things go wrong.

– Erica Bradbury, software developer

Have you ever been in an incident review meeting where half the room is clamouring to take responsibility for what went wrong? I have. Several times. It's weird. As humans, and especially at work, we're so used to people trying to cover up their mistakes, deflect blame or point the finger elsewhere that it's both refreshing and bizarre when the opposite happens. Our retrospective meetings, introduced in Chapter 4, serve not only as a forum for uncovering the root cause of a problem, but also provide an opportunity for personal reflection. When a significant issue arises, it's often the case that many people can point to something they did, no matter how small, that contributed to the issue. For a retrospective to work well, all of these things need to be exposed. In doing so, addressing one incident can often reveal a raft of collective actions that would not only prevent that incident from happening again, but potentially a number of others that we will never know about. As for the meeting I recall, I came to the conclusion that all of my colleagues were wrong. The root cause of that particular incident was a decision I'd made more than two years before. And I said so.

As we said in Chapter 6, with autonomy comes accountability and responsibility. We don't employ dedicated software testing teams or quality control managers. That doesn't mean we don't do these things, but each team is responsible for its own quality and checks, which are performed both within teams and using peers from another team where appropriate. These quality control procedures can be time consuming, so we seek to automate them wherever possible. Knowing that you have to clean up after your own mistakes is a powerful incentive to drive innovation even in quality assurance, and our test coverage becomes more extensive as a result.

Claire, product owner, writes:

I still remember a lightbulb moment from our early days at Mayden, so we're talking well over 10 years ago. We found an issue on one of our servers, a genuine mistake someone made that could have had consequences if we didn't resolve it. We had a new person on the team who hadn't quite picked up on how we worked yet. The company they came from was very hierarchical and there they understood that when someone got into trouble, you cleared out of the blast radius to avoid becoming collateral damage. They said there would even be shouting! I find this very strange; we're not children and you're not my parent, you know? It's like, 'Stop yelling at me, I'm an adult.' But that's the environment they came from.

We needed to find out what had happened, what the impact was, and what we could do about it. We came together, then somebody put their hand up and said: 'It was me. I made a mistake.' The new person was waiting for the bomb to drop, for the person who had taken responsibility to be screamed at and fired on the spot. But Chris M said: 'OK, let's fix it then work out how we make sure that doesn't happen again.' The new person couldn't believe it. It saved so much time because nobody was stressed or anxious or crying in the bathroom for being yelled at. Everyone just got on and sorted it. This error never happened again because we put a process in place to prevent it. You see people who come in from another style of company – at some point they have this moment where they realise it's different here.

Developing an authentic governance regime

For a no-blame culture to work well, it requires a conscientious attitude by employees and a commitment by the company to investigate mistakes and make sure they aren't repeated.

– Erica, software developer

Our lack of hierarchy means no one feels the need to pass the blame down the chain for a mistake. All that matters is fixing the mistake and learning from it. We trust each other to make sure the mistake isn't repeated.

– Dave B, software developer

It's all very well running a company without middle managers, but that doesn't mean it's a free-for-all. What we've previously referred to as scaffolding has to be in place to make the organisation run smoothly. And this equally applies to governance. Like all organisations, Mayden has risk registers, health and safety procedures, employment policies, security regimes for our buildings, and business continuity plans. In that sense, we look no different from the outside to any other company. As we addressed in Chapter 10, we still have a board of directors with overall responsibility for assurance that conforms to what's expected by the outside world, even though it might operate differently on the inside. Mayden has particular governance structures around information, data security and clinical safety that we must abide by since we handle enormous amounts of sensitive patient data. For example, we hold the international ISO27001 accreditation for information security and governance as well as Cyber Essentials Plus. Both are absolutely key to our professional credibility and providing assurance to our customers. Both accreditors and customers expect to see things done a certain way and this is what we must satisfy, even if we have to map them to our own organisational arrangements.

At Mayden, the difference is that our governance regimes consist less of rules and more of lessons. In fact, the word 'rule' is rarely heard in our offices, and when it is, it's usually in the context of something that has been imposed on us from the outside. Even then, we will adapt the rules so that they work appropriately in our context. As we make mistakes and learn from them, our policies and processes evolve to ensure those mistakes can't be repeated. Over time these lessons have supplemented industry best practice to develop a comprehensive governance regime that's built on the real, live experiences and challenges that the company has faced rather than just wisdom that we've garnered from a generic company playbook. Today, every employee has access to a wealth of guidance created by their colleagues to inform safe and robust practice.

As a case in point, our first set of information security and governance policies consisted of eight documents. It has expanded to 30 as we gradually encountered things that we wanted to expand or improve upon in the existing policies. For example, at one point we identified that the patching policy for our server operating systems was not as comprehensive as we would have liked and that this could potentially expose us to a range of emerging security threats. Within a month we'd produced a policy that was considered an 'exemplar' by the British Standards Institute. Yet having such a comprehensive information governance regime can't be considered a badge of honour if it's simply shelved and never looked at. We recognised that no one could realistically read, absorb, digest and then live out the entirety of the 30-document set we had created. So, we simplified and improved the navigation so people could find what they needed easily, and then created a checklist that every employee has to complete each quarter, reminding us of our key responsibilities and pointing to the more comprehensive documents as and when we require more detail.

Rather than policies and procedures being produced from

on high by people who have no direct experience of the area or function they're providing them for, ours are evolved for the teams by the teams. There's perhaps no better example than our testing and deploy processes, which have been adapted over time to ensure we don't deliver faulty software to the customer. At no point did a manager dictate that these improvements should happen; the team gradually evolved the new processes in response to problems they encountered. The term 'evolved' is important here. We learn and adapt. Sometimes the mitigations we put in place to avoid repeating a mistake are the wrong ones: they cause other problems elsewhere. Consequently, it's important that we're just as agile about our governance regime as we are about everything else. It's a dynamic, moving set of guidance, drawn from experience and adapted as change and new experience dictate.

Does it work?

You might be forgiven for thinking that having the freedom to make mistakes means that more mistakes are made. The key test of our no-blame culture and derived governance regime is, of course, precisely this: do we make lots of mistakes and, more importantly, do we make the same mistakes repeatedly? It's impossible to know for sure whether this is true or not; I can't answer the first question accurately without benchmark reference points, but the board and I are satisfied that the level of self-inflicted problems is low, and 20 years of experience indicates that our error rate has reduced. Reflecting back to before we began this journey, for example, the number of bugs we introduced into our own software has reduced significantly. The answer to the second part of the question – whether we make the same mistakes repeatedly – is an emphatic 'no'. I can't remember one retrospective where the root cause identified had been one we were supposed to have addressed previously. As long as we uncover all the lessons to be learned from each mistake that does occur, and act on them, we will be closing the doors on the possibility of future problems.

As our organisation expands, we face new and greater challenges than we have before. We must be confident that we can address these without looking over our shoulder to check that older challenges are still under control. Our governance regime helps us build both capability and resilience, providing us with a safety net that rises with us, even as our no-blame culture continues to create the freedom and confidence to innovate – without fear – as the company grows.

Performance management

So far, I have looked at minimising risk – to the business and the customer. What about maximising value to both? In general, organisations aren't judged on how many mistakes they avoid making. Not getting things wrong is one thing; getting things right is quite another. They are, however, two sides of the same coin, and our approach to performance management is similar to that for governance.

As with our governance regime, on the surface there's little difference between our performance management systems and those of other organisations. At an organisational level, as we saw in Chapter 8, sales revenue and revenue per employee (measured as whole-time equivalents) are key metrics. The amount of income that's recurring is also important for our type of business, and we try to focus on work that generates recurring revenue streams rather than stand-alone projects. During the start-up and scale-up phases of Mayden's growth, profit margins weren't as important as revenue, though we have so far managed to grow organically without ever making a loss. Today we still aim to make a profit – it's crucial to funding future plans so we can achieve our purpose of bringing innovation that changes what possible for our customers – but this isn't what we focus on. If what drives us is our purpose translated into revenue growth, then the internal performance metrics that matter most are those that measure added value. And by added value we mean those activities that deliver what our customers want and are willing to pay for. In other words, are we doing the right things and are we doing those things productively? Our product owners have a mantra that's even shorter: 'Maximise value, minimise risk.'

While our financial key performance indicators (KPIs) provide an objective and quantifiable measure of the company's overall financial progress, internally we depend more on continuous improvement measures than absolute ones. So, from sprint to sprint, we're asking the question: 'Did we do better than the sprint before? If not, why not? And what do we need to do to make the next sprint better still?' If we do the right things as efficiently as possible, we hope this will result in us hitting our short- and long-term financial targets, but there's no explicit link between the two.

In all honesty, performance measurement has been one of the toughest challenges we have met. In software development there's no set of metrics that can reliably provide an accurate, quantifiable measure of productivity consistently. And, of course, we cannot claim to know whether our productivity is better than it would have been under a hierarchical management system. What is important, though, is that this way of working expects teams to own their performance, continually improve, sense that improvement in the absence of hard metrics, and for those improvements to ultimately be reflected in the bottom line. If we have a business plan, and the summation of all the activities and improvements we undertake results in us hitting that plan and the financial ratios I mentioned in Chapter 8, then we're satisfied. Yes, maybe it could have been better, but it could also have been a lot worse. The financial KPIs are currently only reviewed each quarter; if they're off target we ask why and take remedial action as appropriate. The assessment of whether value is being added, however, is repeated by every team at the end of each sprint – typically every two weeks. Tracing direct connections between our activities and our financial performance is only possible to a degree. And as we build our capability over time, it's sometimes the actions that we take today that produce the commercial rewards in the years that follow.

Even so, part of our underlying ethos is to be data driven, so we nevertheless collect and review a wide variety of data in assessing our overall performance. Some of this data, especially relating to activity, time and money, is quantifiable. But we also collect subjective data through forums such as our temperature panel, which seeks to highlight problem areas through the perceptions of individuals, rather than indisputable facts. The panel, made up of whoever attends on the day, meets once a quarter and allocates a score between 1 and 9 to every area of the business against a set of criteria (e.g. do we have the right capacity in that area? is that part of the business transparent to all?). If the panel doesn't agree on the score, then it's the lowest score that gets allocated. Actions are then agreed for the areas with the lowest scores with the intention that those low scores will be eradicated by the next temperature panel meeting. Whether quantifiable or subjective, our transparency value compels us to share all this information widely and it's then down to teams to digest the metrics and determine what action, if any, needs to be taken both within and across the teams.

To address gaps in our performance monitoring, we've recently introduced a series of objectives and key results (OKRs) that we believe will underpin the delivery of our medium-term strategy. The six objectives and associated measurable key results should enable us to check whether our activities are producing the outcomes we desire, over and above the blunt instrument of financial performance. This is important because we believe that the long-term success of the company will depend more on making appropriate investments with our limited resources than on hitting short-term financial targets.

The fourth role of the director

One of the four roles of the directors (Chapter 10) is to seek assurance from the teams that the value we expect is being delivered. Practically, what this means is that our role is to check that teams are indeed monitoring their own performance, or commissioning monitoring systems to fill in gaps, or creating them for themselves. The point is, the directors are responsible for making sure that the information is available, but not for determining what action should be taken. We may be involved in follow-up actions, but only as a voice in the room along with other voices. We don't dictate them. So, both our governance (minimising risk) and performance management (maximising value) regimes are treated in much the same way – as fuel to support a programme of continual, marginal improvement that's ingrained in the culture and operates perpetually at team level and across the business. Our culture, governance and performance evolve together as the company grows and matures. They are by no means a finished product and likely never will be. But the pace of our advancements in these areas appears to be in step with the overall direction of the organisation and its readiness to receive new wisdom.

Conclusion

Elements of our way of working have been around for a long time. But our no-blame culture was one of the things I found the hardest to get my head around when I joined Mayden. Despite hearing the term fairly early on, I don't think I fully understood it, or bought into it, for some time. I remember wondering if it meant no consequences. It didn't. Nor did it mean that people were oblivious to things going wrong. My early understanding was that, in the case of a bad outcome, there would be no assigning fault or heavily criticising an individual.

I kept waiting for the other shoe to drop, thinking that eventually there would be a scenario that didn't stand up to this way of working. But as far as I can recall, that hasn't happened... Eventually it becomes clear. Instead of a culture of blame, we have a culture of agility: iteration, improvement, growth and learning. It's about everyone sharing accountability and responsibility for continuous reflection and improvement, to make sure that we learn from our mistakes and don't repeat them. There's a mindset shift that you go through as you adjust from a more traditional hierarchy.

— **Jen, analyst**

The real test, of course, is whether all of this has also created an organisation that's resilient in the event of a shock. When the pandemic hit in March 2020, we looked on as many hierarchical organisations – including some of our customers – struggled to adapt. Mayden, I'm proud to say, hardly skipped a beat. All of our teams, without exception, continued to complete their sprints despite what was happening, and even responded to changing customer requirements as they arose. Most importantly, our prevailing performance and governance systems stood up to the challenge – as we moved to a period of remote working – largely because they were about how we managed the work and not the people or where they were based.

As we enter the post-pandemic era, we're still learning the lessons that this new world is presenting us with, especially in our understanding of what really drives our culture and makes it tick. The conclusions we draw as we reflect on this unprecedented period will no doubt be used to strengthen both our governance and performance regimes even further, as our culture, in turn, moves into the next stage of its development. What's already clear is that we're not going to get everything right, there are things we need to change, and no one is to blame.

PART 3

The Journey

Chapter 14

Where do I start?

Navigating your own self-management journey

Taryn Burden and Philippa Kindon

Once clear about Mayden's way of working, some can be quick to point out, 'Well, it won't work for an organisation like ours, we're too big/small/controlled by a parent company/high risk [and so on].' You don't have to look too hard, though, to find a variety of companies adopting non-traditional ways of working, including those referenced in Chapter 1. They're all over the world, in different sectors, some highly regulated, and in every size imaginable. Mayden's approach is still rare, but by no means unique. What is unique, we believe, is the way a blend of agile practices with self-management across the whole company has emerged over time in this particular organisational setting.

By now you will have a good understanding of the way Mayden works, from the ethos and foundations it's built upon to the practices and processes we've developed. If, as a result, you are feeling energised to embark on your own journey, we suspect you'll be asking, 'Where do I start?' Given how often we get asked that question, we know there's as much interest in *how* we've done it as *what* we've done. In this final chapter, we aim to shine a light on the *how*.

Chapter 1 told the story of how our journey unfolded. Now we'll take you through how we've worked on it since that staff day in 2016 when we started to be intentional about designing our way of working. Then we'll reflect on the lessons we have learned that could help others embarking on similar journeys and share some of the areas we are working on next. Finally, we'll conclude with some guiding principles that have emerged for us which may be relevant in other settings.

How we work on our way of working

The core team

While we have found it is key to enable the whole organisation to develop its own approach to how we work, the practicalities of achieving this gave rise to us setting up a facilitating core team. Our core team champions the vision and supports efforts to work on our way of working. The team has adopted an agile approach to this, developing a backlog of work, refining user stories relating to our way of working, and prioritising which stories need to be delivered.

Early on, we learned you cannot work on everything all at the same time. As tempting as it is to do as much as possible as soon as possible, we quickly found there's a limit to the organisation's capacity for the amount of organisational development it can tackle at once. The need for high levels of engagement, its continuous nature... there's only so much you can do at once. As the Agile Manifesto reminds us, we need to work at a sustainable pace and reflect regularly in order to make incremental adjustments. The core team played a key role as pace setter. We learned quickly to allow the way of working to emerge and mature at the natural pace of the organisation and its growth, rather than orchestrate an overnight revolution. This was in the context of a fairly sudden change to agile practices in our software teams and some sense of urgency to make things better for everyone after those concerning staff survey results in 2016. Once we regained people's confidence that things were going to get better, we felt free to work at a manageable pace – one that allowed the best way forward to become clear gradually and over time rather than being forced.

The original core team met regularly to curate the work. Ali SD was the lead director, setting overall direction and expectations. Philippa ensured stakeholders' voices (i.e. everyone in the business) were being heard. Taryn ushered the process, keeping the wheels turning smoothly and making sure the work undertaken by the working groups and the core team was visible. From developing the first iteration of our decision-making process to getting to grips with the role of director, and feedback, no pole was left unattended as we constructed our organisational scaffolding. Our experience of working on our way of working has shown that deconstructing and reconstructing the way you organise is highly interconnected, further supporting a more emergent approach. As we started working on a particular piece of the scaffolding, it impacted another in ways that were rarely predictable. We've had to accept and embrace the complexity of a system comprising unpredictable, autonomous humans in which one thing will always lead to an unknown other. Having a core team helped to keep a view of 'the whole'.

Over the years we have made several attempts to draw 'the whole' – to map the different practices, processes, pillars and foundations of our way of working in relation to each other 'on a page' (the scaffolding, if you like, and the couplers that connect the poles together). The practice of depicting our way of working has been a valuable part of the process of identifying the constituent parts and beginning to understand how it all hangs together. While we still feel we've yet to achieve this satisfactorily (perhaps a clue to the complexity of any organisational system!), we have continued to improve our understanding of how all the pieces of the puzzle fit together.

Everyone owning the organisation's development

But the core team should not slip into doing it for everyone else. Ownership is key to creating a way of working that works for all staff and ultimately our customers. By creating a space for everyone to address challenges, employees are more likely to champion change because they care. Working groups and task & finish groups have provided a way for people to get involved and own elements of the scaffolding. These groups can flex to suit current needs. Group members are self-selecting. They are accountable for whether they deliver against the problem they set out to address. Early 2017 was an exciting time. We were seeing effort from most people in the company as they formed working groups to generate new processes, practices, tools and solutions to articulated issues and requirements. There were high levels of engagement; across the business people were invested in making Mayden the company they wanted to work for. Allowing the process to be driven by those with a fire in their belly for the issues in hand put us in a good position to tackle what mattered most throughout the organisation.

However, people are naturally busy with their day jobs. Following an enthusiastic start after the 2016 staff day, involvement began to fall away. The core team started to fill the space in order to keep things moving. We were aware we were beginning to control rather than hold the space. We noticed when 'them and us' language started to creep in, when those of 'us' in the core team started to talk as if we were doing it for 'them' (the rest of the employees). The balance of ownership needed to be checked. Our agile approach helps. It encourages small incremental iterations which make getting involved in change via a working group or other means less of a daunting commitment. When combined with our no-blame culture, it helps people not to be afraid of taking ownership and trying new processes and practices.

Guiding mantras

Over the years several organisational mantras have emerged, such as:

'Manage the work, not the people.'

'What are you going to do about it?'

'Guidelines over rules.'

'Let's be agile about it – try it and change if needed.'

'Act like an owner.'

'Hold the space rather than control the space.'

Generated in dialogue when we are wrangling aspects of our way of working, these phrases tend to stick because they encapsulate something fundamental – either about the scaffolding itself or how to work on the scaffolding. They are often invoked to help us unstick ourselves when the process is stalling.

We gather feedback regularly and work together

We notice that pain points in how we're working naturally bubble to the surface. Being tuned in to these is how we prioritise what to work on next on our way of working. We carry out a regular staff survey that gives us a temperature check as to what's working and what might need our attention next, as well as generally staying tuned in through ongoing conversations across the business. We dedicate time during our biannual staff days to our way of working. Sometimes we focus on something that doesn't seem to be working well; other times it might be about raising awareness of particular aspects of our way of working.

Developing our way of working is a fine balance of coordination, curation, providing a fluid structure while enabling things to emerge, sensing, data-gathering, acting, reflecting, mapping, iterating, listening, refining, challenging and championing. We experienced a bit of a hiatus during the pandemic years, but as

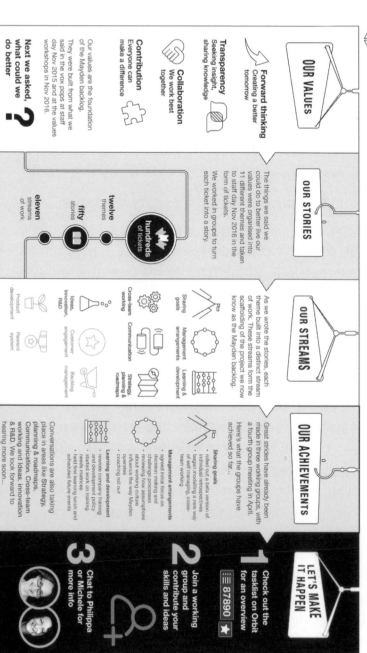

Building for the future The Mayden backlog, Nov 2016-April 2017

OUR VALUES

Forward thinking
Creating a better tomorrow

Transparency
Seeking insight, sharing knowledge

Collaboration
We work best together

Contribution
Everyone can make a difference

Next we asked, what could we do better ?

Our values are the foundation of the Mayden backlog. They were built from what we said in the vox pops at staff day Nov 2015 and at the values workshops in Nov 2016.

OUR STORIES

The things we said we could do to better live our values were organised into 11 different themes and taken to staff day Nov 2016 in the form of tickets.

We worked in groups to turn each ticket into a story.

hundreds of tickets

fifty stories

twelve themes

eleven streams of work

OUR STREAMS

As we wrote the stories, each theme built into a distinct stream of work. These streams form the scaffolding of the project we now know as the Mayden backlog.

Here's what the groups have achieved so far...

Sharing goals
Management arrangements
Learning & development
Communication
Cross-team working
Ideas, innovation, R&D
Strategy, planning & roadmaps
Backlog management
Customer engagement
Reward system
Product development

OUR ACHIEVEMENTS

Great strides have already been made in three working groups, with a fourth group meeting in April. Here's what the groups have achieved so far...

Sharing goals
· rolled out a beta version of individual retrospectives
· began modelling a new way of self managing, cross-team working

Management arrangements
· agreed initial focus on decision making and challenge processes
· reviewing how assumptions about working culture influence the way Mayden operates
· coaching roll out

Learning and development
· rewrote company training and development policy
· started work on training needs matrices
· held first learning lunch and scheduled future events

Conversations are also taking place in areas like Strategy, planning & roadmaps, Communication, Cross-team working and ideas, innovation & R&D. We look forward to hearing more soon...

LET'S MAKE IT HAPPEN

87890

1 Check out the tasklist on Orbit for an overview

2 Join a working group and contribute your skills and ideas

3 Chat to Philippa or Michele for more info

How we worked on our way of working in 2016/17. This poster was created to communicate to all employees the work we were doing and how they could get involved.

256

we write this book we feel as if we're getting back on track with being able to fully re-engage with this rewarding and challenging work. Meanwhile, the way of working we'd created by March 2020 proved its worth as the whole company transitioned to a fully remote operation incredibly seamlessly.

Lessons learned

The lessons we have learned from working on our way of working present themselves as five pairs of tensions we've had to balance. We share them here in the hope that anyone thinking of embarking on becoming a self-managing organisation will benefit from an awareness of some challenges they might face.

Find your own way, but don't travel alone

The first thing is, don't try to do what we've done! Not because we think we've done it wrong, but because by definition your organisation needs to find its own way (see Tenelius & Gill 2020). If teams are to manage themselves, it follows that they need to be free to self-manage how they self-manage, not have a blueprint imposed on them by any perceived authority, internal (e.g. the board) or external (i.e. experts). That's not to say that directors or external experts don't have a say or a role to play – far from it. We've found that the role of directors and the input we've received from outside the organisation to be crucial in creating our way of working. It's important to have the support of those in the formal leadership roles. They too need to hold the space to allow self-management. This requires them to step back to create that space so this cannot work without their support.

As with most challenging journeys, companionship can be a tonic. We have benefited from personal guidance from many in our network who we've come to think of as critical friends, as well as published practitioners and thinkers referenced throughout this book. We've attended conferences as delegates and speakers, hosted events for business students, leaders and practitioners. We (Taryn and Philippa) also became coordinators, along with Brett Sadler (the UK Leadership Academy) and Ben Simpson (Organisational Vitality) of our local 'Reinventing Work' group in our home city of Bath (reinventing.work). It has been exciting to weave together theory and practice around new ways of working as interest, resources and our own experience grow. You don't necessarily have to speak at conferences about your way of working, but we have found that opportunities to be quizzed about why we work the way we do always helps clarify our own thinking. As we expected at the beginning, writing this book has been no exception!

One example of this was our conversations with academic, consultant and coach Jürgen Scherer (2022). We connected with Jürgen via Corporate Rebels when he called for 'navigators' to come forward. Navigators are characterised by a 'triad of skills and traits, which can be described as a balanced portfolio of head, heart and hand'. This means they can vision, plan, map, figure stuff out, take people along with them and overcome hurdles to get stuff done. We have come to realise that Mayden benefits from a prevalence of navigators. The organisational conditions are favourable to supporting them to bring their proactive best, day in, day out. We can tap into our creativity to forge the futures we want for ourselves (see Heffernan 2020).

Encourage those who believe in this way of working *and* embrace those who don't

Even inside Mayden there have been people who broadly agree with our approach and those who disagree. Embracing rather than quashing resistance and scepticism, we suspect, has been an important factor in being able to make the cultural and process-related shifts needed towards our way of working. We have come to see those who disagree as the grit in the oyster that makes our pearl. Paying attention to doubts and misgivings provides important perspectives. Sincere challenges about the way we work help us to learn, iterate and improve. These challenges also remind us that we don't choose to work in this way for the sake of it but because we believe it's better for our people, purpose and customers. They also keep us from dogmatically following a formula; rather, we are constantly appraising what is best for the employees, business and customer.

Generate a deep understanding of your 'here' but accept you'll never get 'there'

When people ask 'Where do I start?', the answer we give is 'From where you are'. It's the ONLY place you can start from. The important thing is to *recognise and understand* where you are. We found that exploring what we call the ethos of the business has been helpful in understanding our starting point. This was about recognising how the beliefs of Chris M, our founding director, informed the underpinning ethos of the business. This ethos provided the fertile ground for self-managing to unfold, rooted in underlying beliefs that fundamentally people can be trusted to operate as autonomous adults in the workplace.

By asking two questions at the values workshops in 2016 ('Where are we living by our values?' and 'Where could we be better at living by our values?') we were able to generate the data we needed to understand what needed to change. It gave us a clear picture of our 'here', and a reasonable idea of where we wanted to get to (even though at the time we didn't fully appreciate how much getting 'there' was a fallacy).

We've found that working at being self-managing is a never-ending quest. We're always reaching for the next iteration and improvement. It's not possible to reach an endpoint. As circumstances change, we adjust and adapt our tools and practices to meet new challenges. We've come to realise it's about the journey, not the destination. You'll start, but you'll never finish. This takes commitment, determination and courage, but is also exciting, rewarding and humanising.

Know your mind *and* leave your ego at the door

'Physician, heal thyself.'

'Charity starts at home.'

'You can only change yourself.'

'Be the change you want to see in the world.'

You'll no doubt have heard some of these sayings, but what do they mean in this context? Whatever your role in the organisation, or the change you're trying to achieve, it starts with you. Once again, we find ourselves agreeing strongly with Lisa Gill and Karen Tenelius (2020) that mindset is the most important. Everyone's mindset influences how the organisation is shaped (both in support of and resistance to the organisation's ethos) through how it affects behaviours and the way we interact with one another. 'Managing the work, not the people' isn't just about implementing the right tools and practices; it's about a mindset about the capability and trustworthiness of your people that fundamentally impacts how they and their work are organised.

Chris M highlighted a number of mindset shifts in Chapter 3, including around people's trustworthiness. Many of us have been conditioned through years of education and previous employment that you come to work to do a job, you're not necessarily trusted, you need to be managed, you have to fight to survive, and it doesn't matter if you stand on someone's head and hands climbing the ladder. We know that some of these statements sound extreme and may not be your reality, but we're sure we have all experienced some element of them. It takes a bit of time to rewire that thinking.

We've found that a self-managing journey isn't just about the processes, practices, tools and policies (although the impact these have are important). It's about raising awareness of underlying assumptions and mindsets. We believe organisations can tend to sleepwalk into how they organise themselves based on the norm, the way it has always been done, the accepted wisdom and conventional mindsets. By paying attention to your way of working and intentionally challenging yourself to uncover the assumptions that guide the tools, policies, practices and structures that are implemented, it's possible to find your own way. And as well as being conscious of your own mind, we encourage everyone to be themselves, whether introvert or extrovert, whether bubbly, bold, quiet or serious. We want them to be their best self and bring all of their personality, experience, skills, wisdom and creativity into the workplace.

Knowing your own mind and being yourself doesn't mean unchecked egos, nor that the biggest egos get to have the most impact. Organisational and team processes enable all voices to be heard. As one of our software developers, Martin Watts, once said to Philippa: 'Mayden is the first organisation I've worked for where I had a seat at the table and my voice was valued from day one.' Once you know you have nothing to prove, you can just get on with doing a great job for your team, your company and your customer.

Have fun *and* get stuff done

Having fun (and cake) has been important to us. People are human beings with emotions, feelings, energies, faults and foibles. If people are happy at work, they get on better with their work, with one another and with overcoming hurdles. This isn't about 'corporate fun'. It's about employee-led initiatives such as our Unofficial Christmas Party (the one with quizzes, movies and bring-your-own drinks that the employees organise, as opposed to the official one laid on by the company as a thank you for the hard work over the year), planting trees, and permission to spend (some) company time getting to know one another as human beings, not just colleagues – or, as Taryn says, 'frolleagues' (friend-colleagues).

As with cost control, the amount of time spent on the lighter side of organisational life is self-moderated, in balance with the overall need to get work done, serve our customers and take the safety and security of our system and the data that sits on it very seriously. We've found that when you trust people to do the right thing, they tend to do the right thing.

Ministry of Fun

Hannah, social media marketer, writes:

One December, a few colleagues who are big on Christmas wanted to get a committee together to 'deck the halls'. There was no budget and no constraints, just a goal to bring some cheerfulness to our colleagues. We donned our elf tights and planned which set of fairy lights should glitter which staircase, wondered how many trees we could get away with putting up and discussed whether or not we could convince a director to dress up as Santa. (We failed on that one!) Fuelled by mince pies and mulled cider, we brought Christmas to Mayden.

The Ministry of Fun was officially born.

We decided to take on the task of bringing cheer throughout the year, not just at Christmas. Pretty soon a calendar emerged of regular events, plus some ad hoc activities when we felt the company needed a lift. Since 2018, we've celebrated each Easter with office-wide chocolate egg hunts, marked Bonfire Nights with an evening of apple bobbing, a fire pit and s'mores, decorated for Halloween and have tested our fair share of different gins at our summer gin-tasting parties.

Just as we announced our Pancake Day plans in 2020, the Covid-19 pandemic hit. For a company so used to being together as friends, not just colleagues, many found this sudden isolation from teammates very difficult. For the Ministry of Fun, we had the challenge of helping to keep company morale high while dealing with all the personal anxieties and fears that come with a worldwide pandemic. Ministry members reported for duty (virtually) and threw around the usual ideas for remote fun – quizzes, online games etc. Our two most successful ideas proved to be a monthly Mayden Bake-Off (we introduced this just as Paul and Prue were back on our screens) and 'Fun Surprises' where we picked a colleague's name out of a hat and sent a gift to their home address.

We're incredibly lucky to be part of a company that sees the benefit of having happy staff. Being given time in our working day to think up ways we can have more of a laugh sets the tone for the whole of Mayden. That tone? Have some fun, get stuff done.

Now we'd like to share what we believe we need to work on next.

Is Mayden there yet?

This is, of course, a trick question. We said earlier that we'll never get 'there', but 'there' can also mean being in the flow of self-managing. Accepting that we're in flow when it comes to our way of working, we recognise that there's still work to be done. We also talked about how issues bubble up and set the agenda for what needs attention next. Two practices (decision making and progression) and two processes (embedding and scaling) are currently calling for our attention.

Decision making

In Chapter 7 we considered why decision making is one of the most fundamental processes within a self-managing organisation. As we write this book, we are working on the third iteration of our decision-making process. For us this is about getting the balance right between the high-level, broad guidelines of the first iteration (the orange hands poster) and a more granular process that was introduced in the second. We continue to work on improving the speed of decision making, making who the decision maker is clearer, minimising the number of times decisions are made by a director, and optimising the number (enough but not too many) of people involved in decisions.

Progression

In Chapter 12 we summed up our philosophy towards progression and promotion as being about growing (your role) not climbing (the hierarchy). We recognise the need to provide more structure and support to role growth. We have more than 100 people and an ever-evolving range of opportunities. We need to ensure everyone has a personal understanding of what progression could look like for them, with transparent and fair processes to help them move into those opportunities. Some of our people have been with us many years and have evolved considerable roles for themselves in terms of their complexity and the work they own and are accountable for. Finding individual paths that continue to stretch, challenge and provide progression, equivalent in stature to managing teams of people or departments, will be part of this.

Embedding

We've successfully embedded many tools and practices as a result of developing our way of working, such as working groups, toolbox talks, C-Me colour profiles and coaching. There are other things, however, that have been worked on, released but not yet embedded, such as a skills radar that helps individuals map their progress against different dimensions and plan their next area for development. We will look to cycle back to this tool in the coming months to see how it might be iterated and embedded to support progression.

Scaling

We're growing – sustainably, organically and in line with a manageable trajectory in terms of people and financial turnover. We're conscious that there are likely to be challenges as we grow – including the temptation to introduce layers of hierarchy, perhaps sneak in the odd middle manager to take the pressure off the directors and their line management duties. As we've said throughout this book, we're not completely against hierarchy – it can, and obviously does, work for many organisations. What we'd like to stay true to, however, is our ambition to scale how we manage the work and not to engage middle managers to start managing the people.

Will we be able to operate in this way when we have 150 staff? How about 200? What about 1,000? We know that businesses much larger than we imagine we'll ever be work well with a flat structure, such as some mentioned in Chapter 1. We believe we have shifted our mindsets far enough that we'll be able to scale our way of working. We may have to change some of the tools we're currently using and review some of the new processes implemented, but that's OK. We may even find we have not yet been radical enough! We wonder if at the scale we are currently, we are too easily able to fall back on an old system that relies too much on line managers, rather than enable and allow self-management as much as we could. We trust that we can return to our ethos, our values, our guiding principles and mindset, and figure out together how all this works as we grow.

The future of work?

Becky Minton, director of clinician engagement and innovation at ieso, and formerly IAPT service improvement manager and senior therapist at Camden and Islington NHS Foundation Trust, writes:

I'm really interested in the way that Mayden works and how we can use some of the learning in healthcare teams. For many years, I worked as a therapist, manager and service improvement lead in psychological therapy services in the NHS. A couple of years ago, I spent a day with Mayden teams, along with clinicians and managers from other healthcare services, finding out more about their way of working. The key takeaway for me was how their teams continuously reflect on work in order to improve things. As clinicians, it's so important that we continuously improve the care we provide and do the best we can for our patients.

The fact that there are so few line managers at Mayden, that everyone coaches and challenges each other to come to decisions, I think is really interesting too. I'd love to see that happen more in all organisations. It made me want to inspire my whole team and get them thinking about what they could do. As managers we could use more of a coaching approach with colleagues and help everyone to be responsible for the work and the decisions that are made in healthcare services.

While this book has provided a unique case study of Mayden, and we've encouraged you to consider your own business, we'll finish by considering the future of this way of working more generally. It's wonderful when someone in our network like Becky is inspired to look at possible applications in their own workplace. But what is transferable? We said at the start that we did not intend to provide a playbook because each organisation is unique, and it's as much about the process of how a particular

266

team arrives at their own approach meaning no two approaches will be the same.

Does this mean there are no generalisations to be drawn? Our contribution here is a single case study, written by busy people with day jobs who felt wholeheartedly that they wanted to help others (and ourselves) figure out how to make workplaces the best they can be. From our own experience, and reading the popular literature in the field, we think the following are examples of what could be fairly universal in flatter organisational forms that succeed:

+ Believe in your people and trust them to do a good job.
+ Ensure information transparency.
+ Have a decision-making process.
+ Foster a no-blame culture.
+ Invest in facilitation and coaching.
+ Achieve buy-in from the formal leadership, e.g. the board.

But are we right? And what about all the other questions? What makes one way of working better than another and under what conditions? Does size, scale or sector make a difference? What does success look like? In the Introduction I mentioned the number of university schools of management that have established centres for 'the future of work' whose agenda includes new organisational forms. We encourage academics and practitioners to keep going with the research. This is an area of growing importance, but understanding is not yet where it needs to be (see Lee & Edmondson 2017).

Meanwhile, we'll continue on our journey. We hope you make a start on yours. And we hope that we will all continue to share what we learn to help one another create organisations that are fit for the future.

Glossary

Agile – Agile can be described as an iterative approach to software development, but is now used in other industries too, articulated by a set of values and principles, as set out in the Agile Manifesto.

Backlog – see: Product backlog.

Black Box – a repository used at Mayden for coding-related information and standards.

Campaign owner – is responsible for planning and delivering specific marketing campaigns for the business.

Coach (individual) – a trained person who helps a person to arrive at the answer to a question or issue rather than giving them the answer. See also: Team coach.

Core curriculum – tools and skills available to all at Mayden to enable them to manage themselves, their relationships with others and their work.

Daily scrum – a short (15-minute) daily event where the scrum team inspects its sprint progress and produces a plan of action for the day.

Epics – large, unrefined chunks of potential work.

EPR – electronic patient record. An IT system that supports healthcare teams to manage their patients' care and clinical notes digitally.

Feature owner – similar to product owner but responsible for specific features offered by the software.

HiPPO – highest paid person's opinion.

IAPT (Improving Access to Psychological Therapies) – An NHS programme launched in 2008 aimed at transforming the treatment of mental health conditions such as anxiety disorders and depression in England.

iaptus – Mayden's customisable electronic patient record (EPR) system originally built to support psychological therapy services.

IG – information governance. Making information assets available to those who need it while ensuring compliance and streamlining management.

KPI – key performance indicators. A quantifiable measure of performance over time for a specific objective.

Mayden backlog – a prioritised list of things we want to improve about our way of working.

Mayden Credo – a statement of beliefs drafted during Mayden's exercise to define its culture in 2013; it was not formally adopted.

Mayden Manifesto – our first attempt to deliberately work on our culture in 2013.

Mayden Village – a visual map we've created to provide early orientation for new starters around the business and our way of working.

One Place – Mayden's employee intranet.

Orbit – Mayden's customer relationship management system (CRM), technology used to manage interactions with customers, potential customers and employees.

Product backlog – a prioritised list of desired improvements for, and value to be added to, a product in order to achieve the product's goals.

Product owner – a person who represents the customer within the team. They are responsible for shaping and communicating the product vision and goals, for maximising the value (or return on investment) of the product and for prioritising the product backlog. Effectively they are responsible for *what* is going to be worked on, *who* it is for and *why* it is worthwhile; they are not responsible for *how* work will be done.

Retrospective – see: Sprint retrospective.

Roadmap – an intended plan of future work to be done.

Scrum – a lightweight framework of roles (product owner, scrum master and developers), practices and events (sprint planning, daily scrum, sprint review and sprint retrospective) that helps teams deliver products in short cycles (sprints), enabling frequent and regular feedback, continual improvement, and the ability to adapt to change.

Scrum master – serves the developers, product owner and wider business by training and coaching agile and scrum practices and adoption. They guide the scrum team to higher levels of self-management, cross-functionality and effectiveness and work to remove anything impeding the team's progress. They're coaches, facilitators and champions of teamwork.

Scrum team – a small, self-managing group of people consisting of a scrum master, a product owner and developers. The team should have all the skills necessary to successfully deliver the work it commits to each sprint. Although there are different roles within a scrum team, there are no hierarchies.

Sprint – a short, fixed period of time (a month or less in length) during which a scrum team commits to delivering product backlog items. They are cyclical in that a new sprint starts immediately after the end of the previous sprint and are of the same length.

Sprint planning – an event, marking the start of a sprint, where the scrum team determines which product backlog items they are going to commit to delivering in the sprint and how they are going to deliver them.

Sprint retrospective – a meeting at the end of each sprint where the team reflects and inspects and adapts its practices, processes, behaviours, interactions and attitudes. A chance to increase quality, effectiveness and team health.

Sprint review – an opportunity for the scrum team and stakeholders to inspect the outcome of the sprint, the progress made towards the product goals and adapt the product backlog in response.

Stand-up – see: Daily scrum.

Strategy stack – Mayden's purpose, credo for healthcare (beliefs about the future of healthcare), vision, strategy, and objectives and key results (OKRs) for the company, business plan and a set of differentiators (what sets us apart from the competition in our customers' eyes).

Story – see: User story.

Task & finish groups – a short-life working group spun up to address a specific issue or project. See also: Working groups.

Team coach – a person who unlocks the potential of a team by guiding, challenging, facilitating and reflecting to enable them to see things differently and improve their working practices, helping them to develop safe and trusting relationships.

Tech stack – a technology stack, also called a solutions stack, technology infrastructure or a data ecosystem, is a list of all the technology services used to build and run one single application.

Toolbox talks – a series of short talks to help educate and inform on a wide range of topics.

User story – a short description of a desired improvement to a product written from the perspective of an end user or customer. They articulate how the improvement will add value and promote conversation. They're not part of the scrum framework, but originated with Extreme Programming (XP) and are often adopted by agile teams.

Working groups – groups of people who come together to discuss a topic.

Appendix

A. Agile principles

In the Introduction we provided a brief introduction to agile, including the Agile Manifesto statement. Here are the 12 principles that accompany the manifesto. This can all be found at agilemanifesto.org.

'We follow these principles:

Our highest priority is to satisfy the customer through early and continuous delivery of valuable software.

Welcome changing requirements, even late in development. Agile processes harness change for the customer's competitive advantage.

Deliver working software frequently, from a couple of weeks to a couple of months, with a preference to the shorter timescale.

Businesspeople and developers must work together daily throughout the project.

Build projects around motivated individuals. Give them the environment and support they need, and trust them to get the job done.

The most efficient and effective method of conveying information to and within a development team is face-to-face conversation.

Working software is the primary measure of progress.

Agile processes promote sustainable development. The sponsors, developers, and users should be able to maintain a constant pace indefinitely.

Continuous attention to technical excellence and good design enhances agility.

Simplicity – the art of maximising the amount of work not done – is essential.

The best architectures, requirements, and designs emerge from self-organising teams.

At regular intervals, the team reflects on how to become more effective, then tunes and adjusts its behaviour accordingly.'

B. The Mayden Credo (unadopted)

The following was drafted during Mayden's exercise to define its culture as part of the Mayden Manifesto in 2013 but was not formally adopted.

cre·do/'krēdō/ (n) a statement of the beliefs or aims that guide someone's actions.

1. We value initiative, judgement and the ability to take informed action.

2. Everyone is a trusted member of the company. We believe they want to do the right thing, work hard, and pull in the same direction. They take personal responsibility for our success.

3. Everyone should know what's going on (unless it's personally sensitive or confidential), and be involved in deciding things.

4. Everyone has permission and is welcome to challenge and question the way we do things.

5. Our clients deserve our understanding, respect, and best endeavours. We will always put their needs first, even when this means putting ourselves out, or telling them things they don't want to hear.

6. We work on a 'minimum spec' basis. Everyone can expect a clear set of requirements and objectives, then the freedom to organise themselves and get on with it the way they see best.

7. More experienced colleagues are available and delighted to provide wisdom, direction and support.

8. Team working, collaboration and networking constitute our default operating model.

9. Internal budgets for projects and tasks are negotiated and agreed with the client, project owner and project team – then managed to.

10. Long hours are sometimes necessary, like when there is a deadline. Long hours all the time is a sign there is something wrong, which we need to sort out.

11. The tension between efficiency and creativity is a fact of life. We want both, and we're comfortable with the paradox.

12. We take risks and try things out in order to get a better result than we would have done otherwise, but we're not ridiculous or selfish about it.

13. Innovation is how we future proof. Everyone is expected to use their whole brain – that includes the right hemisphere – and to entertain new ideas, whoever they come from. See Appendix 'Left & Right braininess'.

14. Mistakes, wrong turns and dead ends are inevitable consequences of creating things, so we expect them and learn from them. Ignoring the evidence, feedback from others, and repeatedly making the same mistakes is dumb and is not acceptable.

15. We accept that uncertainty and change are features of the world we work in, but we will still have a system for anticipating, agreeing and communicating changes when they occur.

16. Everyone takes responsibility for their continuous learning and development, resourced and cheered on by the company.
17. We will never 'get there'. Dissatisfaction and frustration are enduring emotions.

C. Salary and individual bonus-setting criteria

See Chapter 12.

Job role

+ Regional market rates for the core job role, including level/experience (external benchmarking).
+ Criticality of the job role to Mayden.
+ Usual pay band for job role at Mayden.

Responsibilities: the work they take ownership of

+ Range, complexity and importance of issues they own and take a lead on.
+ Drives progress until 'done'.
+ Contributes beyond immediate team – inter-team and companywide responsibilities.
+ Does not neglect core responsibilities of job role, nor immediate team, in the process.
+ Makes themselves accountable to others for work, progress and decisions in areas of responsibility.
+ Has a demonstrable impact on the commercial performance of the business.

Personal attributes

+ Knowledge, experience and skills:
  ◇ Qualifications.
  ◇ Specialist and technical experience, knowledge and skills in their field (directly relevant and transferable to Mayden).
  ◇ Domain knowledge (sector specific) – healthcare, healthcare IT.
  ◇ Domain knowledge (unique to Mayden), e.g. iaptus, our particular processes.
  ◇ Project management skills.
+ Continuously engaged in self-improvement – seeks, receives, reflects and effectively acts upon feedback; actively engaged in learning, development and training; makes effective use of coaching and training budget.
+ Works hard, but not too hard (see 'able to manage oneself' below).
+ Productive – output has demonstrable value and impact.
+ Able to manage oneself – organise, prioritise and deliver work; takes the initiative; manages their own contribution.
+ Forward thinking – critical thinking, problem-solving, ideation, realisation, strategic thinker, sees the bigger picture, innovation differentiator.
+ Customer-centric – customer service differentiator.
+ An ambassador for Mayden outside the business – develops network, relationships and partnerships and promotes Mayden to the outside world (brand differentiator).

+ Behaves like an owner.
+ Builds respect and trust.

Team working attributes

+ Positive impact on teams they are in, team player, collaborates well with others.
+ Amplifies the contribution of others. Scrum master/ team coach has particular opportunities to do this, but not limited to people in those roles.
+ Improves team processes and effectiveness.
+ Takes people with them – engages and influences others in order to see progress.
+ A respected voice – aligns views, is the voice of reason.
+ Helps, teaches, mentors and develops others; gives feedback effectively.
+ Flexible, responsive and willing.
+ Gives and receives challenge constructively.
+ Transparent – shares information and communicates well.
+ Practises and champions Mayden's ways of working and all the values (culture differentiator).

Consistency

Performance against criteria demonstrated consistently over time (not just in short term), or level of performance consistently expected in any new salaried role.

References and further reading

Argyris, C. (1982). 'The executive mind and double-loop learning'. *Organizational dynamics* 11(2).

BEIS (2021). 'Business population estimates for the UK and regions 2021: statistical release'. URL: gov.uk/government/statistics/business-population-estimates-2021/business-population-estimates-for-the-uk-and-regions-2021-statistical-release-html

Berne, E. (1968). *Games People Play: The psychology of human relationships.* Penguin UK.

Bodell, L. (2020). 'Why T-Shaped Teams Are the Future of Work'. *Forbes*, 28/8/2020. URL: forbes.com/sites/lisabodell/2020/08/28/futurethink-forecasts-t-shaped-teams-are-the-future-of-work/?sh=25cc5c7c5fde

Brown, B. (2018). *Dare to Lead.* Vermilion.

Budworth, M.H., Latham, G.P. & Manroop, L. (2015). 'Looking forward to performance improvement: A field test of the feedforward interview for performance management'. *Human Resource Management.* 54(1).

Cain, S. (2013). *Quiet: The power of introverts in a world that can't stop talking.* Penguin.

Clark, D.M. (2018). 'Realising the Mass Public Benefit of Evidence-Based Psychological Therapies: The IAPT Program'. *Annual Review of Clinical Psychology.* No. 14, 7 May 2018. URL: ncbi.nlm.nih.gov/pmc/articles/PMC5942544

Daisley, B. (2019). *The Joy of Work: 30 ways to fix your work culture and fall in love with your job again.* Penguin.

Fromm, E. (2001). *The Fear of Freedom.* Routledge.

Gabriel, Y. (2015). 'Narratives and stories in organizations: A longer introduction'. URL: yiannisgabriel.com/2015/11/narratives-and-stories-in-organizations.html

Gascoigne, J. (2014). 'The 4 Benefits of Transparency We've Seen at Our Startup'. URL: buffer.com/resources/why-transparency/

Graves, C.W. (2005). *The Never Ending Quest.* ECLET.

Griffiths, E.R. (1983). 'NHS Management Inquiry: Griffiths Report on NHS'. SHA. URL: navigator.health.org.uk/theme/griffiths-report-management-nhs

Haidt, J. (2012). *The Righteous Mind: Why good people are divided by politics and religion.* Vintage.

Hastings, R. & Meyer, E. (2020). *No Rules Rule: Netflix and the culture of reinvention.* Penguin.

Heffernan, M. (2020). *Uncharted: How to map the future*. Penguin.

Herrero, L. (2008). *Viral Change*. 2nd Ed. Meetingminds.

HMRC (2022). 'Employee Share Schemes statistics'. URL: gov.uk/government/statistics/employee-share-scheme-statistics/employee-share-schemes-statistics-commentary

Karpman, S. (1968). 'Fairy tales and script drama analysis'. *Transactional Analysis Bulletin*. 7(26).

Laloux, F. (2014). *Reinventing Organizations: A guide to creating organizations inspired by the next stage in human consciousness*. Nelson Parker.

Lee, M.Y. & Edmondson, A.C. (2017). 'Self-managing organizations: Exploring the limits of less-hierarchical organizing'. *Research in Organizational Behavior*. Vol. 37, 2017.

Lencioni, P.M. (2002). *The Five Dysfunctions of a Team*. Jossey-Bass.

Marquet, D. (2016). 'Turn the Ship Around'. URL: youtube.com/watch?v=HYXH2XUfhfo.

Marquet, L.D. (2020). 'What is the power gradient?'. URL: intentbasedleadership.com/what-is-the-power-gradient

McGregor, D. (1960). *The Human Side of Enterprise*. McGraw-Hill.

Morgan, G. (1986). *Images of Organization*. Sage Publications.

Pink, D.H. (2011). *Drive*. Canongate Books.

Robertson, B.J. (2015). *Holacracy: The revolutionary management system that abolishes hierarchy*. Portfolio Penguin.

Scherer, J. (2022). 'The Role of Navigators in Travelling Organizations' in: Kempf, Michael; Kühn, Frank (eds) (2022). *Navigating a Travelling Organization: Insights, ideas and impulses from the 3-P-model*. Cham.

Semler, R. (1993). *Maverick: the success story behind the world's most unusual workplace*. Warner Books.

Sutherland, J. (2014) *Scrum: The art of doing twice the work in half the time*. Crown Business.

Sutton, R.I. (2007). 'Why I Wrote the No Asshole Rule'. *Harvard Business Review*. URL: hbr.org/2007/03/why-i-wrote-the-no-asshole-rule

Taylor, F.W. (1911). *The Principles of Scientific Management*. Harper & Brothers.

Tenelius, K. & Gill, L. (2020). *Moose Heads on the Table*. TUFFleadershiptraining.

Wiseman, L., & McKeown, G. (2010). *Multipliers: How the best leaders make everyone smarter*. HarperBusiness.

Yoshida, S. (1989). 'The Iceberg of ignorance', at International Quality Symposium, Mexico City – see Yenice, S. (2018). 'Organizational Culture and Managing Change. Rejuvenating Pathology'. *International Federation of Clinical Chemistry and Laboratory Medicine*. See also corporate-rebels.com/iceberg-of-ignorance/

Zook, C. & Allen, J. (2011). 'The great repeatable business model'. *Harvard Business Review*. 89(11).

Useful websites and resources

Corporate Rebels: corporate-rebels.com

Decision making: see reinventingorganizationswiki.com/en/theory/decision-
making; corporate-rebels.com/distribute-decision-making; enliveningedge.org/
tools-practices/do-try-this-work-6-advice-process

Kirstie Sneyd: linkedin.com/in/kirstiesneyd

Reinventing Work: reinventing.work

Scrum Guides: scrumguides.org

Will James: linkedin.com/in/will-james-coach

Paul Goddard: agilify.co.uk/paul-goddard

Happy: happymanifesto.com

TrustWorks: trust-works.co.uk

The Human Organising Co: hoco.humanorganising.co

GreaterThan: greaterthan.works/academy

Chapter 4 reading list

Derby, E., Larsen. D. & Schwaber, K. (2006). *Agile Retrospectives: Making Good Teams Great (Pragmatic Programmers)*. Pragmatic Bookshelf.

Parton, J. & Economy, P. (2014). *User Story Mapping: Discover the Whole Story, Build the Right Product*. O'Reilly Media.

Pichler, R. (2010). *Agile Product Management with Scrum: Creating Products that Customers Love*. Addison-Wesley Professional.

Sutherland, J. & Coplie, J. (2019). *A Scrum Book: The Spirit of the Game*. O'Reilly.

Sutherland, J. & Schwaber, K. (2020). 'The 2020 Scrum Guide'. URL: scrumguides. org

Sutherland, J. & Sutherland, J.J. (2014). *Scrum: The Art of Doing Twice the Work in Half the Time*. Currency.

Watts, G. (2017). *Product Mastery: From Good to Great Product Ownership*. CreateSpace Independent Publishing Platform.

Watts, G. (2021). *Scrum Mastery: From Good to Great Servant Leadership*. Independently published.

Acknowledgements

Writing this book has been much harder than any of us ever imagined. We knew we were being ambitious in adopting the multivocal approach we have. In the end it involved eight chapter authors collating contributions from over 30 other employees in order to tell our story from a variety of perspectives, not a single one. Ultimately, we feel richly rewarded for our endeavour as it came to mirror the organisational journey itself. Our thanks go to everyone who took the time to tell of their experiences, many of which you find in the boxes and other references and quotations throughout the book. Some got us reminiscing, others made us laugh out loud, while others literally made us cry (in a good way!) – we thank you all.

Given the scale of the editorial challenge inherent in the approach, we are grateful to everybody at The Right Book Company, especially Beverly Glick, Andrew Chapman and Paul East. Thank you for your belief in us, your patience, willingness to adapt to our unusual approach and your continuous support. Special thanks go to our panel of external reviewers who shared their wisdom, feedback and suggestions which helped us create the book in the format you read it in today, including Dr Graham Abbey, Dr Karla Benske, Denis Bourne, Dr Humphrey Bourne, Mark Eddlestone, Jane Ginnever, Paul Goddard, Caroline Gourlay, Margaret Heffernan, Will James, Dr Richard Longman, Becky Minton, Britt MacFarlane, Brendan Martin, Hazel Nendick, Jon Ross, Ceri Newton-Sargunar, Kirstie Sneyd, Dr Jürgen Scherer, Ben Simpson and Henry Stewart. Your encouragement for what we were doing kept us going. Suggestions to improve our readers' navigation and experience, particularly from Dr Graham Abbey and Dr Richard Longman, were invaluable. Thank you to Helen Barnes for your comprehensive review and wise counsel, and to Ali Bisping for your ever reliable proofreading. The book would not be here at all without the meticulous project management provided by Taryn Burden and Ali Bisping.

Of course there would be no story without those who helped create and inspire a different way of working. We are indebted to many inside and outside Mayden – to everyone within the business who has given their time and thought to how we can create a better workplace, with special thanks to Taryn Burden for her tenacity in keeping us moving forward and coordinating all our efforts to improve our way of working, and to our external champions – Paul Goddard, who has inspired and challenged us in our agile and scrum journey, and Kirstie Sneyd and Will James for their help with coaching deserve particular mention. We have been encouraged and championed by many, and special mention must go to Henry Stewart at Happy and the Corporate Rebels.

Lastly but not least, Chris May – what can we say? Without your vision and abiding ethos there would have been no Mayden and no story to write! Thank you for believing in us all and trusting us with the business.